The ANTI-CAPITALISM READER

Imagining a Geography of Opposition

EDITED BY

Joel Schalit

AKASHIC BOOKS
NEW YORK

Published by Akashic Books
©2002 Joel Schalit

Design and layout by Courtney Utt
Cover image by Winston Smith (www.winstonsmith.com)
Photography/painting/performance by Eric Brown, Jimmy Chen, Tim Gordon, Lisa Knowles, Ultra-red, and Courtney Utt
Indexing by Spencer Sunshine

ISBN: 1-888451-33-5
Library of Congress Control Number: 2002106600
All rights reserved
First printing

Printed in Canada

Akashic Books
PO Box 1456
New York, NY 10009
Akashic7@aol.com
www.akashicbooks.com

For my big sister Naomi,
who called me a Groucho Marxist when I was in college.

In short, this left-wing radicalism is precisely the attitude to which there is no longer, in general, any corresponding political action. It is not to the left of this or that tendency, but simply to the left of what is in general possible. For from the beginning all it has in mind is to enjoy itself in a negativistic quiet. The metamorphosis of political struggle from a compulsory decision into an object of pleasure, from a means of production into an object of consumption—that is this literature's latest hit.

—Walter Benjamin, "Left-Wing Melancholy"

Table of Contents

CASH IS
THE KING

VISA

MasterCard

VISA

MasterCard

SWITCH SOLO

Acknowledgments

I can't even begin to formulate a proper thanks to all the people who helped assemble this book of essays. Indeed, given the number of folks involved in this book's production, rather than indulge in specifics, I'll try and summarize your value to me in as few words as possible.

First off, I want to thank all of the contributors for putting so much work into their essays. All of you did an absolutely terrific job, using time that wasn't neccessarily yours to give. In between your jobs, partners, and children, you put in an unbelievable amount of effort into this project.

Secondly, I want to thank a number of generous folks who either made themselves available for interviews or allowed us to reprint their work: Naomi Klein, Slavoj Zizek, Wendy Brown, Ramsey Kanaan, Colin Robinson, Giuseppe Cocco, Doug Henwood, Maurizion Lazzarato, and Thomas Frank. Equal gratitude is extended to Michael Hardt for providing us with the fantastic interview with Toni Negri, and to Kathleen Devereaux for the fabulous French-English translation. Aaron Shuman gets ten free dinners in Oakland for all the article-solicitation assistance he provided. And Charlie Bertsch gets the free Sony 17" for his advice,

11

SOHO, LONDON, DECEMBER 2001
COURTNEY UTT

his energy, and the extremely large number of crucial interviews he pulled out of his proverbial hat for this book.

There's always the subject of presentation to contend with. No collection of excellent political writing would be complete without equally imaginative artwork. Winston Smith made a dream come true when he generously provided us with the faux Norman Rockwell cover image. Having been a fan of his Dead Kennedys/Jello Biafra album jackets since I was a teenager, it was a great honor to have him contribute this image. Also worthy of high praise are photographers Eric Brown, Lisa Knowles, and Ultra-red, painter Jimmy Chen, and performance artist Tim Gordon, who provided wonderful documentary, impressionistic, and incendiary pieces.

Finally, I want to extend deep gratitude to my publisher Johnny Temple, and to this book's designer, art director, and contributing photographer, Courtney Utt. This is the second time we've done this in a year, kids. Praise be the two of you for putting up with me and investing so much of your hearts, so much of your time, and every ounce of your patience into our shared projects. I adore and respect the both of you immensely. I think that says it all.

Introduction

When I was in the seventh grade, I was fortunate enough to have an older sibling in college to help provide the framework for my own intellectual endeavors. A university senior finishing up a joint degree in Religious Studies and Politics, Naomi had amassed a considerable library that reflected her academic curiosities as a young Jewish leftist. Although I was too young to discriminate between the volumes on her shelves, there were two books with titles that lodged in my mind in the same way that the names of albums circumscribe the imagination of dedicated music fans: Karl Marx and Friedrich Engels's legendary *Communist Manifesto,* and Rudolf Bahro's 1978 work, *The Alternative in Eastern Europe.*

To this day, I can only begin to surmise why these book titles were so fascinating to me. Perhaps it was because this was the start of the last decade of the Cold War and it was impossible to avoid every name and phrase associated with the conflict becoming a potential gateway to some great realm of ideas. After all, to an inquisitive adolescent living in the United States just before the dawn of the Reagan years, what could have been more compelling than two books outlining the possibilities for utopia from the perspective of communism and the former Soviet Bloc? Even though my reading skills were poor, this much I could intuit. I revelled in the mysterious impenetrability of these two books, knowing somewhere, deep down, that I was holding in my hands the ideological equivalent of forbidden fruit. They felt good. They reminded me of my favorite Black Sabbath records.

It would not be until I actually bought my own copies as an undergraduate student in the late 1980s that I'd move beyond the countercultural mystique these rather awkward books held for me and actively try to understand them. By that time, the pro-democracy movement had already started to take root in Eastern Europe, and Bahro's anti-Stalinist notion of a "third way" for socialism would not figure prominently until the mid-1990s, when it became a catch-all phrase employed by former communists in Western Europe to describe their new-found appreciation of the free market.

"What are these books about?" I once asked Naomi in the spring of 1980.

"Oh," she replied, "that first book inspired most of the communist revolutions over the past hundred years, and the book by Bahro is about what went wrong, and how a more humane socialism might be achieved."

Looking at the trajectory of my own interests over the years, I find it highly ironic how two volumes I became fascinated with as a teenager came to metaphorically book-end the parameters of my own political thinking, as well as the opinions and perspectives espoused by most of the essays herein. While the historical circumstances informing the basis of this collection are entirely different than those of Marx and Engels during the late 1840s (and those of the German Democratic Republic in the late 1970s), what they have in common is a suspicion about the limitations that market economies impose on people's freedom, and a decidely heterodox Marxist slant, informed by the varieties of progressive intellectual currents which contributed to the rearticulation of materialist thinking after the 1960s.

The underlying theme which ties this book together is a sense that a healthy respect for democracy requires an appreciation of the forces that inhibit its realization and prevent its logic from being extended to every sector of modern society.

This is not meant to suggest that this book is a nostalgic invocation of Marxism. *The Anti-Capitalism Reader* is not intended to be a comprehensive representation of the varieties of anti-capitalist movements making themselves felt around the world. To accomplish that task would require a far different, more exhaustive, multivolume set than this modest collection could ever hope to achieve. Rather, these pieces are contemporary reflections on the role that the market continues to play in our lives, on the ways in which we might construe critical responses to it.

This collection is broken up into four sections. The first, *My Definition Is This,* concerns itself with defining "anti-capitalism." The second, *Done By the Forces of Nature,* attempts to break down the ways in which some people critically interrogate the political effects of the market in terms of revolutionary social movements; struggles for national self-determination; popular conceptions of the "freedoms" granted to indviduals by the market; the redefintion of imperialism and sovereignty in a post-9/11 world; as well as the insufficiency of historical discourses about human rights.

Section three, *Open Up the Iron Gate,* grapples with how it is that people react to the market, both in terms of progressive forms of resistance—developing alternative methods of economic exchange, engaging in creative and symbolic forms of protest, and reconsidering the language that the left uses to express itself—to more alienated, and yet no less critical forms of anti-market social movements and ideologies, such as religious fundamentalism. After all, anti-capitalism is not the sole domain of the left. If anti-capitalism has any articulation equally eloquent to that made by progressives, it is in religion.

The focus of the fourth and final section, *Culture and the Angels of History,* is devoted exclusively to what more orthodox, labor-oriented leftists have historically stressed as the least important zone for anti-market activism: culture. As many a scientific, facts-and-numbers-driven revolutionary continues to insist—and here it is worth echoing the words of James Carville, quoted again in Charlie Bertsch's essay, "Anti-Capitalist Taste"—"it's the economy, stupid!" According to the contributors to this concluding portion of the book, this dynamic has always been true. Culture is consistently conditioned by the economic and historical circumstances in which it is produced, and like any symbolic reflection of the world, it is more often than not deployed to mystify inequality and represent the perennially unjust status quo as though it were natural.

But to allude to two highly influental intellectuals cited in this volume—Jürgen Habermas and Antonio Gramsci—culture is also a synonym for the social space in which critical reflection can and must take place, because culture can always become a material force. This insight is already taken for granted by those critics of cultural activism who choose only to read culture as a consistently symbolic realm of total affirmation. Like many materialist theorists of culture before them, and in the tradition of good dialectical analysis, this section's contributors consistently reverse this equation, because they rightly believe that culture is the space where it remains possible to have something resembling a public sphere—a space for exchanging critical thoughts, a space where it is still possible to create new constellations of ideas and beliefs in order to critically influence the common sense of our age.

In essence, this sums up exactly what this book is about.

Joel Schalit
San Fransisco, August 2002

In this society, all human relationships transcending immediate encounter are not relations of happiness: especially not relations in the labor process, which is regulated with regard not to the needs and capacities of individuals but rather to profit on capital and the production of commodities. Human relations are class relations, and their typical form is the free labor contract. This contractual character of human relationships has spread from the sphere of production to all social life. Relationships function only in their reified form, mediated through the class distribution of production to all social life.

—Herbert Marcuse, "On Hedonism"

My Definition Is This

KENTISH TOWN, LONDON, JANUARY 2002
COURTNEY UIT

What Is Anti-Capitalism?
J.C. Myers

*E*very socially necessary task eventually gives birth to its own cadre of specialists. And surely, by now, the issuing of proclamations every twenty years or so declaring capitalism's permanent victory over all conceivable opposition has become the work of dedicated professionals. Before Francis Fukuyama's announcement of the End of History in 1989, a generation of aging European intellectuals had already danced on the grave of "modernity," pronouncing dead all questions of inequality and exploitation and turning instead to probe the more marketable mysteries of "the gaze" and "the body." The first years of the 1960s, some may recall, were supposed to have marked the End of Ideology, and we all know how that turned out. Fifty years earlier still, Max Weber was predicting the imminent demise of communist internationalism when it was only just getting started. To be sure, when the European uprisings of 1848 were turned back by bayonets and musket balls, some thoughtful representative of the Holy Alliance must have remarked that finally all this nonsense about a workers' revolution was finished, once and for all.

But each time the Captains of Industry had been tucked safely into their beds, the words of the happy fairy tale still soothing them to sleep, the echoes of massed voices rose again in the streets and the sea of bodies and banners rolled back in like the tide. The

25

demonstrations that have confronted every major meeting of world trade and finance officials in recent years are, if nothing else, yet another reminder that the grievances of millions upon millions of people against capitalism have not gone away. In December 1999, when protesters battled riot police outside the World Trade Organization's ministerial talks in Seattle, the demonstration's underlying sentiment was widely described as "anti-globalization." But as a movement began to take shape, it became increasingly clear that its target was not the connection of all parts of the globe to one another, but the domination of that process—and of the world itself—by the forces and the logic of capitalism.

The results of capitalism's successes in the 1980s could not be more patent. The total number of people around the world living on less than two dollars a day rose from 2.5 billion in 1987 to 2.8 billion in 1998.[1] And while the gap between rich and poor countries unquestionably expanded, it was not simply a matter of the West benefiting at the expense of the Rest, but of a global capitalist class benefiting at the expense of a global working class. Nothing about the world economy in the last two decades of the twentieth century can be understood without including in the picture the fact that material inequality grew not only *between* rich and poor countries, but *within* the rich countries themselves. In 1983 the top 1% of all households in the United States owned 33.8% of the country's wealth, while the bottom 60% owned 6.1%. By 1998 the share of national wealth held by the top 1% had expanded to 38.1% while the portion owned by the bottom 60% had fallen to 4.7%. The worst losses were sustained by the bottom 40% of U.S. households who saw their share of the country's assets drop from 0.9% in 1983 to just 0.2% in 1998.[2] When the workers of the rest of the world found themselves losing ground, American laborers found themselves caught in the same downward spiral. Market forces may respect many principles, but nationality is clearly not one of them.

Nor is rationality. Market decisions are the result of buyers and

26

sellers pursuing their immediate interests, and while free markets have proven to be astoundingly effective at offering up a mind-boggling array of consumer goods, they have also proven to be singularly disastrous at ensuring social equity or planning for the future. To take just one example, the continued dependence of developed economies on fossil fuels, despite the looming threat of global warming, has nothing to do with the science available to us. We have—and have had for many years—cleaner, more sustainable methods of generating power for homes, industries, and vehicles. Why do we fail to use them? Because it would mean cutting into the profits enjoyed by the board members and shareholders of the oil industry, the electric power industry, and the auto industry. Shifting to a less profitable but more sustainable technology is a decision that market forces will never make. Only political power can force such a change.

The anti-capitalist movements have always known this. Unemployment, poverty, social deterioration, and environmental degradation have all been addressed, at one time or another, within capitalist societies. But they have never been remedied by the fundamental mechanisms of capitalism itself. This is the reason why anti-capitalist movements rose in the past and the reason why they will continue to rise, again and again, until a better way of life is won.

27

What Was Anti-Capitalism?

The precise origins of capitalism remain a subject of debate among historians. But whether shifts in trade patterns or legal structures gave rise to its basic dynamics, capitalism—as a way of life—first took shape during the Industrial Revolution. Tempting as it is to associate that hundred-year transformation first and foremost with the introduction of new technology, the innovations really responsible for making the Industrial Revolution what is was came in the organization of production. Through most of the eighteenth century, manufacturing was a small-scale affair, carried out by individual craftspeople in their homes or workshops, using hand tools they owned themselves. But if industries like cloth-weaving and iron-forging were going to make use of steam engines or water-powered looms, what was required was not only the technology itself, but a new way to use it: factories large enough to house the gigantic machines and accommodate the numbers of workers needed to operate them. Similarly, the whole factory system would have been impossible without urbanization: the growth of cities large enough to house, feed, and clothe this new industrial working class.

Yet, while the basic outlines of the Industrial Revolution—factory production and urbanization—were determined by the technique of production being employed, the character of social life in this brave new world was set by the way in which its resources were owned. There is nothing inherent in the nature of factory production that requires it to be nightmarishly grueling and dangerous, nor is there any immutable law demanding that city life be unhealthy, degrading, and cruel. There is, however, a direct trade-off between the conditions experienced by ordinary working people in factories and cities, and the profits to be made by factory-owners and urban landlords. In other words, the Industrial Revolution created poverty and misery not because it was an *industrial* revolution, but because it was a *capitalist* revolution: a mobilization of industrial technology in the interests of the few at the expense of the many.

The many responded to this brutal transformation of the world with apathy, alcoholism, and religious revivals, but also with political struggles. At one end of the continuum, workers destroyed machines and organized unions within individual firms; at the other end, they began to envision and to fight for a social transformation as sweeping as the one they were already living through. What sort of transformation was this to be? If the poverty and misery of the Industrial Revolution were caused by the fact that the bulk of productive resources was owned and operated by private individuals for their own benefit, then the key to transforming soci-

28

ety in a more positive direction would be to bring those resources under public control for the benefit of the society as a whole.

Precisely how that reorganization was to be accomplished drew the dividing line between two camps of social revolutionaries. Socialism, communism, and social democracy (essentially interchangeable terms in the nineteenth century) built their political vision around three pillars: a critique of private property as the central principle of economic life; a corresponding critique of market-commodity exchange as the dominant force in social life; and a belief in the capacity of a democratic state to step in and improve things where private property and the market had created chaos and misery.[3] Anarchism largely agreed with the first two ideas, but disagreed strongly with the last. For nineteenth-century anarchists, all forms of political authority were to be rejected in favor of voluntary and spontaneous forms of social organization.

Yet, in this respect, the anarchists shared a core belief with the apostles of capitalism: Both argued that the best form of society would arise from the spontaneous interaction of individuals freed from government interference. For both camps, the question of the proper relationship between state and society proved to be a haunting one throughout the twentieth century. If for socialists, communists, and social democrats the problem was one of insuring that a strong state with control over the economy remained meaningfully democratic, for anarchists the problem was exactly the reverse: maintaining effective control over private property without any form of state at all.

29

One further difficulty confronted the forces of social revolution: While capitalism did in fact give birth to its gravediggers, it fought with every weapon at its disposal to keep them at bay. Karl Marx, the single greatest analyst and critic of early capitalism, has often been ridiculed for predicting a future marked by the rise of anti-capitalist workers' revolutions, yet this is precisely what actually happened. In the nineteenth and twentieth centuries, every corner of the globe was touched by social revolution, from Central Europe in 1848 to

Central America in 1979. What did not occur frequently, easily, or unproblematically was the victory of those revolutions over their adversaries. In the highly developed capitalist countries, the ability of ruling classes to offer temporary compromises—institutionalized collective bargaining and social welfare benefits—often derailed the drive for more sweeping transformations. In the lesser-developed countries, the sheer lack of resources and the constant pressure exerted by the capitalist world (in both military and economic forms) damaged and deformed the revolutions that did come to power. It is worth remembering, though, that Marx had predicted two possible outcomes to the era of class struggle: a revolutionary transformation of society or the collective ruin of all those involved.

What Isn't Anti-Capitalism?

So large did anti-capitalism loom on the horizon of the twentieth century that virtually every opposition movement seemed in one way or another to become associated with it. While for a time this helped to foster a sense of momentum—even inevitability—in anti-capitalist politics, it also had the gradual effect of confusing anti-capitalism with other, decidedly different, political agendas.

30

This occurred perhaps most often with the various expressions of anti-colonial nationalism. Even prior to the turn of the century, some social revolutionary thinkers had begun to develop a critique of colonialism, and by the end of WWI, opposition to imperialism had become an accepted element of anti-capitalist politics. More importantly, though, as independence movements arose in the colonized world (largely after WWII), they readily adopted for themselves the imagery and discourse of social revolution. On the one hand, this earned them practical benefits: a ready-made political theory and, in many cases, material assistance from the Soviet Union. On the other hand, however, the commitment of anti-colonial movements to anti-capitalist politics was not always a deep or lasting one. Once in power, anti-colonial leaders often jettisoned their critique of capitalism in favor of a more economically flexible vision of national strength and unity.

Why was this transformation such a seemingly effortless one? Although many anti-colonial movements expressed an opposition to capitalism for its exploitation of people as workers, the primary purpose of any anti-colonial effort is the expulsion of outsiders from what is to be an independent nation-state. This is to say that what is most central to an expression of anti-colonial nationalism (like any other kind of nationalism) is a claim about identity: the existence of a unique, exclusive people and that people's right to political self-determination. In the context of colonial domination this may represent an important form of emancipation, but nothing about it suggests a critique of capitalism as such. If foreign exploiters are bad because they are foreign, indigenous exploiters may be perfectly acceptable. Thus, for many anti-colonial nationalists, a national capitalist class is something to be promoted rather than overthrown.

A similar set of circumstances and dynamics might also be said to have connected anti-capitalism to the politics of cultural identity. As with the struggles against imperialism, anti-capitalists have often been counted among the strongest allies of the movements opposed to racial, ethnic, and sexual oppression. When Marx and Engels drafted the *Communist Manifesto* in 1848, they felt compelled to respond within the text to one set of critics who had already identified the anti-capitalist movement with early feminist thought. In the U.S., for most of the twentieth century, the only political organization with a majority "white" membership to take an uncompromising, active stand against racism was the Communist Party. But while anti-capitalists have regularly filled the ranks of the movements for civil rights and gender equality, there has never been any good reason to assume that the relationship was a reciprocal one. As historian Eric Hobsbawm has argued, however just their struggles, identity groups are ultimately motivated by particularistic interests and exclusive

31

claims. At the end of the day, they are for themselves and no one else.[4]

Like nationalism and identity politics, both fascism and religious fundamentalism have at times found capitalism to be an occasional inconvenience—challenging its tendency to trade moral fiber for consumer hedonism—yet both have always made their peace with it in the end. Hitler railed against "Jewish bankers" at the same time that he depended upon corporate giants like Krups to build his short-lived empire. Christian fundamentalists in the United States and Islamic fundamentalists in the Middle East often bemoan the commodification of sex while offering no similar critique of the commodification of labor-power. Anti-capitalism, by contrast, is a universalistic movement. It is not a complaint about *who* owns the banks and the factories, but about the *way* in which banks and factories are owned. It is not a criticism of the fact that women or Hispanics end up in the lower ranks of the working-class, but of the fact that any person should end up spending his or her life as little more than a worker. Anti-capitalists are opposed not only to the exploitation of racialized groups or religious minorities, but to the exploitation of all human beings.

Curiously enough, this is also the reason why anti-capitalism must be distinguished from environmentalism. The latter is, to be sure, a universalistic belief: environmentalists are for the preservation of the Amazon rainforest and the California redwoods alike. But environmentalism, particularly in its more radical forms, is ultimately uninterested in human beings. Thus, at one end of the spectrum, the Sierra Club bourgeoisie can comfortably accommodate a love for both endangered species and expanding markets, while at the other end, Earth First! activists can accept a thoroughgoing critique of capitalism without giving any substantial consideration to what sort of economic arrangements should replace it.

Of course, environmentalists might have good reason to be suspicious of anti-capitalist intentions. "Industrializing socialism" in Eastern Europe and the Third World was notoriously unconcerned with environmental protection and sustainable development. Yet, one fact we can note about defense of the environment in capitalist countries is that it has always and everywhere been an initiative of the state against the market. No firm in private industry would willingly incur the costs required to reduce their output of pollutants without government regulations forcing them to do so. So-called "green products" (i.e., unbleached toilet paper, non-aerosol sprays) have found small niche markets among enlightened consumers, but for most shoppers, price will win out over extra-economic appeal. Thus, while anti-capitalism does not in and of itself guarantee that the natural environment will be protected, it does offer the only set of tools with which we might realistically do so, while simultaneously looking after the needs and aspirations of humanity as a whole.

What Is Anti-Capitalism?

Anti-capitalism, then, begins with a commitment to the idea that capitalism cannot produce societies fit for all or even most of the people who live in them, and follows with a commitment to a realistic, achievable alternative. That alternative would necessarily mean the planned use of major economic resources to achieve a society in which all human beings could live more fully human lives. What would such a society look like? Some might suggest that what is most important about human beings is their radical individuality, and that any planned effort to provide for their needs and desires would only result in a massive hubristic fiasco. Others might argue, in a similar vein, that if a post-capitalist future is to be a democratic one, little if anything could be said in advance about how such a society would be organized. What such criticisms ignore, however, is that the ability to pursue individual desires and to participate in democratic institutions is rooted in a set of basic needs all people share. Someone dying of hunger has little use for the freedom to choose from thirty-seven varieties of soda in order to select the one most expressive of his or her unique personality. Likewise, someone able to meet their basic needs and still have time left over in the day for other activities might be better able to develop and express their individuality than someone barely able to make ends meet with a full-time job. Further still, the quality of some individual rights and freedoms might be meaningfully improved by the provision of certain fundamental goods. Freedom of speech might be more useful to someone who was also provided with a decent level of health care, just as the right to vote might be more useful to someone who was also provided with a high-quality education.

In its history, capitalism has done an outstanding job of providing a relatively small number of people with both the foundational goods (food, shelter, health care, education) and the time away from work to experience something we might call freedom. Anti-capitalism seeks to take that freedom away from no one. Rather, anti-capitalism, first and foremost, is a call for society to be reorganized in such a way as to provide the greatest amount of freedom for all; to use our resources and our technology to provide people with their needs so as to allow them to pursue their desires. For all but a handful, capitalism has failed. For the rest of us, anti-capitalism remains our only hope.

34

Endnotes:

1. Source: *Global Economic Prospects and the Developing Countries*, World Bank, 2001.
2. Source: "Recent Trends in Wealth Ownership 1983–1998," Edward N. Wolff, Jerome Levy Economics Institute, 2000.
3. Two caveats apply here: (1) Private property, in this sense, refers to productive resources rather than personal property, i.e., factories and farms rather than shirts and shoes. (2) Socialists, communists, and social democrats did not necessarily reject all market mechanisms, but were critical of the increasing dominance of markets and market principles in all aspects of life.
4. Hobsbawm, Eric, "Identity Politics and the Left," *New Left Review*, May/June, 1996.

Does It Mean Anything to be a Leninist in 2001?
Doug Henwood

For the conference "Towards a Politics of Truth: The Retrieval of Lenin,"
Essen, Germany, Feburary 4, 2001

When I was asked to present a topic for discussion at this conference, I chose the question, "Does it mean anything to be a Leninist in 2001?" I really had no idea of an answer then, but was convinced I'd come up with something in the intervening eight weeks. I'm not sure I have, even though most of this conference is now behind us.

One reason I picked the title is that over the years I've asked self-identified Leninists for their definition. I can't say that I've gotten a memorable answer yet—or one that isn't a literal transposition of Lenin's own writings into the present, like some case of ideological time travelling. I just don't see how a revolutionary doctrine that was devised for a lightly industrialized, semi-peripheral monarchy, remains relevant to highly industrialized metropoles where censorship and the police operate in much more subtle, often unconscious ways.

I've heard some efforts at definition over the last couple of days. One set of suggestions held that Lenin serves as a reminder of the centrality of politics, the crucial importance of a good analysis,

35

and the indispensability of The Party. The first two seem fairly obvious to me, and so general that Margaret Thatcher or the people who thought for Ronald Reagan would have assented to them.

Lenin's emphasis on the centrality of The Party seems like a dead idea to me. Like it or not, the notion of a vanguard party in the Leninist model, operating on quasi-military principles of discipline and hierarchy, has less than zero appeal to all but a handful of relics today. It is, I'm fairly certain, beyond any hope of revival. To speak that language today, to an audience not already in basic sympathy to your program, is to condemn yourself to irrelevance.

So much for the Leninist style of politics. There is also the matter of Lenin as icon, the successful revolutionary who keeps alive the possibility of revolution today. I'm susceptible to this appeal; I even have a picture of Lenin hanging in my kitchen. There's no denying that he is a great image. But again, I doubt the breadth of that appeal. The other week I asked a friend of mine who is a professor of English at a major American university, whose allegiance to Marxism has almost certainly hurt his career, what he thought of Lenin. His answer was that he was a philosophical cretin and a political gangster. I'm sure almost everyone in this room would disagree with this characterization. But if you get this kind of response from a Marxist intellectual, I'd say Lenin's image problem borders on the fatal.

I'm certainly not endorsing this view of Lenin. However, in politics you have to work with the hand you've been dealt, and Lenin's face isn't even in the deck these days. A more possible project might be the retrieval of Marx, a topic I'll return to a bit later. Nevertheless, I have to dissent from Slavoj Zizek's picture of the Old Man's growing respectability, at least from my experience in the U.S. Aside from a handful of universities, Marxism has disappeared from American economics departments. In fact, I know of only one Marxist who's been hired by a major U.S. department in the last twenty years—John Roemer, by Yale. That was a joint appointment with the Political Science department, and it was Poli

36

Sci that was the driving force behind the hire. Yes, things are a bit better in the humanities, but many of my friends in the Marxist Literary Group have severe publication and employment problems.

There are very few Marx-o-philes on Wall Street. I know of one exception, though I think he's rather paranoid about having this be known: Bruce Steinberg, the chief economist at Merrill Lynch. Steinberg was on the editorial board of the *Review of Radical Political Economics* about twenty years ago, and has been heard saying that his study of Marx helped him immensely. I strongly suspect he was the unnamed Wall Streeter who was quoted in John Cassidy's article on the Marx revival in *The New Yorker* in October 1997. But that's about it. My own Marxist book on Wall Street—though our friends the Spartacists will dispute its Marxism—was received mainly with silence by financiers, though the financial weekly *Barron's* described it as "loopy" and "repellent." A member of the business staff of the *Los Angeles Times* characterized it as mapping out the road to the gulag (of course). Some years ago, the former executive editor of the *Wall Street Journal* told me that I am "sick and twisted," and added that it's tragic that I exist. But that's Wall Street. The exuberant reception for Verso's 150th anniversary latte-table edition of the *Communist Manifesto* and Cassidy's *New Yorker* article suggest a broad willingness to listen to Marx, now that memories of the USSR are fading and the moment of capitalist triumphalism is starting to feel hollow. Perhaps even false.

Aside from media evidence, my own experience of talking to popular audiences in the U.S. has been that people are quite willing to listen to a Marxian analysis, especially if they don't know that's what they're hearing—and that younger audiences don't even have any problem with the name. With Lenin's name, though, they most certainly do.

What about Lenin as a political analyst? The essay on imperialism has come up a lot here, and it so happens that I just reacquainted myself with it, after a long separation, to prepare for this conference.

37

It's certainly of great historical interest. But unfortunately, too many self-identified Leninists take it and apply it unmodified as an analytical template for today. That just won't do. One very serious problem is the prominence of Hilferding's analysis of finance capital, a book that has long afflicted Marxian analyses of finance in general. First, let me start with the achingly obvious: the era of high colonialism is over. Right now, Kautsky's ultra-imperialism seems a like a not-bad characterization of the world in the early twenty-first century, even if he was very wrong about the early twentieth century.

Yes, there are contradictions in the system; yes, there are rivalries among the major imperialist powers; yes, the three metropoles, the U.S., the EU, and Japan, each have their own geographic spheres of particular influence. But conceding all that, it's amazing how peaceful the coexistence is among the imperial powers. The members of the EU fought among themselves over who would be the first head of the European Central Bank, but they ended up with a nominee. The major powers fought over who would head the WTO and the IMF, but they ended up with nominees. The U.S. is the major investor in Latin America, but the EU is the major investor in Brazil and Argentina. Yet all parties pretty much get along. The U.S. is in the process of economically annexing Mexico, but you'll find Sony and Volkswagen plants operating happily there.

After all, in *The Economic Consequences of the Peace*, John Maynard Keynes wrote that an upper-class Londoner around 1910 regarded the then-prevailing freedom of trade and capital flows as (freer by many measures than the present, I should add):

> normal certain and permanent, except in the direction of improvement, and any deviation from it as aberrant, scandalous, and avoidable. The projects and politics of militarism and imperialism, of racial and cultural rivalries, of monopolies, restrictions, and exclusion, which were to play the serpent to this paradise, were little more than the amusements of his daily newspaper, and

appeared to exercise almost no influence at all on the ordinary course of social and economic life, the internationalization of which was nearly complete in practice.

Maybe there's a serpent waiting to pounce sometime in the future, but not right now. Right now it sure looks like a truly global ruling class is constituting itself through public institutions like the IMF and private ones like the Davos World Economic Forums.

And then there's the stuff about cartels and banks. I often hear self-described Leninists apply these concepts to the present with almost no modification. The word "monopoly" is thrown around, as if J.P. Morgan were still walking the earth. First off, lets take cartels. For the last twenty years, it has been the policy of many governments around the world to promote competition, through deregulation and the dismantling of import barriers. The executive committee of the bourgeoisie realized that the comfy world of the 1950s and 1960s, the one described with some admiration by John Kenneth Galbraith and with considerable hostility by Paul Baran and Paul Sweezy, had led to systemic sclerosis. Nor is there any compelling evidence of a trend toward monopoly. A study of twenty industrial sectors published last summer in the *Harvard Business Review* found increased concentration of market share in only one, semiconductors. All others saw a decline or no change. It also found that cross-border mergers imparted no competitive advantage on the new entities, a result confirmed by other studies showing that multinationals are no more profitable than domestic firms.

To complicate the picture even further, contrary to Lenin's assertion that profits are higher in poor countries, data on American multinationals shows returns on Latin American investments to be lower than those in Canada or Western Europe, and returns in Taiwan to be higher than those in China. Furthermore, over two-thirds of the total stock of U.S. foreign direct investment is in countries with incomes roughly comparable to the home country's.

39

Throw in the four classic Asian Tigers and you've got over three-quarters of the total. I'm not entirely sure what this all means theoretically, but it does suggest that some serious rethinking of received wisdom—received wisdom to which Lenin's Imperialism contributed no small amount—is in order.

And as for the banks, well, to quote the Velvet Underground, those were different times. Lenin, following Hilferding, declared that the stock exchange was an institution in serious decline. It's not. In the U.S., the power of stockholders has grown enormously over the last twenty years, and other countries are following suit. One of the vastly under-appreciated aspects of the Euro project is to create more American-style financial markets, and to weaken the hold of German-style bank ownership. The point is to expose companies to the constant public discipline of profit maximization.

There's been a lot of talk about Michael Hardt and Antonio Negri's *Empire* over the last couple of days. I've only begun to think about the book, but there's a lot to consider in it. I think they overdo the assertion that today's Empire has no Rome—Washington, Wall Street, and Hollywood are a lot more central to the structure than they allow—but their point about the dispersion of power in the new order is absolutely right, I think. Empire today is a much more collective and dispersed affair than it was in Lenin's day, what with the UN and NATO acting the part of imperial enforcers, and stock markets arranging ownership and discipline. No, the nation state isn't dead, and yes, financial power is still concentrated—but too much attention to Lenin will only confuse us.

★ ★ ★

Having doubted the relevance of Lenin for the last two thousand-some words, I'll now invoke the clichéd Leninist question: What is to be done? I wish I had a good answer, or even several approximations of the beginning of an answer. Certainly the state of official electoral politics everywhere is dismal. European leftists can kvetch about the "Third Way," but we've just inaugurated a reactionary moron who didn't really even win the election. It's almost enough to make me nostalgic for Bill Clinton.

But outside the electoral realm, there are some new-ish and very exciting political movements for which "Seattle" has become the shorthand. I understand there's quite a dispute going on between the British Socialist Workers Party and its U.S. subsidiary, the International Socialist Organization, on just what these movements are all about, with the SWP calling them "anti-capitalist," and the ISO calling them "anti-corporate." In part this may be a geographical difference. I've noticed that the European press uses the term "anti-capitalist" to describe them. The U.S. press calls the demonstrators "anti-corporate" or "anti-globalization," both because they can't even imagine how anyone could object to capitalism and because we don't have much of a native strain of anti-capitalism in our political tradition—but we do have a populist, petit-bourgeois, small business one. All these names, you'll observe, begin with the word "anti-," which suggests that they've got a pretty good idea of what they're against, and a much vaguer idea of what they're for. That criticism has been made here, and its truth has to be conceded. But after twenty or twenty-five years of political torpor, this is some serious progress.

Even though I said that "Seattle" is the shorthand for these movements, it's important to remember that they weren't born there. You can trace them back at least a few years earlier. There was the worldwide mobilization against the Multilateral Agreement on Investment, which was being negotiated in effective secrecy by the major powers—until a draft text of the treaty was leaked and posted on the web in January 1997. Within weeks, an anti-MAI movement was formed, in large part through websites and email lists, and not all that much later, the MAI talks collapsed in April 1998. Part of the problem was that the major powers had some differences

41

among themselves, but the popular movement contributed a lot to the failure. Then there were the coordinated worldwide demonstrations around the G-7 summit on June 18, 1999. At the time, almost no one paid serious attention to these summits. However, J18 was marked by scores of protests from New York to Nairobi. The front page of the *Financial Times* carried an inspiring picture of a shirtless protester hurling a rock at some cops; the city of London was effectively shut for the day.

Then, of course, there was Seattle. There was a lot that was unique and irreproducible about that event. For one, the authorities were caught off guard; for two, it's a liberal city whose government wanted to be as tolerant of protest as possible; and for three, the local police just weren't up to the task. At the end of the protest week, I walked up to a group of cops and said, "I'm from New York, and believe me, this couldn't have happened there. The mayor would have surrounded the meeting site with 40,000 cops and no one but the delegates would have gotten close." One of the cops replied, "Yes, but the NYPD has lots of experience with crowd control. We don't."

A few months later, in Washington, DC, the cops were plenty prepared for the April 16 protests against the World Bank and the IMF—but the meetings were still disrupted, and virtually the entire center of the city was shut down. But of more political importance, the Bank and the Fund had to junk their prepared agenda and instead talk unconvincingly about their deep concern for the world's poor. If hegemony consists in part by establishing the terms of discourse—as they say in the opinion-management business, we can't tell the public what to think, but we can tell them what to think about—then something is happening here. We were telling them what to think about.

I could list some more names: Melbourne, Davos, Porto Alegre, and, in two months, Quebec City. That kind of catalog would point out one of the risks of this movement—that, in the words of the Canadian writer Naomi Klein, it threatens to devolve into serial protest. But since I'm trying to be more optimistic these days, I'll say that hasn't happened yet because it's still a young movement, trying to find its feet.

Related to this movement is an explosion over the last three years in the level of political activism on U.S. campuses, most prominently the anti-sweatshop movement. (Anti- again, but it's having serious real-world effects.) Maybe I'm a bit biased about this because I live with its leading journalistic chronicler, Liza Featherstone, but this is profoundly inspiring stuff. Here's an example of what it's up to: A few weeks ago, a South Korean-owned firm that does contract work for Nike fired some workers who were trying to organize an independent union. The students heard about it, and within days they were on the scene in Mexico—and at home, they started publicizing the fight. Just the other day, Nike, fearful of bad publicity, forced the Korean firm (whose managers had claimed that it was an acceptable form of labor discipline to hit lagging workers in the head with a hammer) to rehire the organizers. Maybe this is just temporary; maybe it's a PR coup that will soon be quietly undone. Maybe this is all too media-driven. News that MTV is working on a special about "Revolution" confirms anxieties that the system is, in the words of Tom Frank and his colleagues at *The Baffler* magazine, commodifying our dissent. But better MTV is doing a special on revolution than on apathy. Again, we're telling them what to think about.

Some of the many exciting things about these recent movements is that they're global, they're fast, and they've had an impact. They couldn't exist without technologies like the web and the cellphone, things that were only recently the stuff of capitalist triumphalism. Organizationally, they're flexible yet disciplined, serious yet good-humored. Their structure has more to do with Spanish anarchism of the 1930s than with the Bolsheviks of 1917. Soon after I got back from Seattle, I was part of a panel reporting on the events to the New York City chapter of the Labor Party. After I was

43

done, a voice arose from the audience to complain that what I was talking about sounded more like a carnival than politics, and then it launched into what sounded like a computer-generated Leninist diatribe about imperialism. How especially odd it seemed to hear that; it was as if the speaker wasn't, as the doctors say, properly oriented in time and space. The kids wouldn't have listened to him for a second. And the carnival was absolutely wonderful, one of the greatest weeks of my life.

So, is there a role for Marxist intellectuals in these new movements? Yes, absolutely, I'd say. It's true that they're theoretically unsophisticated (though Michael Hardt told me that some of the anti-sweatshop activists at Duke, where the movement started in 1997, are really liking his class on *Kapital*). Seattle, the new revolutionary icon, was ideologically a very mixed bag, with nationalist Steelworkers mingling with topless lesbians, petit-bourgeois Greens, and some unaffiliated socialists—and the infamous Black Bloc of anarchists, who marched around chanting things like "Capitalism, no thanks/We will burn your fucking banks!" The new activists tend to focus on extreme abuses like sweatshops, or on state institutions like the IMF and WTO—though it's easy to understand that institutional focus, because such institutions give Empire something like a home address. But in my experience of talking to the protesters (and I don't want to give the impression that they're all young, though they mostly are), they're extremely open to a radical analysis.

The ISO has been spending a lot of time around the anti-sweatshop movement. From what I'm told, the kids are grateful to hear a coherent analysis of how the parts of the system fit together. However, they're extremely wary of furtive takeover attempts. Vanguardists have this distressing habit of trying to take over movements that they had no role in starting. It reminds me of the American poet A.R. Ammon's line (which I'm quoting from memory, so I may not have it exactly right) that the way to look like a leader is to get in front of a moving crowd and start waving your arms. That's not very helpful, and it will give Marxism a very bad name at a moment when its prospects look better than they have in a very long time. It seems like it would be far more efficacious for Marxist intellectuals to talk with the protesters, to engage them in conversation with some modesty, perhaps even a touch of awe.

A few months ago, I interviewed the Columbia University economics professor Jagdish Bhagwati for an article I co-wrote on the anti-sweatshop movement that will appear imminently in the academic gossip magazine *Lingua Franca*. Bhagwati was very disturbed by the events in Seattle, and came back from there to organize his free-trading comrades into a protest group of their own, the Academic Consortium on International Trade. Bhagwati recalled a chat he had with a masked young woman in Seattle. He asked her if the mask signified that she was a Zapatista. She said no, she was an anarchist. He just didn't know what to make of her, or the crowd she was part of, but he was quite shaken up. The ruling class is rather unnerved by this new generation of protest, and that can only be a good thing. I'm almost tempted—especially given the lack of a female presence on the platform throughout this conference—to nominate the anonymous masked woman as the Lenin of our time. That wouldn't be quite accurate, I know, but it's still mighty tempting.

45

What News from Genoa? Varieties of Anti-Capitalist Experience
Paul Thomas

For Barbara Lee and in memory of Michael Rogin.

*W*hat is the price of anti-capitalism in the twenty-first century? In answering this question, we should not allow the dramatic events of September 11, 2001 to overshadow or displace the drama of what happened in Genoa two months earlier. For one thing, July and September have already been joined, officially and authoritatively, from the right. John Ashcroft—not the first U.S. Attorney General for whom the sobriquet "dyed-in-the-wool" might actually have been coined—acted with all due dispatch retroactively to define and brand as a "terrorist" anyone who had taken to the streets in Genoa or Seattle to protest the G-8 Summit or the WTO (though not, of course, those who took to the streets in uniform to hunt them down). Add to this a reprise of the old McCarthyite logic— if you're not against terrorism as we define it, you're pro-terrorist— and what comes out is the no-less-ominous observation that while European communism may be a spent force, the American National Security State is alive and well. It's an ill wind, as has frequently been observed, that blows nobody any good.

All of a sudden, the crowing triumphalism that attended the fall of European communism has started to look dated, shopworn, and distant. The line connecting the Battle in Seattle to Fortress Genoa, a line that passes through Gothenburg, Quebec, and Prague, shows that the fall of the Berlin Wall did not pull down with it the prospects of further anti-capitalist protest. To the contrary, it would appear that Genoa changed the rules of the anti-capitalist game (and perhaps the coordinates of capitalism itself) decisively and irreversibly. It is unlikely that the leaders of industrialized countries will be able to meet together any time soon other than in off-season, remote Canadian ski-resorts (with Sergeant Preston of the Yukon nearby, scanning the horizon nervously).

What was distinctive about Genoa was not that it was organized by email and cellphones (Seattle was too) but that both sides in the street battle were so amply prepared. The death of Carlo Giuliani was an unwelcome surprise, to be sure. But much of the rest was elaborately prepared for. Millions of dollars were spent on pre-Summit restoration, more than 16,000 soldiers, policemen, and Carabinieri assigned for the sake of "security," a six-square-mile "red zone" within which the G-8 leaders could meet, and an airport closed for the duration of the Summit. The scale of the preparedness was impressive—the more so if we recall that the SDS (Students for a Democratic Society) did not shut down Chicago in 1968 even for an afternoon. (I know, I was there.) And yet, as Michael Hardt and Antonio Negri put the matter in their July 20, 2001 op-ed piece in the *New York Times*, "What the Protesters in Genoa Want":

47

> A new species of political activist has been born with a spirit that is reminiscent of the paradoxical idealism of the 1960s—the realistic course of action today is to demand what is seemingly impossible, that is, something new . . . One of the most remarkable characteristics of these movements is their diversity: trade unionists together with ecologists together with priests and communists. We are beginning to see a multitude emerge that is defined not by any single identity, but can discover communality in its diversity.

So defined, anti-capitalist protesters seem to fall all too neatly into the category of New Social Movements as these were celebrated by Ernesto Laclau and Chantal Moffe in *Hegemony and Socialist Strategy* (Verso, 1977). Here, the destabilization of identities and multiplication of politicized spaces tends toward the dissolution of what Mouffe and Laclau call "the differential positivity of the social" and the explosion of "the idea and reality . . . of a (singular) unique space for the constitution of the political." New social movements, we are given to understand, multiply along the lines of intersection of various concerns and social forces or spaces; they are not regulated by any singular concept of political subjectivity, and, accordingly, do not occupy the space, the topos, of "politics" as conventionally defined. They have been critical in mobilizing opposition and alternative cultures within major capitalist states. Such mobilizations have been all too facilely labeled as self-destructive left-sectarianism by members of the erstwhile New Left (as in Todd Gitlin's *The Twilight of Common Dreams*). Alternatively, they have been celebrated for being sporadic, discontinuous, fragmented, and jagged by observers of a "post-modernist" persuasion, observers who have a vested, anti-essentialist interest in such adjectives. It looks likely that NSMs, including anti-capitalist protesters, have gained their momentum and mobility from their transgressions of the normative divisions of political state and civil society in ways that are difficult for states to contain. As Paul Gilroy has remarked, where the new movements keep their distance from the institutions of the political system, the distinction between human emancipation and the formal freedoms guaranteed by politics is constantly underlined.

This in turn entails a point made by David Lloyd and myself in our book *Culture and the State* (Routledge, 1997). We put forth the argument that the success of the modern, "hegemonic" state presupposed the acceptance not of "human" but precisely of "political"

48

emancipation, much as Karl Marx had presciently outlined and jux-taposed these categories in his 1843 essay, "On the Jewish Question." Such untoward acceptance involved the retraction of democratic aspirations (which had been marked among the British Chartists) into the mere capacity "to be represented." If this is so, then what we are witnessing today is a return of the repressed. The openings for social movements have multiplied, as civil society has become more porous. Diverse social spaces have opened up for alternative cultural formations that owe precious little to class membership or to political subjectivity as this is conventionally understood. The force, the élan, of these movements derives from the fact that they have not succumbed to pre-given differentiations. Laclau and Mouffe believe that the path to radical democracy "lies not in the abandonment of the democratic terrain, but, on the contrary, in the extension of the field of democratic struggles to the whole of civil society and the state." This forces Laclau and Mouffe to endorse the already-constituted political and social subject-divisions of liberal, representative democracy, the very subject-positions that NSMs themselves are engaged in transgressing. Struggles now seem to follow pre-given, and rather too constricted, lines of distinction (race, gender, class), and get represented by "anti" movements: anti-racism, anti-sexism, and, for that matter, anti-capitalism. Negative definition that takes its lights from what is to be opposed, and from nothing else, may be unhelpful or even self-defeating. *Culture and the State* suggested that social movements like Chartism were transgressive of such categories even before the spaces and subject positions associated with "the social," "the economic," "the political," and "the educational," had established themselves. This in turn would entail that, shorn of their connection with twentieth-century "identity politics," new social movements may in fact not be so very new after all.

All the more reason, then, to take the broader view, armed in the certainty that there have been anti-capitalist movements and

49

doctrines throughout the history of capitalism, from its very beginnings and even (on the part of those, like the French Sans-Culottes or the British Chartists, who read the writing on the wall) on the eve of the triumph of capitalism. It is these apparently kaleidoscopic responses and reactions that cry out for categorization and theorization. That they are kaleidoscopic but in no way random or scattershot can be seen more clearly if we acknowledge, right off the bat, the centrality of socialism in general—and Marx in particular—to their sequence and their patterning. Marx, of course, was not alone in having advocated revolution or in having believed in the need for drastic change in order to attain human autonomy, as the merest glance at the wonderland of nineteenth-century revolutionism will reveal. But his sense of the tension between the depravity and the promise of capitalism was unique. It is no doubt easier to imagine a world without Marx than a world without capitalism, communism, socialism, and revolution. But in the world we actually inhabit, these facts of life still have to be seen through Marx.

It is to Marx that we owe an entire vocabulary, consisting of *proletariat, class* (including *class consciousness* and *class struggle*), *ideology,* and *alienation* (including the fetishism of commodities). These terms were arrayed alongside the new economic vocabulary of *use-value, exchange-value, surplus-value,* and the *falling rate of profit.* The point here is not just that we owe to Marx the main elements of the method Engels and others were to term "historical materialism"—true and important though this is. It is that one would be hard put to analyze capitalist society—let alone oppose it—without recourse to the above inventory. Indeed, the very idea that effective opposition to capitalism must be rooted in a solid intellectual analysis of how capitalism works, from the point of production outwards, is an idea of distinctly Marxian provenance. It is hard to overestimate its importance. Marx's central convictions, that "the production of material life," the organization of productive activities, should have pride of place in the investigation of social structures and historical

50

development, and that "the mode of production conditions the social, political, and intellectual life-process in general," always have been, and still remain open to interpretation and disputation. But they cannot be ignored, or passed over rough-shod. It is for this very reason that even though there are elements in the compound of what came to be known as "historical materialism" that were not, strictly speaking, Marx's at all—it's worth remembering that we would have had capitalism, communism, socialism, revolution, and even the labor theory of value if Marx had not written a word— they continue to be elements on which Marx left his own distinctive imprint.

What stands out most distinctively about Marx is his unsurpassed sense of the enormous potential (alongside the actual depravity) of capitalism. This double-edged characterization was one that Marx could proffer without either lapsing into a purely moralistic critique or subscribing to the romantic attitude (one that was far from uncommon among Marx's contemporaries) that capitalism had disrupted a pre-industrial idyll. It is to Marx we owe the insight that under capitalism the capacity to produce expands, and might exceed all known bounds, while ownership of the means of production contracts (relatively or absolutely). We are not yet done with the sheer usefulness of this insight into an asymmetry or maladjustment that is not accidental but built-in. It was Marx's distinction of forces from relations of production that enabled him, and may still enable us today, to deny that physical production and material growth depend by their very nature on the maintenance and furthering of capitalism. Marx contended that if capitalism is not understood genetically— understood, that is to say, as it arose, when it arose, and at no other time—we have no way of accounting for its historical specificity. Capitalism would then be falsely and uncritically understood as the universal norm and standard by which all earlier modes of production could be judged, and found wanting. Conversely, these earlier modes of production would be,

51

again falsely and uncritically, regarded as though they were nothing but early, immature, faltering, and tentative approximations of capitalism itself. While it is unlikely that more modern scholars will fall as neatly into this particular trap as did those "political economists" who were Marx's near-contemporaries, the trap itself—the trap, that is, of falsely absolutizing capitalism as the summit of human endeavor or the be-all and end-all of human existence—has widened considerably over the span of time that separates us from Marx. Capitalism is not unassailable, whether or not what Marx called "revolutionary activity, practical-critical activity" will suffice as assailant. The chain of causality that undergirds capitalism, according to which human relationships have become phenomena of the market, can in principle (like the crust of custom) be broken. Capitalism, that is to say, has its enabling assumptions, and these in turn have practical effects; should these cease to operate, capitalism could not and (Marx hastened to add) would not persist.

What Marx bequeathed to his followers was a revolutionary doctrine and movement, as well as a method of social, economic, political, and historical argument. While the combination was nothing if not fertile, it could be argued, of course, that doctrine, method, and movement have never yet found their proper mix (if indeed there is a proper mix to be found). To adjudicate this question we must proceed at this juncture to a consideration not of the centrality of Marx in particular but of the centrality of socialism in general to the continuum of anti-capitalist movements.

The word "socialism" first appeared in Robert Owen's *Co-operative Magazine* in 1827, *"le socialisme"* in the Saint-Simonian journal *Le Globe* in 1832. It meant a projected socio-political alternative to capitalism, not a political movement or demand. In early socialist doctrine there is not a word about the proletariat, the class system, or revolution. While John Stuart Mill's *Principles of Political Economy* (1848) regarded socialism and communism not as political movements but as theories, Marx and Engels's *Manifesto of the*

Communist Party (1848) identified communism as a movement that would render socialism utopian in the sense of being impracticable. It was communism, not socialism, that carried with it the idea of revolutionary struggle and human agency. A new and better society could not be wished or legislated into existence by benevolent doctrinaires, but had to await the advent of a politically conscious labor movement.

Years were to pass before Marx and Engels dropped the communist label and consented to having their cause described as "socialist." A politically oriented labor movement that was self-consciously socialist did emerge in Marx's name later in the nineteenth century, by which point the meaning of socialism had changed. Today, the word can mean a social or political doctrine or a political movement or system. In view of this latitude, it is not surprising that "socialism" in social-science literature often becomes a noun qualified by an adjective—as in utopian socialism, scientific socialism, state socialism, revolutionary socialism, evolutionary socialism, Fabian socialism, democratic socialism, parliamentary socialism; or as in actually existing socialism (until recently) or market socialism. Similarly, the adjective "socialist" can act as a pendant qualifying or characterizing a noun, as in socialist internationalism, socialist economics, socialist realism, or socialist feminism.

These junctures are not just convenient subdivisions, but successive attempts at spot-welding that can readily be arrayed in historical sequence. Utopian socialism dates from the 1830s, Fabian or evolutionary socialism from the late nineteenth and early twentieth centuries, Guild socialism from the period between the world wars. Socialist internationalism peaked, then bottomed out, in the period before 1914; socialist realism (like socialism in one country) belongs to the Stalinist period; socialist feminism to Western scholarship of a later date. Each instance of spot-welding affected the coordinates of its successors. Anarchism, syndicalism, and their offshoots (whether revolutionary or not) are kinds of socialism that were

53

elaborated in opposition to state socialism. Engels contrasted scientific with utopian socialism. Lenin defined Bolshevism, then communism as he understood the term, against the parliamentary, reformist socialism of the pre-1914 German SPD (and by extension the Second International). His successors proceeded to counterpose Soviet socialism in one country against the socialist internationalism that the First and Second Internationals had espoused.

All in all, it is not the tidiest of pictures. But there is a patterning to the galaxy, with Marxism as its lode star. Leszek Kolakowski's ambitious survey, *Main Currents of Marxism* (Oxford, 1979) rightly calls attention to "the surprising diversity of views expressed by Marxists in regard to Marx's so-called historical determinism." What is "surprising," however, is not this diversity itself but Kolakowski's pontifical belief that he could "schematize with precision the trends of twentieth-century Marxism." Kolakowski's failure to attain the desired precision serves as a salutary warning to anyone attempting to characterize the broader and much more diverse terrain of socialism, of which Marxism—nineteenth- or twentieth-century Marxism—is itself but a "main current." Whether or not present-day anti-capitalist protesters would describe themselves as Marxists or socialists, and whether or not they are aware of their own ancestry, they have distinguished precursors. It has long been distressing to see the same tired labeling of Marx's thought as determinist and authoritarian by certain feminists, ecologists, radicals, community activists, and opponents of racism and imperialism—some of the very people who would have most to gain from a constructive, open-ended encounter with his real legacy. Jean-Paul Sartre commented that so many attempts to move beyond Marx end up occupying a position not ahead of but behind Marx. This admonition has not yet lost its pertinence or its poignancy.

The Public Sphere in the Era
of Anti-Capitalism
John Brady

At the risk of offending prose stylists, I'm starting this essay with a cliché. What's perhaps worse, I'm starting off with a cliché from Marx. I thus risk embodying the most hackneyed of leftist stereotypes: the Marx-quoting writer who, like some cook with a zealous affinity for one particular spice, liberally mixes Marx citations into his work to give it intellectual heft and improve its "redness," as it were. But in an essay about language, especially the language actors deploy in the public realm, the risks are worth it, I think, if only because they focus our attention on the importance of not only what we say, but how we say it.

So here's the cliché: "Men make their own history, but they do not make it just as they please; they do not make it under circumstances chosen by themselves, but under circumstances directly encountered, given, and transmitted from the past." The passage is from *The 18th Brumaire of Louis Bonaparte*, Marx's study of the coup d'état led by Napoleon Bonaparte. Oft cited, commentators take from the passage an insight about the structural constraints imposed on political action by the past and the relative freedom political actors do or do not have to move within these constraints.

A perfectly justifiable reading, to be sure. But commonly over-

55

looked is that this passage is part of a more detailed meditation about not only history, but also language and its relationship to realizing fully the political possibilities of the present. Marx goes on:

> The tradition of all the dead generations weighs like a nightmare on the brain of the living. And just when they seem engaged in revolutionizing themselves and things, in creating something new that never yet existed, precisely in such periods of revolutionary crisis they anxiously conjure up the spirits of the past to their service and borrow from them names, battle cries, and costumes in order to present the new scene of world history in this time-honored disguise and this borrowed language.

In the paragraphs that follow, similar references to language recur as Marx underlines the significance of the symbolic dimension of political struggle. Thus, the use of "Roman costume and . . . Roman phrases" by the leaders and masses of the French revolution helped them in "glorifying the new struggles . . . and of finding once more the spirit of revolution . . ." However inspiring such a move may be, the reliance on previously produced symbols brings with it certain dangers. Indeed, one of the ways in which the dead weigh upon the living, Marx suggests, is in the use of an antiquated political language to dress up struggles in the present. In deploying such language, the politicos of the present risk deluding themselves and, importantly, also their followers about the true nature of their movement. Taking political metaphors from ancient Rome, France's revolutionaries glorified their revolution to be sure, but they also "conceal[ed] from themselves the bourgeois limitations of the content of their struggles . . ." The working-class revolutionaries of the nineteenth century, Marx concludes, cannot give in to the temptation of such symbolic appropriation of the past. This revolution "cannot draw its poetry from the past, but only from the future."

In the *Brumaire's* opening pages, Marx reminds us that the question "How and what are we going to say?" is just as important as the more often posed "What is to be done?" Along with formulating the appropriate political strategy, any emancipatory social movement must also formulate a new language, one capable of expressing the sufferings and the deprivations, but also the hopes and desires that motivated the movement's adherents to cross the threshold of their private worlds and engage in collective action in the first place. In short, the movement needs a language for its content.

One of the sites for producing this political language is the public sphere, the network of political spaces in which citizens appear in order to raise new themes and concerns or to debate issues of common concern already raised by others. At present, one of the more significant developments in the public arena has been the anti-capitalist movement. The movement has thematized the underside of globalization, giving voice to the social costs and political injustices lurking just beneath the global market's glitzy veneer. This essay explores the political vocabulary the movement has deployed in its mobilization against global capitalism, searching it for traces of both borrowed language and future poetry.

The Public Sphere: Between Democracy and Domination

In the West, the public sphere arose in the wake of feudalism's decline. The emerging bourgeoisie, debating in coffeehouses and penning essays in literary and political journals, began to contest the authority of kings and princes to regulate social, economic, and political affairs without first hearing the voice of the "public." From the start, the public sphere has been a site of critique, reason, and solidarity. *Critique* in the sense that social movements have mobilized in public to cast a critical light on the illegitimate use of power by state actors, and later on the colonizing power of the market. *Reason* in the sense that the rational exchange of opinions, instead of the mobilization of prejudice or the frank assertion of power and status, has always been the ideal medium of communication in public debate. And finally, *solidarity* in the sense that through intervening in

57

the public sphere, previously excluded groups like workers, women, and minorities have been able to fashion strong political bonds as they pushed to democratize their societies.

But let's not paint too rosy a picture. The public sphere has been fragile, too. Although providing a space for the mobilization of democratic critique, the public sphere has also served as a platform on which the powerful have stood in order to manipulate popular opinion and conjure up the aura of legitimacy for their policies and political programs. They have exploited the public's accessibility to repress or at least marginalize opposition groups and emancipatory movements and stymie their attempts to democratize political debate. In these cases, ideological spectacle replaces rational critique as the medium of public communication. And instead of forging bonds of solidarity which can serve as the foundation for future collective action, the domination of the public sphere by special interests aims to produce political passivity and civic privatism among citizens.

In short, public politics have always swung between democracy and domination.

And it is no different now with anti-capitalism. The loose coalition of associations, affinity groups, revolutionary cells, unions, and civic and political organizations that together make up the anti-capitalist movement has accomplished a surprising amount considering the relatively short time it has been in the public eye. Capitalism's cantankerous *other,* the movement, not unlike capitalism itself, has been global, mobile, and spontaneous. Protesters have staged simultaneous demonstrations across the world, giving real meaning to the term "global public." They've hounded world leaders and the representatives of the status quo from one meeting to the next regardless of national borders, enlarging with mobile protest modernity's political space. And they've engaged in refreshing forms of creative, extemporaneous protest, reinvigorating the public sphere as a site of participatory politics, not managed political spin.

In performing this task, the movement has shaken the cultural edifice that has supported the neo-liberal revolution. On the one hand, the movement has articulated a meaningful cosmopolitanism. This is not the glib cosmopolitanism of consumer culture, the cosmopolitanism that celebrates global difference because it sells things faster. No, this is a global perspective more in the tradition of progressive internationalism, one that attempts to forge solidarity across the artificial boundaries of nationality in order to highlight the connections between Western consumption and Third World suffering.

And even more importantly, the movement has contested the hegemony of the market, thus denting neo-liberalism's ideological armor. As commentators have pointed out, neo-liberalism was unusual for a conservative movement. Instead of trying to preserve the past, it aggressively moved to revolutionize the present.[1] This has included re-naturalizing the market, that is, offering the market as the natural arbiter of not just economic relationships, but *all* social relationships. By giving voice to the obvious suffering and global inequities caused by the intensification of market relationships, the anti-capitalist movement has interrupted this ideological process.

In reaction to this activism, the state and other defenders of the capitalist status quo have not sat idly by. While surprised in Seattle, state actors have recovered quickly, moving not only to disrupt the protests, but to undermine the very possibility of protest by disrupting the organization and leadership structures of the various groups participating in direct action. Deploying the time-tested arsenal of spying, harassment, the exaggerated show of force, and the swinging baton, the police and the state have attempted to seal off access to the public sphere. As many in both the mainstream and independent press have rightly pointed out, these actions amount to the criminalization of free speech, the denial of rights, and the creation of a hostile, repressive political climate. We can add some-

59

thing more to this list: the erosion of political solidarity. Then, in undermining the public arena of free debate, the police and the courts also deny citizens access to the political solidarity that debate, discussion, and dissent produce. Like the others, this is a harm that tears at the fabric of democracy.

Throughout all of this, there has been no shortage of new words, concepts, and metaphors to describe the politics of anti-capitalism: global grassroots democracy, the perpetual protest machine, the rise of the multitude and the posse, a global carnival against capital, the convergence of an international social movement, a new world social alliance, and on and on. Indeed, so fast and furious has been the production of potential elements of anti-capitalism's political imaginary that some have worried whether it will at all be possible to form a coherent language of global democracy, one able to express the needs and desires of the globe's emerging citizenry. While certainly a concern, I am not sure that such diversity can be avoided at this particular developmental juncture in the movement's history. After all, the mobilization against global capital is still in its infancy. And while the idea of a cosmopolitan republic has long fascinated moderns, its possible institutional infrastructure exists, if at all, in only the barest of outlines. Indeed, the global anti-capitalist movement is less a movement, and more a loose collection of disparate groups who, in certain cases (unions and environmentalists spring most immediately to mind), have quite different agendas. They are acting in a political arena with no real center or structure. Given this protean, even contradictory state of affairs, it will take time for the movement to distill its myriad concerns into a focused collection of issues around which a political language of democratic anti-capitalism can crystallize. In the interim, expect symbolic inflation.

Thus, in the present fluid situation, I think it is more useful to explore the *terms* of anti-capitalism's symbolic/conceptual production. It is more fruitful to examine, in other words, the conceptual

60

frameworks and ideological assumptions that guide the left's construction of its political vocabulary. To what extent is this production burdened by questionable ideological inheritances? To what extent is it necessary to alter these frameworks and assumptions in order to avoid repeating some of the left's previous mistakes (i.e., anti-democratic sectarianism, elitist vanguardism, pseudo-revolutionary violence). It isn't only the right that can fall victim to the perils of traditionalism. The left, too, has not always found it easy to leave ossified concepts behind. As a result, it is worthwhile to explore whether—to return to Marx—the movement, as it finds its political voice, speaks in language borrowed from the past.

The Levers of Power

The suddenness with which the anti-capitalism movement emerged has been breathtaking. In the space of five short days in Seattle, the movement went from operating at the margins of the world's consciousness to *sitting-in* in its center. Demonstrating communicative savvy, the movement successfully negotiated the corporate mediasphere's rules to become an attention-grabbing political spectacle. But, of course, anti-capitalist activists have done more than create compelling visuals for the evening news. More importantly and more substantively, they have subjected global capitalism's political and economic elites, who for so long have acted without much resistance or even much attention, to the public's critical gaze. The demos stood up to the dominant. Much to the satisfaction of movement activists, the dominant have reacted in part by seemingly going on the defensive. They have shielded their meetings from anti-capitalist forces with lines of riot police, clouds of tear gas, miles of chain-link fences, even going so far as to meet in far-away locales beyond the protesters' reach.

Movement activists have read this defensiveness as a useful illustration of the anti-democratic, authoritarian face of the emerg-

61

ing global order. In this reading one hears echoes of earlier leftist critique. In the 1960s and 1970s, many on the left argued that protest, especially militant protest, forced the state to reveal its true violent character and, importantly, contributed to the popular mobilization against the state apparatus and capitalism. The purported link between protest, state authoritarianism, and popular mobilization is not at all obvious to me. Provoking state violence can just as easily lead to political resignation and fear among an emerging movement. But questionable logic aside, a revival of this earlier perspective is to my mind also problematic because it obscures another, more politically productive reading of elite reaction to anti-capitalism. In retreating behind the riot police and chain-link fences and into the Canadian wilderness, the representatives of global capital have exercised one of the oldest prerogatives of power: the privilege to ignore the powerless, or, in the case of the anti-capitalist movement, the relatively powerless. Given their superior political resources, it has always been possible for the powerful to insulate themselves from protest in the public sphere. It is no different now. Global political and economic elites surrounded themselves with riot police because they can, because that's power.

This suggests that the anti-capitalist movement cannot only rely on the streets and the power of popular mobilization in the public sphere to achieve its goals. It may be possible to combat capitalism by revealing its authoritarian soul. But more effective is subjecting it to democratic control. And here we must simply concede a central weakness of public politics. Effective as an arena for generating awareness and political influence, the public sphere is far removed from the actual levers of power and political decision-making—levers which control not only the decision to deploy riot police, but also control the policy decisions shaping the global and economic and political arena. The path to these levers travels through political parties, parliament, and the state administration. And this is the path the anti-capitalist left must follow.

I think it is fair to say that since the '60s, most of the radical democratic left's energy has been focused on the public sphere and civil society. There has been less of an effort to mobilize within the electoral arena. Up to this point, much of the current politics of anti-capitalism has replicated this pattern. Yet, if the second reading of the elite reaction to anti-capitalism is correct, the left cannot neglect political parties and electoral politics. After all, in modern democracies the will of the people is expressed most directly through elections. Electoral politics, of course, is slow, demands a longterm commitment, and often involves painful choices (just ask the German Greens). But it also confers political legitimacy on a movement's agenda and further exposes it to a wider audience of potential supporters. And electoral politics forces a movement to test its ideas before the court of critical public opinion, thereby giving it the opportunity to temper the more unworkable and outlandish elements of its agenda. Most importantly, if successful, an electoral strategy places a party and its supporters in a position to concretely wield power and make, not just influence, political decisions.

Fashioning a more just and equitable future is clearly a complex task. The anti-capitalist political response should reflect this complexity in part by expanding its conception of the legitimate arenas for political action. Entering the electoral arena, speaking the language of party politics, is one of the more obvious directions to move in this regard.

Democracy and Democrats

At the end of *Empire*, Michael Hardt and Antonio Negri draw a striking and evocative picture of the multitude, that dynamic mass of people that is simultaneously the product of Empire's economic and political forces and the collective political subject of this same Empire's possible transformation into a just and humane global order. Hardt and Negri by no means assume that such a transformation will be automatic: indeed, although hopeful, they note that any victory of the multitude will be the result of a long, bitter struggle. Part of theory's task at this historical juncture, Hardt and Negri argue, is to explore this struggle and reveal the conditions shaping the rise of this "new political subjectivity, [this] insurgent multitude against imperial power." The two authors take up this task with gusto. Not content to tinker with old concepts, gerry-rigging them to fit the imperial age, they search for a new theoretical language with which to capture the changes wrought by the latest incarnation of global capitalism. Such creativity and daring is refreshing. Yet with respect to the multitude and the political struggle to transform imperial capitalism, they make one serious mistake that the anti-capitalist movement cannot duplicate. They assume the multitude's democratic credentials. They take for granted that when the multitude mobilizes, it will do so on the side of enlightenment values and democratic justice.

The terrorist attacks of September 11, 2001 revealed many things. They demonstrated the ease with which the emerging discourse about global justice can be eclipsed by a discourse of much older provenance: the discourse of retribution, punishment, and military justice. Of more importance for the anti-capitalist movement, the attacks revealed what some activists were just beginning to recognize: the superficiality of the globe's democratic consciousness.[2] While before September 11 the talk of a global grassroots democracy seemed rather premature, if only because the movement was so new, such talk now seems downright utopian because there seem to be so few progressive democrats the world over.

In America and across the West, popular sentiment has been quickly and successfully diverted away from a critical engagement with the events, and mobilized instead for the Bush administration's militarized solution. Outside the West, the attacks re-introduced the world to the public sphere of the "Arab street," in which one of the louder voices communicates less through democratic demands for justice and global citizenship and more through the anti-modern, moralistic argot of religious fundamentalism.

From the left's response to the attacks, there seems to be little indication that this fact has been taken to heart. Instead of reflecting on what the attacks have revealed regarding the relative absence of a constituency supportive of a transformative project of global democracy, the left has fallen back on an older pattern of denouncing U.S. imperialism. This critique is justified, to be sure, but risks missing the larger picture. U.S. hegemony is a constant and will continue to be so for the foreseeable future. No doubt, it represents a real impediment to democratic progress. But so, too, does a lack of democrats. After all, democracy must be popular, although not necessarily populist, if it is to succeed, and democratic institutions need a democratic political culture in which to take root.

Taking this fact seriously necessitates a significant shift in the anti-capitalist project from one of critique to one of democratization. To this point, the anti-capitalist movement has communicated in the medium of critique, offering compelling indictments of sweatshop labor, global environmental destruction, world poverty, and now U.S. imperialism. The implicit claim has always been that in offering this critique, the movement speaks for the world's people, a people who share the movement's democratic aspirations. But in the wake of September 11, this claim seems questionable at least and hollow at worst. What has become apparent is the necessity of coupling critique with cultural production. The anti-capitalist movement faces the task of deepening the democratic consciousness across the globe so that it can cash in on its claim to represent the wider global citizenry. This demands communicating in a new medium: the medium of democratic values and norms. The cultivation of these values and norms is an enormous, but not impossible task. The left already possesses significant resources—its activist networks, its tradition of fostering popular participation—that can

65

help accomplish this. In today's world, it is now a matter of deploying these resources to cultivate an enduring commitment to democratic norms and values in the same creative, spontaneous manner the movement has used to construct its public sphere of anti-capitalist protest.

Democracy's Open Horizon

There are no formal requirements to enter the public sphere, no elections to be won, no degrees to attain before speaking. Money helps, of course, but a well-conceived protest or a well-organized campaign of consciousness-raising can offset some of the political advantages of wealth. Compared to other institutions in society—the state or parliament—the barriers to participation in the public sphere are low; it takes relatively little to garner publicity and recognition there. This accessibility is the public sphere's weakness and strength.

Weakness, because in the absence of high barriers to participation, it is just as likely that the powerful will enter the public arena as the powerless. Once there, they can deploy their superior resources to dominate debate and extract political loyalty and legitimacy from the citizenry. In such cases, the democratic norms we usually expect to govern political debate—equality, reciprocity, accountability, transparency—prove to be flimsy guards against political manipulation. Yet this absence is also a strength. It opens up a space for democratic agency and creativity. Like the powerful, the relatively powerless have the opportunity to organize and enter the public sphere where they can actualize the public's democratic potential by thematizing new issues and sensitizing their fellow citizens about pressing problems of common concern. Because there are few rules of behavior or pre-defined roles to play, these actors can and do realize this potential in a myriad of creative ways, from street theater to street parties to civil disobedience to direct action to public education campaigns to . . . the next innovation in popular politics.

As the anti-capitalist movement progresses and attempts to realize the regulative ideals of democratic participation and social justice in concrete policies and institutions, it needs to maintain horizons as open as those of the public sphere. This is necessary not just for strategic reasons—not only to give the movement maximum flexibility in order to adjust to new situations and changing political conditions. It is a demand of democracy itself.

At democracy's heart is the ideal of self-determination. The people should determine the laws and conditions that shape their collective lives. But this ideal tells us relatively little about how democratic politics should be organized. How, for example, should representation be organized in a democracy? The ideal of self-determination also tells us relatively little about the relationship between the democratic process and other political institutions such as rights and constitutional norms. To what extent must the democratic process be constrained by individual and human rights in order to ensure the fair and equal treatment of all people? How can we protect against the tyranny of the majority? These are fundamental questions that must be answered through deliberation and debate. So far, the anti-capitalist movement has done an admirable job publicizing the unfairness of global capitalism and the suffering it engenders. As the movement develops, it should work to create a similarly vibrant discourse about the possible institutional outlines of a future global democracy.

Because, after all, the whole world is watching. This chant, a favorite of social movements since television became the dominant medium of political communication, has, of course, been applied to the police and other detachments of the state apparatus in an effort to remind them that their brutal tactics will not go unobserved. But the chant's sentiment applies directly to the anti-capitalist movement as well. Certainly one of the worst inheritances of the left tra-

67

dition has been the tendency of political radicals to believe that they possess the sole authoritative conception of the end of democratic politics. The audience observing the police also observes the anti-capitalist protesters, watching for an indication of whether this new generation of leftists have shaken off their tradition's doctrinaire past, watching to see if the movement is something they wish to support or even to join, watching to see if the movement can include their needs and concerns. By self-consciously maintaining open horizons with regard to its issue agenda and its conception of democracy, the anti-capitalist movement can demonstrate its attractiveness as an emancipatory political project.

★ ★ ★

In anticipating the language of the workers' revolution he never lived to see, Marx argued that unlike past revolutions, this revolution's content must go "beyond the phrase." This is a rather cryptic remark. Marx seemed to suggest that the workers' revolution will be so radical, so total, and so unique, or, in other words, so modern, that it will exhaust the expressive power of society's existing stock of metaphors, images, and concepts used to describe its political life. Although Marx didn't explicitly say so, this would demand that society develop a new language with which to capture the essence of the revolution and its results.

With over a century's worth of hindsight, we can remark with both irony and sadness that it has been capitalism, and neither the workers' nor any other social movement, that has more often than not revolutionized society's content beyond the phrase. The capitalist mode of production has produced both affluence and suffering to degrees that defy categorization. It has torn apart the fabric of countless communities and traditional ways of life in modes that strain our ability to capture symbolically the ensuing loss and absence. And it continues to push the calculus of profit maximization into areas of human life and experience at a dizzying pace. We struggle even now to describe these developments, as evidenced most simply by our inability to find a term to characterize the present era. Globalization? Neo-liberalism? Empire? The End of History, or, simply, Capitalism as Usual? In a tangible way, we lack the words to express the reality of our situation.

It is also with hindsight that we can question Marx's faith in total revolution. But this does not entail giving up his hope in a more democratic future. After all, the history of modernity has not simply been the history of capitalist victory. It has been punctuated, too, by significant victories on the part of social movements, victories that have realized modernity's own potential for increased political freedom and social justice. And so with Marx, we should continue to hope for and organize toward the moment when the demos can once again gain power over the phrase and content of social progress.

Endnotes

1. Eric Hobsbawm with Antonio Polito, *On the Edge of the New Century* (New York: The New Press, 2000), 97.

2. See Aiden Enns's brief article about the evolution of the indymedia network, "Indy Nation: the Whole World is Watching—Really," in *Adbusters* 38 (Nov/Dec 2001).

Interview with Slavoj Zizek
Doug Henwood, with Joel Schalit
Introduction by Charlie Bertsch

It's hard to become a superstar in the world of scholarly publishing. Most of the people who can read its products can also write them. To stand out in a crowd this smart requires both luck and perseverance. Slavoj Zizek has demonstrated plenty of both. When he first burst onto the American intellectual scene at the end of the 1980s, his "obscure" origins proved a perfect marketing tool. When Yugoslavia started to break up in 1990 in the aftermath of the Cold War, pristine Slovenia was the first of its republics to declare independence. As one of Slovenia's leading thinkers, Zizek basked in an aura of novelty that had yet to be overshadowed by the realization that independence movements always have a dark side. We were excited to be witnessing the rebirth of "nations" that had disappeared into Germany, the Soviet Union, or, in the case of Slovenia, first the Austro-Hungarian empire and then Yugoslavia. Remaking our global map filled us with hope for the future.

A decade later, we have seen how quickly that hope turned into despair. But Zizek's star hasn't dimmed. If anything, it has grown brighter. For anyone who has tired of the dumbing down of mainstream political discourse in the West, who wants to critique global capitalism without falling back on faded Marxist slogans,

Zizek's work flashes the promise of something better. From his groundbreaking 1989 book *The Sublime Object of Ideology* to his trenchant 1999 critique of Western governments' intervention in the former Yugoslavia in NATO as *the Left Hand of God?*, Zizek has never failed to stimulate thinking. As Zizek himself suggests in this interview, philosophy helps us not by "purifying" our thought, but by making it more complex.

What really sets Zizek apart from other major scholars is his willingness to take risks. If you were to read all of his books in rapid succession, you would find that they sometimes contradict one another. But you would also see how the tension between them reflects Zizek's real purpose: to allow us see the world with fresh eyes. He roots around in the realm of ideas looking for whatever will prove useful. It doesn't matter if his findings come from different intellectual traditions, or if they are, in some sense, philosophically incompatible—Zizek forces them to collaborate. Marx, Freud, Hegel, Kant, Lacan . . . and Alfred Hitchcock, David Lynch, and the Slovenian electronic agit-prop band Laibach all come together in a delightful mix. It's one thing to illuminate contemporary political concerns with the help of dense philosophical points; it's another entirely to make that insight enjoyable to read.

Left Business Observer editor and *Wall Street* author Doug Henwood talked with Zizek prior to the September 11 terrorist attack on the Pentagon and World Trade Center, with a small number of additional questions not long thereafter. In the days following the attack, Zizek's take on its significance—put forth in an incredibly moving essay titled "Welcome to the Desert of the Real"—circulated on email lists worldwide. Unlike the vast majority of commentators, Zizek was not content to express disbelief and outrage. His words offered an antidote to the mindless drivel on the major networks, CNN, and Fox News. Reflecting on the many "previews" of the tragedy in American movies, Zizek refused to blunt his critical edge.

71

September 2001

DH: In general, anarchism plays a big role in American radical politics and countercultures. Do you have any thoughts on this influence?

SZ: I certainly can understand where the appeal of anarchism lies. Even though I am quite aware of the contradictory and ambiguous nature of Marx's relationship with anarchism, Marx was right when he drew attention to how anarchists who preach "no state, no power" in order to realize their goals usually form their own society which obeys the most authoritarian rules. My first problem with anarchism is always, "Yeah, I agree with your goals, but tell me how you are organized." For me, the tragedy of anarchism is that you end up having an authoritarian secret society trying to achieve anarchist goals. The second point is that I have problems with how anarchism is appropriate to today's problems. I think if anything, we need more global organization. I think that the left should disrupt this equation that more global organization means more totalitarian control.

DH: When you speak of a global organization, are you thinking of some kind of global state, or do you have non-state organizations in mind?

SZ: I don't have any prejudices here whatsoever. For example, a lot of left-wingers dismissed talk of universal human rights as just another tool of American imperialism, to exert pressure on Third World countries or other countries America doesn't like, so it can bomb them. But it's not that simple. As we all know, following the same logic, Pinochet was arrested. Even if he was set free, this provoked a tremendous psychological change in Chile. When he left Chile, he was a universally feared, gray eminence. He returned as an old man whom nobody was afraid of. So, instead of dismissing the rules, it's well worth it to play the game. One should at least strategically support the idea of some kind of international court and then try to put it to a more progressive use.

America is already concerned about this. A few months ago, when the Senate was still under Republican control, it adopted a measure prohibiting any international court from having any jurisdiction over American citizens. You know they weren't talking about some Third World anti-imperialist court. They were talking about the Hague court, which is dominated by Western Europeans. The same goes for many of these international agencies. I think we should take it all. If it's outside the domain of state power, okay. I think the left should overcome this primordial fear of state power, that because it's some form of control, it's bad.

DH: You describe the internal structure of anarchist groups as being authoritarian. Yet, the model popular with younger activists today is explicitly anti-hierarchical and consensus-oriented. Do you think there's something furtively authoritarian about such apparently freewheeling structures?

SZ: Absolutely. And I'm not bluffing here; I'm talking from personal experience. Maybe my experience is too narrow, but it's not limited to some mysterious Balkan region. I have contacts in England, France, Germany, and more—and all the time, beneath the mask of this consensus, there was one person accepted by some unwritten rules as the secret master. The totalitarianism was absolute in the sense that people pretended that they were equal, but they all obeyed him. The catch was that it was prohibited to state clearly that he was the boss. You had to fake some kind of equality. The real state of affairs couldn't be articulated. Which is why I'm deeply distrustful of this "let's just coordinate this in an egalitarian fashion." I'm more of a pessimist. In order to safeguard this equality, you have a more sinister figure of the master, who puts pressure on the others to safeguard the purity of the non-hierarchic princi-

73

ple. This is not just theory. I would be happy to hear of groups that are not caught in this strange dialectic.

DH: We've seen over the last few years the growth of a broad anti-capitalist movement, a lot of it organized according to anarchist principles. Do you think these demonstrations are a sign of any left revival, a new movement?

SZ: Mixed. Not in the sense of being partly good and partly bad, but because the situation is undecided—maybe even undecidable. What will come out of the Seattle movement is the terrain of the struggle. I think it is *precisely now*—after the attack on the World Trade Center—that the "Seattle" task will regain its full urgency. After a period of enthusiasm for retaliation, there will be a new (ideological) depression, and *that* point will be our chance!

DH: Much of this will depend on progressives' ability to get the word out.

SZ: I'm well aware of the big media's censorship here. Even in the European big media, which are supposed to be more open, you will never see a detailed examination of the movement's agenda. You get some ominous things. There is something dark about it. According to the normal rules of the liberal game, you would expect some of these people to be invited on some TV talk shows, confronted with their adversaries, placed in a vigorous polemic—but no. Their agenda is ignored. Usually they're mocked as advocating some old-fashioned left-wing politics or some particularism, like saving local conditions against globalism. My conclusion is that the big powers must be at least in some kind of a panic. This is a good sign.

DH: But much of the movement has no explicit agenda to offer. Why is the elite in such a panic?

SZ: It's not like these are some kind of old-fashioned left-wing idiots, or some kind of local traditionalists. I am well aware that Seattle, etc. is still a movement finding its shape, but I think it has potential. Even though there is no explicit agenda, there is a kind of outlook reproaching *this* globalization for being too exclusionary, not a true globalization but only a capitalist globalization.

DH: At the same time this movement was growing, there was a string of electoral victories for the right—Silvio Berlusconi's Forza Italia in Italy, Jorg Haider's Freedom Party in Austria, our own Bush. What do you make of these?

SZ: They're not to be underestimated. I'll put it in my old-fashioned Stalinist terms: there are two deviations to be avoided here, left and right. The right-wing deviation is to fully endorse their liberal opponents, to say, "Okay, we have our problems with Gore or Blair but they're basically our guys, and we should support them against the true right." We should also avoid the opposite mistake, which is to say that they're all the same, that it doesn't really matter if it's Gore or Bush. From this position, it's only one step to the position that says, "So it's even better we have Bush, because then we see the true enemy."

We should steer the middle course: while maintaining our critical distance toward the moderate left, one shouldn't be afraid when certain issues are at stake, to support them. What is at stake is the following: it looked in the 1990s that after the disintegration of socialism, the Third Way left represents the universal interests of capital as such (to put it in the old Marxist way), and the right-wing parties represent only particular interests. In the U.S., the Republicans target certain types of rich people, and even certain parts of the lower classes—flirting with the Moral Majority, for example. The problem is that right-wing politicians such as Austria's Haider are playing the global game. Not only do we have a Third Way left, we now have a Third Way right, too, which tries

75

to combine unrestrained global capitalism with a more conservative cultural politics.

Here is where I see the longterm danger of these right wingers. I think that sooner or later the existing power structure will be forced more and more to directly violate its own formal democratic rules. *[Ed. Note: Such as the new emergency powers granted to the U.S. government for domestic surveillance purposes after the WTC/Pentagon attacks, which suspend habeas corpus rights for immigrants, and allow security services to monitor telecommunications activities and student and bank records without permission from a judge.]* In Europe, the tendency behind all these movements, like Holocaust revisionism and so on, is an attempt to dismantle the post–World War II ideological consensus around anti–fascism, with a social solidarity built around the welfare state. It's an open question as to what will replace it.

DH: What about the transition from Clinton to Bush? What's significant about this from your point of view?

SZ: The sad thing is that Clinton left behind him a devastated, disoriented Democratic Party. There are people who say that his departure leaves some room for a resurgence of the party's left wing, but that will be difficult. The true problem of Clinton is his legacy, which is that there is none. He didn't survive as a movement, in the sense that he left a longterm imprint. He was just an opportunist and now he's simply out. He didn't emerge as a figure like Thatcher or Reagan who left a certain legacy. Okay, you can say that he left a legacy of compromise or triangulation, but the big failure is at this ideological level. He didn't leave behind a platform with which the moderate liberals could identify.

DH: A lot of readers of American underground zines like *Punk Planet* read Noam Chomsky and Howard Zinn, and the publications coming out of small anarchist presses. What would they get from reading your work that they might be missing?

SZ: Martin Heidegger said that philosophy doesn't make things easier, it makes them harder and more complicated. What they can learn is the ambiguity of so many situations, in the sense that whenever we are presented by the big media with a simple opposition, like multicultural tolerance vs. ethnic fundamentalism, the opposition is never so clear-cut. The idea is that things are always more complex. For example, multiculturalist tolerance, or at least a certain type of it, generates or involves a much deeper racism. As a rule, this type of tolerance relies on the distinction between us, multiculturalists, and intolerant ethnic others, with the paradoxical result that anti-racism itself is used to dismiss, *in a racist way,* the other as a racist. Not to mention the fact that this kind of "tolerance" is as a rule patronizing. Its respect for the other cannot but remind us of the respect for naïve children's beliefs: We leave them in their blessed ignorance so as not to hurt them . . .

Or take Chomsky. There are two problematic features in his work—though it goes without saying that I admire him very much. With all his criticism of the U.S., Chomsky retains a certain commitment to what is the most elemental ingredient of American ideology, individualism, a fundamental belief that America is the land of free individuals, and so on. So in that way he is deeply and problematically American.

DH: Chomsky and some others seem to think that if we just got the facts out there, things would almost take care of themselves. Why is this wrong? Why aren't "the facts" enough?

SZ: Let me give you a very naïve answer. I think that basically the facts are already known. Let's take Chomsky's analyses of how the CIA intervened in Nicaragua. Okay, he provides a lot of details, yes, but did I learn anything fundamentally new? It's exactly what I'd expected—the CIA was playing a very dirty game. Of course it's more convincing if you learn the dirty details. But I don't think that we really learned anything dramatically new there. I don't think that merely "knowing the facts" can really change people's perceptions.

To put it another way: Chomsky's own position on Kosovo, on the Yugoslav war, shows some of his limitations, because of a lack of a proper historical context. With all his facts, he got the picture wrong. As far as I can judge, Chomsky bought a certain narrative—that we shouldn't put all the blame on Milosevic, that all parties were more or less to blame, and the West supported or incited this explosion because of its own geopolitical goals. All are not the same. I'm not saying that the Serbs are guilty. I just repeat my old point that Yugoslavia was not over with the secession of Slovenia. It was over the moment Milosevic took over Serbia. This triggered a totally different dynamic. It is also not true that the disintegration of Yugoslavia was supported by the West. On the contrary, the West exerted enormous pressure, at least until 1991, for ethnic groups to remain in Yugoslavia. I saw former Secretary of State James Baker on Yugoslav TV supporting the Yugoslav army's attempts to prevent Slovenia's secession.

DH: Years ago, you were involved with the band Laibach and its proto-state, NSK (*Neue Slovenische Kunst*). Why did you get involved with them?

SZ: The reason I liked them at a certain moment (which was during the last years of "really existing socialism") was that they were a third voice, a disturbing voice, not fitting into the opposition between the old communists and the new liberal democrats. For me, their message was that there were fundamental mechanisms of power which we couldn't get rid of with the simple passage to democracy. This was a disturbing message, which was why they got on everyone's nerves. This was no abstract theoretical construct. In the late 1980s, people got this message instinctively—which is why Laibach was more strongly repressed by the new democratic, nationalist powers in Slovenia than previously by the communists. In the early 1980s, they had some trouble with the communists, but from the mid-1980s onward, they didn't have any trouble. Then they did again with the transition of power. With their mocking rituals of totalitarian power, they transmitted a certain message about the functioning of power that didn't fit the naïve belief in liberal democracy. The miracle was that they did it through certain stage rituals. Later, they tried to change their image (to put it in marketing terms) and they failed.

DH: You talk and write a lot about popular culture, particularly movies. How does your thinking about pop culture relate to your thinking about politics?

SZ: We can no longer, as we did in the good old times (if they were really good), oppose the economy and culture. They are so intertwined not only through the commercialization of culture but also the culturalization of the economy. Political analysis today cannot bypass mass culture. It's there that what we are ideologically is fought for, is staged. For me, the basic ideological attitudes are not found in big-picture philosophical statements, but instead in lifeworld practices—how do you behave, how do you react—which aren't just reflected in mass culture, but which are, up to a point, even generated in mass culture. Mass culture is the central ideological battlefield today.

79

DH: You have recently been speaking about reviving Lenin. To a lot of politically active young people, Lenin is a devil figure. What do you find valuable in Lenin, or the Leninist tradition?

SZ: I am careful to speak about not repeating Lenin. I am not an idiot. It wouldn't mean anything to return to the Leninist working-class party today. What interests me about Lenin is precisely that after World War I broke out in 1914, he found himself in a total deadlock. Everything went wrong. All of the social democratic parties outside Russia supported the war, and there was a mass outbreak of patriotism. After this, Lenin had to think about how to reinvent a radical, revolutionary politics in this situation of total breakdown. This is the Lenin I like. Lenin is usually presented as a great follower of Marx, but it is impressive how often you read in Lenin the ironic line that "about this there isn't anything in Marx." It's this purely negative parallel. Just as Lenin was forced to reformulate the entire socialist project, we are now in a similar situation. What Lenin did, we should do today, at an even more radical level.

For example, at the most elementary level, Marx's concept of exploitation presupposes a certain labor theory of value. If you take this away from Marx, the whole edifice of his model disintegrates. What do we do with this today, given the importance of intellectual labor? Both standard solutions are too easy—to claim that there is still real physical production going on in the Third World, or that today's programmers are a new proletariat. Like Lenin, we're deadlocked. What I like in Lenin is precisely what scares people about him—the ruthless will to discard all prejudices. Why not violence? Horrible as it may sound, I think it's a useful antidote to all the aseptic, frustrating, politically correct pacifism.

Let's take the campaign against smoking in the U.S. I think this is a much more suspicious phenomenon than it appears to be. First, deeply inscribed into it is an idea of absolute narcissism, that whenever you are in contact with another person, somehow he or she can infect you. Second, there is an envy of the intense enjoyment of smoking. There is a certain vision of subjectivity, a certain falseness in liberalism, that comes down to "I want to be left alone by others, I don't want to get too close to the others." Also, in this fight against the tobacco companies, you have a certain kind of politically correct yuppie who is doing very well financially, but who wants to retain a certain anti-capitalist aura. What better way to focus on the obvious bad guy, Big Tobacco. It functions as an ersatz enemy. You can still claim your stock market gains, but you can say, "I'm against tobacco companies." Now I should make it clear that I don't smoke. And I don't like tobacco companies. But this obsession with the danger of smoking isn't as simple as it might appear.

DH: You've also left some of your readers scratching their heads over the positive things you've been writing about Christianity lately. What is it in Christianity you find worthy?

SZ: I'm tempted to say, "the Leninist part." I am a fighting atheist. My leanings are almost Maoist. Churches should be turned into grain silos or palaces of culture. What Christianity did, in a religiously mystified version, is give us the idea of rebirth. Against the pagan notion of destiny, Christianity offered the possibility of a radical opening, that we can find a zero point and clear the table. It introduced a new kind of ethics, not that each of us should do our duty according to our place in society—a good King should be a good King, a good servant a good servant but instead, that irrespective of who I am, I have direct access to universality. This is explosive. What interests me is only this dimension. Of course, it was later taken over by secular philosophers and progressive thinkers. I am not in any way defending the Church as an institution, not even in a minimal way.

Let's take Judith Butler, and her thesis that our sexual identity isn't part of our nature, but is socially constructed. Such a statement, such a feminist position, could only occur against a background of a Christian space.

DH: Several times you've used the word "universalism." For trafficking in such concepts, people you'd identify as forces of political

81

correctness have indicted you for Eurocentrism. You've even written a radical leftist plea for Eurocentrism. How do you respond to the PC camp's charges against you?

SZ: I think that we should accept that universalism is a Eurocentrist notion. This may sound racist, but I don't think it is. Even when Third World countries appeal to freedom and democracy, when they formulate their struggle against European imperialism, they are at a more radical level endorsing the European premise of universalism. You may remember that in the struggle against apartheid in South Africa, the ANC always appealed to universal Enlightenment values, and it was Buthelezi, the regime's black supporter in the pay of the CIA, who appealed to special African values.

A more crucial point is that my opponent here is the widely accepted position that we should leave behind the quest for universal truth—that what we have instead are just different narratives about who we are, the stories we tell about ourselves. So, in that view, the highest ethical injunction is to respect the other story. All the stories should be told; each ethnic, political, or sexual group should be given the right to tell its story, as if this kind of tolerance toward the plurality of stories with no universal truth value is the ultimate ethical horizon.

I oppose this radically. This ethics of storytelling is usually accompanied by a right to narrate, as if the highest act you can do today is to narrate your own story, as if only a black lesbian mother can know what it's like to be a black lesbian mother, and so on. This may sound very emancipatory, but the moment we accept this logic, we enter a kind of apartheid. In a situation of social domination, all narratives are not the same. For example, in Germany in the 1930s, the narrative of the Jews wasn't just one among many. This was the narrative that explained the truth about the entire situation. Or today, take the gay struggle. It's not enough for gays to say, "We want our story to be heard." No, the gay narrative must contain a universal dimension, in the sense that their implicit claim must be that what happens to us is not something that concerns only us. What is happening to us is a symptom or signal that tells us something about what's wrong with the entirety of society today. We have to insist on this universal dimension.

The question is whether Europe will use the second chance it now has for the civilizing of the earth, for breaking out of the desperate circulatory process of imperialistic power politics.

. . . Europe must use one of its strengths, namely its potential for self-criticism, its power of self-transformation, in order to relativize itself far more radically vis a vis the others, the strangers, the misunderstood. That's the opposite of Eurocentrism. But we can overcome Eurocentrism only out of the better spirit of Europe.

—Jürgen Habermas, *The Past as Future*

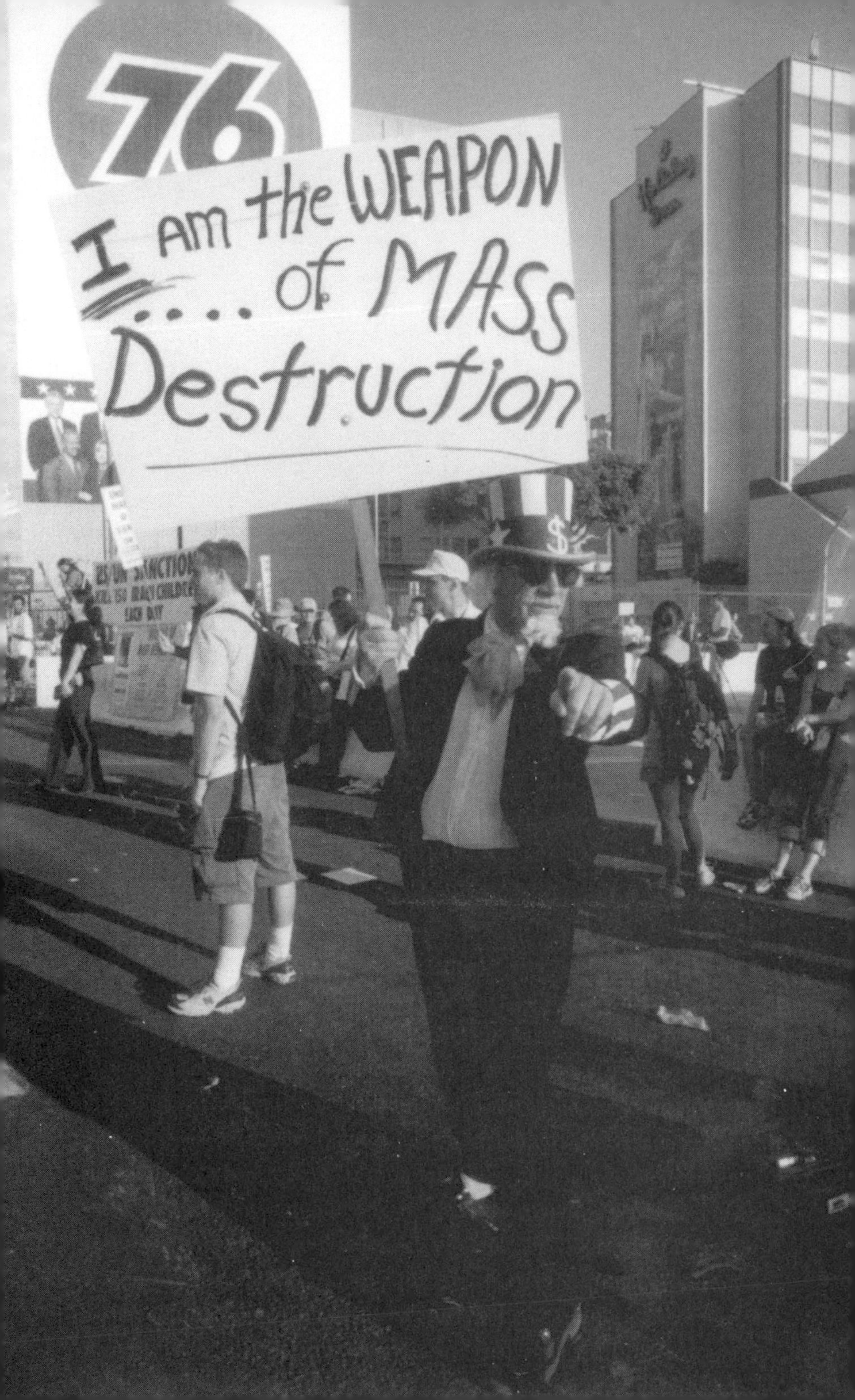
76
I am the WEAPON
.... of MASS
Destruction

Done By the Forces of Nature

The Unknown Icon
Naomi Klein

This article originally appeared in The Guardian *(UK), March 3, 2001.*

I've never been to Chiapas. I've never made the pilgrimage to the Lacandon jungle. I've never sat in the mud and the mist in La Realidad. I've never begged, pleaded, or posed to get an audience with Subcomandante Marcos, the masked man, the face of Mexico's Zapatista National Liberation Army. I know people who have. Lots of them. In 1994, the summer after the Zapatista rebellion, caravans to Chiapas were all the rage in North American activist circles: friends got together and raised money for secondhand vans, filled them with supplies, then drove south to San Cristobal de las Casas and left the vans behind. I didn't pay much attention at the time. Back then, Zapatista-mania looked suspiciously like just another cause for guilty lefties with a Latin American fetish: another Marxist rebel army, another macho leader, another chance to go south and buy colourful textiles. Hadn't we heard this story before? Hadn't it ended badly? Last week, there was another caravan in Chiapas. But this was different. First, it didn't end in San Cristobal de las Casas; it started there, and is now crisscrossing the Mexican countryside before the planned grand entrance into Mexico City on March 11. The caravan, nicknamed the "Zapatour" by the Mexican press, is being led by the council of twenty-four Zapatista commanders, in full uniform and masks (though no weapons), including Subcomandante Marcos himself. Because it is unheard of for the Zapatista command to travel outside Chiapas (and there are vigilantes threatening deadly duels with Marcos all along the way), the Zapatour needs tight security. The Red Cross turned down the job, so protection is being provided by several hundred anarchists from Italy who call themselves *Ya Basta!* (meaning "Enough is enough!"), after the defiant phrase used in the Zapatistas' declaration of war. Hundreds of students, small farmers, and activists have joined the roadshow, and thousands greet them along the way. Unlike those early visitors to Chiapas, these travellers say they are there not because they are "in solidarity" with the Zapatistas, but because they are Zapatistas. Some even claim to be Subcomandante Marcos himself—they say we are all Marcos.

Perhaps only a man who never takes off his mask, who hides his real name, could lead this caravan of renegades, rebels, loners, and anarchists on this two-week trek. These are people who have learned to steer clear of charismatic leaders with one-size-fits-all ideologies. These aren't party loyalists; these are members of groups that pride themselves on their autonomy and lack of hierarchy. Marcos— with his black wool mask, two eyes, and pipe—seems to be an anti-leader tailor-made for this suspicious, critical lot. Not only does he refuse to show his face, undercutting (and simultaneously augmenting) his own celebrity, but Marcos's story is of a man who came to his leadership not through swaggering certainty, but by coming to terms with political uncertainty, by learning to follow.

Though there is no confirmation of Marcos's real identity, the most repeated legend that surrounds him goes like this: An urban Marxist intellectual and activist, Marcos was wanted by the state and was no longer safe in the cities. He fled to the mountains of Chiapas in southeast Mexico to convert the poor indigenous masses to the cause of armed proletarian revolution against the bourgeoisie. He said the workers of the world must unite, and the Mayans just stared at him. They said they weren't workers and, besides, land wasn't property but the heart of their community. Having failed as a Marxist missionary, Marcos immersed himself in Mayan culture. The more he learned, the less he knew. Out of this process, a new kind of army emerged, the EZLN, the Zapatista National Liberation Army, which was not controlled by an elite of guerrilla commanders but by the communities themselves, through clandestine councils and open assemblies. "Our army," says Marcos, "became scandalously Indian." That meant that he wasn't a commander barking orders, but a subcomandante, a conduit for the will of the councils. His first words said in the new persona were: "Through me speaks the will of the Zapatista National Liberation Army." Further subjugating himself, Marcos says that he is not a leader to those who seek him out, but that his black mask is a mirror, reflecting each of their own struggles; that a Zapatista is anyone anywhere fighting injustice, that "We are you." He once said, "Marcos is gay in San Francisco, black in South Africa, an Asian in Europe, a Chicano in San Ysidro, an anarchist in Spain, a Palestinian in Israel, a Mayan Indian in the streets of San Cristobal, a Jew in Germany, a Gypsy in Poland, a Mohawk in Quebec, a pacifist in Bosnia, a single woman on the Metro at 10 p.m., a peasant without land, a gang member in the slums, an unemployed worker, an unhappy student, and, of course, a Zapatista in the mountains."

"This non-self," writes Juana Ponce de Leon, who has collected and edited Marcos's writings in *Our Word Is Our Weapon*, "makes it possible for Marcos to become the spokesperson for indigenous communities. He is transparent, and he is iconographic." Yet the paradox of Marcos and the Zapatistas is that, despite the masks, the non-selves, the mystery, their struggle is about the opposite of anonymity—it is about the right to be seen. When the Zapatistas took up arms and said *Ya Basta!* in 1994, it was a revolt against their

91

invisibility. Like so many others left behind by globalization, the Mayans of Chiapas had fallen off the economic map. "Below in the cities," the EZLN command stated, "we did not exist. Our lives were worth less than those of machines or animals. We were like stones, like weeds in the road. We were silenced. We were faceless." By arming and masking themselves, the Zapatistas explain, they weren't joining some Star Trek–like Borg universe of people without identities fighting in common cause; they were forcing the world to stop ignoring their plight, to see their long-neglected faces. The Zapatistas are "the voice that arms itself to be heard, the face that hides itself to be seen."

Meanwhile, Marcos himself—the supposed non-self, the conduit, the mirror—writes in a tone so personal and poetic, so completely and unmistakably his own, that he is constantly undercutting and subverting the anonymity that comes from his mask and pseudonym. It is often said that the Zapatistas' best weapon was the Internet, but their true secret weapon was their language. In *Our Word Is Our Weapon*, we read manifestos and war cries that are also poems, legends, and riffs. A character emerges behind the mask, a personality. Marcos is a revolutionary who writes long meditative letters to Uruguayan poet Eduardo Galeano about the meaning of silence; who describes colonialism as a series of "bad jokes badly told," who quotes Lewis Carroll, Shakespeare, and Borges. Who writes that resistance takes place "any time any man or woman rebels to the point of tearing off the clothes resignation has woven for them and cynicism has dyed gray." And who then sends whimsical mock telegrams to all of "civil society": "THE GRAYS HOPE TO WIN. STOP. RAINBOW NEEDED URGENTLY."

Marcos seems keenly aware of himself as an irresistible romantic hero. He's an Isabelle Allende character in reverse—not the poor peasant who becomes a Marxist rebel, but a Marxist intellectual who becomes a poor peasant. He plays with this character, flirts with it, saying that he can't reveal his real identity for fear of disappointing his female fans. Perhaps wary that this game was getting a little out of hand, Marcos chose the eve of Valentine's Day this year to break the bad news: he is married, and deeply in love, and her name is *La Mar* ("the Sea"—what else would it be?).

This is a movement keenly aware of the power of words and symbols. Rumor has it that when the twenty-four-strong Zapatista command arrive in Mexico City, they hope to ride downtown on horseback, like indigenous conquistadors. There will be a massive rally, and concerts, and they will ask to address the Congress. There, they will demand that legislators pass an Indigenous Bill of Rights, a law that came out of the Zapatistas' failed peace negotiations with Mexican President Ernesto Zedillo, who was defeated in recent elections. Vicente Fox, his successor who famously bragged during the campaign that he could solve the Zapatista problem "in fifteen minutes," has asked for a meeting with Marcos, but has so far been refused—not until the bill is passed, says Marcos, not until more army troops are withdrawn from Zapatista territory, not until all Zapatista political prisoners are freed. Marcos has been betrayed before, and accuses Fox of staging a "simulation of peace" before the peace negotiations have even restarted. What is clear in all this jostling for position is that something radical has changed in the balance of power in Mexico. The Zapatistas are calling the shots now—which is significant, because they have lost the habit of firing shots. What started as a small, armed insurrection has in the past seven years turned into what now looks more like a peaceful and mass movement. It has helped topple the corrupt seventy-one-year reign of the Institutional Revolutionary Party, and has placed indigenous rights at the center of the Mexican political agenda.

Which is why Marcos gets angry when he is looked on as just another guy with a gun: "What other guerrilla force has convened a national democratic movement, civic and peaceful, so that armed struggle becomes useless?" he asks. "What other guerrilla force asks

93

its bases of support about what it should do before doing it? What other guerrilla force has struggled to achieve a democratic space and not take power? What other guerrilla force has relied more on words than on bullets?"

The Zapatistas chose January 1, 1994, the day the North American Free Trade Agreement (NAFTA) came into force, to "declare war" on the Mexican army, launching an insurrection and briefly taking control of the city of San Cristobal de las Casas and five Chiapas towns. They sent out a communiqué explaining that NAFTA, which banned subsidies to indigenous farm cooperatives, would be a "summary execution" for four million indigenous Mexicans in Chiapas, the country's poorest province.

Nearly one hundred years had passed since the Mexican revolution promised to return indigenous land through agrarian reform; after all these broken promises, Nafta was simply the last straw. "We are the product of five hundred years of struggle . . . but today we say *Ya Basta!* Enough is enough." The rebels called themselves Zapatistas, taking their name from Emiliano Zapata, the slain hero of the 1910 revolution who, along with a rag-tag peasant army, fought for lands held by large landowners to be returned to indigenous and peasant farmers.

In the seven years since, the Zapatistas have come to represent two forces at once: first, rebels struggling against grinding poverty and humiliation in the mountains of Chiapas, and, on top of this, theorists of a new movement, another way to think about power, resistance, and globalization. This theory—*Zapatismo*—not only turns classic guerrilla tactics inside out, but much of left-wing politics on its head.

I may never have made the pilgrimage to Chiapas, but I have watched the Zapatistas' ideas spread through activist circles, passed along second- and third-hand: a phrase, a way to run a meeting, a metaphor that twists your brain around. Unlike classic revolutionaries, who preach through bullhorns and from pulpits, Marcos has

94

spread the Zapatista word through riddles. Revolutionaries who don't want power. People who must hide their faces to be seen. A world with many worlds in it.

A movement of one "no" and many "yeses."

These phrases seem simple at first, but don't be fooled. They have a way of burrowing into the consciousness, cropping up in strange places, being repeated until they take on this quality of truth—but not absolute truth: a truth, as the Zapatistas might say, with many truths in it. In Canada, where I'm from, indigenous uprising is always symbolized by a blockade: a physical barrier to stop the golf course from being built on a native burial site, to block the construction of a hydroelectric dam, or to keep an old-growth forest from being logged. The Zapatista uprising was a new way to protect land and culture: rather than locking out the world, the Zapatistas flung open the doors and invited the world inside. Chiapas was transformed, despite its poverty, despite being under constant military siege, into a global gathering place for activists, intellectuals, and indigenous groups.

From the first communiqué, the Zapatistas invited the international community "to watch over and regulate our battles." The summer after the uprising, they hosted a National Democratic Convention in the jungle; six thousand people attended, mostly from Mexico. In 1996, they hosted the first *Encuentro* (or meeting) for Humanity and Against Neo-Liberalism. Some three thousand activists travelled to Chiapas to meet with others from around the world.

Marcos himself is a one-man web: he is a compulsive communicator, constantly reaching out, drawing connections between different issues and struggles. His communiqués are filled with lists of groups that he imagines are Zapatista allies, small shopkeepers, retired people, and the disabled, as well as workers and campesinos. He writes to political prisoners Mumia Abu Jamal and Leonard Peltier. He is pen-pals with some of Latin America's best-known novelists. He writes letters addressed "to the people of world."

95

When the uprising began, the government attempted to play down the incident as a "local" problem, an ethnic dispute easily contained. The strategic victory of the Zapatistas was to change the terms: to insist that what was going on in Chiapas could not be written off as a narrow "ethnic" struggle, and that it was universal. They did this by clearly naming their enemy not only as the Mexican state but as the set of economic policies known as "neoliberalism." Marcos insisted that the poverty and desperation in Chiapas was simply a more advanced version of something happening all around the world. He pointed to the huge numbers of people who were being left behind by prosperity, whose land and work made that prosperity possible. "The new distribution of the world excludes 'minorities,'" Marcos has said. "The indigenous, youth, women, homosexuals, lesbians, people of color, immigrants, workers, peasants; the majority who make up the world basements are presented, for power, as disposable. The distribution of the world excludes the majorities."

The Zapatistas staged an open insurrection, one that anyone could join, as long as they thought of themselves as outsiders. By conservative estimates, there are now 45,000 Zapatista-related websites, based in twenty-six countries. Marcos's communiqués are available in at least fourteen languages. And then there is the Zapatista cottage industry: black T-shirts with red five-pointed stars, white T-shirts with EZLN printed in black. There are baseball hats, black EZLN ski masks, Mayan-made dolls and trucks. There are posters, including one of Comandante Ramona, the much loved EZLN matriarch, as the Mona Lisa.

It looked like fun, but it was also influential. Many who attended the first *"encuentros"* went on to play key roles in the protests against the World Trade Organization in Seattle and the World Bank and IMF in Washington, DC, arriving with a new taste for direct action, for collective decision-making and decentralized organizing. When the insurrection began, the Mexican military was

convinced it would be able to squash the Zapatistas' jungle uprising like a bug. It sent in heavy artillery, conducted air raids, mobilized thousands of soldiers. Only, instead of standing on a squashed
bug, the government found itself surrounded by a swarm of international activists buzzing around Chiapas. In a study commissioned
by the U.S. military from the RAND Corporation, the EZLN is
studied as "a new mode of conflict—'netwar'—in which the pro-
tagonists depend on using network forms of organization, doctrine,
strategy, and technology." This is dangerous, according to RAND,
because what starts as "a war of the flea" can quickly turn into "a
war of the swarm."

The ring around the rebels has not protected the Zapatistas
entirely. In December 1997, there was the brutal Acteal massacre in
which forty-five Zapatista supporters were killed, most of them
women and children. And the situation in Chiapas is still desperate,
with thousands displaced from their homes. But it is also true that
the situation would probably have been much worse, potentially
with far greater intervention from the U.S. military, had it not been
for this international swarm. The RAND Corporation study states
that the global activist attention arrived "during a period when the
United States may have been tacitly interested in seeing a forceful
crackdown on the rebels."

So it's worth asking: What are the ideas that proved so powerful that thousands have taken it upon themselves to disseminate
them around the world? A few years ago, the idea of the rebels travelling to Mexico City to address the Congress would have been
impossible to imagine. The prospect of masked guerrillas (even
masked guerrillas who have left their arms at home) entering a hall
of political power signals one thing: revolution. But Zapatistas aren't
interested in overthrowing the state or naming their leader, Marcos,
as president. If anything, they want less state power over their lives.
And, besides, Marcos says that as soon as peace has been negotiated
he will take off his mask and disappear.

97

What does it mean to be a revolutionary who is not trying to stage a revolution? This is one of the key Zapatista paradoxes. In one of his many communiqués, Marcos writes that "it is not necessary to conquer the world. It is sufficient to make it new." He adds: "Us. Today." What sets the Zapatistas apart from your average Marxist guerrilla insurgents is that their goal is not to win control, but to seize and build autonomous spaces where "democracy, liberty, and justice" can thrive.

Although the Zapatistas have articulated certain key goals of their resistance (control over land, direct political representation, and the right to protect their language and culture), they insist they are not interested in "the Revolution," but rather in "a revolution that makes revolution possible."

Marcos believes that what he has learned in Chiapas about non-hierarchical decision-making, decentralized organizing, and deep community democracy holds answers for the non-indigenous world as well—if only it were willing to listen. This is a kind of organizing that doesn't compartmentalize the community into workers, warriors, farmers, and students, but instead seeks to organize communities as a whole, across sectors and across generations, creating "social movements." For the Zapatistas, these autonomous zones aren't about isolationism or dropping out, '60s-style. Quite the opposite: Marcos is convinced that these free spaces, born of reclaimed land, communal agriculture, resistance to privatization, will eventually create counter-powers to the state simply by existing as alternatives.

This is the essence of Zapatismo, and explains much of its appeal: a global call to revolution that tells you not to wait for the revolution, only to stand where you stand, to fight with your own weapon. It could be a video camera, words, ideas, "hope"—all of these, Marcos has written, "are also weapons." It's a revolution in miniature that says, "Yes, you can try this at home." This organizing model has spread throughout Latin America, and the world. You can see it in the anarchist squats of Italy (called "social centers") and in the Landless Peasants' Movement of Brazil, which seizes tracts of unused farmland and employs them for sustainable agriculture, markets, and schools under the slogan *"Ocupar, Resistir, Producir"* (Occupy, Resist, Produce). These same ideas were forcefully expressed by the students of the National Autonomous University of Mexico during last year's long and militant occupation of their campus. Zapata once said the land belongs to those who work it; their banners blared, "WE SAY THAT THE UNIVERSITY BELONGS TO THOSE WHO STUDY IN IT."

Zapatismo, according to Marcos, is not a doctrine but "an intuition." And he is consciously trying to appeal to something that exists outside the intellect, something uncynical in us, that he found in himself in the mountains of Chiapas: wonder, a suspension of disbelief, myth, and magic. So, instead of issuing manifestos, he tries to riff his way into this place with long meditations, flights of fancy, dreaming out loud. This is, in a way, a kind of intellectual guerrilla warfare: Marcos won't meet his opponents head on, but instead surrounds them from all directions.

A month ago, I got an email from Greg Ruggiero, the publisher of Marcos's collected writings. He wrote that when Marcos enters Mexico City next week, it will be "the equivalent of Martin Luther King Jr.'s March on Washington." I stared at the sentence for a long time. I have seen the clip of King's "I Have a Dream" speech maybe ten thousand times, though usually through adverts selling mutual funds, cable news, or computers and the like. Having grown up after history ended, it never occurred to me that I might see a capital-H history moment to match it.

Next thing I knew, I was on the phone talking to airlines, cancelling engagements, making crazy excuses, mumbling about Zapatistas and Martin Luther King. Who cares that I dropped my introduction to Spanish course? Or that I've never been to Mexico City, let alone Chiapas? Marcos says I am a Zapatista and I am sud-

99

denly thinking, "Yes, yes, I am. I have to be in Mexico City on March 11. It's like Martin Luther King Jr.'s March on Washington." Only now, as March 11 approaches, it occurs to me that it's not like that at all. History is being made in Mexico City this week, but it's a smaller, lower-case, humbler kind of history than you see in those news clips. A history that says, "I can't make your history for you. But I can tell you that history is yours to make."

It also occurs to me that Marcos isn't Martin Luther King; he is King's very modern progeny, born of a bittersweet marriage of vision and necessity. This masked man who calls himself Marcos is the descendant of King, Che Guevara, Malcom X, Emiliano Zapata, and all the other heroes who preached from pulpits only to be shot down one by one, leaving bodies of followers wandering around blind and disoriented because they lost their heads.

In their place, the world now has a new kind of hero, one who listens more than speaks, who preaches in riddles not in certainties, a leader who doesn't show his face, who says his mask is really a mirror. And in the Zapatistas, we have not one dream of a revolution, but a dreaming revolution. "This is our dream," writes Marcos, "the Zapatista paradox—one that takes away sleep. The only dream that is dreamed awake, sleepless. The history that is born and nurtured from below."

No Justice, No Peace
Ali Abunimah

An Israeli-Palestinian peace based on justice and equality between the two societies must address the economic disparities between them. The architects of the Oslo accords did not shy away from such debates. Rather, they appropriated the language of economic reform and regional integration to mask and deflect attention from the wholly unequal political situation facing Palestinians. Simultaneously advancing an economic agenda that would allow Palestinian, Jordanians, and other Arab populations to become sources of disempowered, cheap labor for exporting industries based in Israel, the United States, and Europe, there was nothing new about the ideology being employed here.

Borrowed from the post–Cold War language of "economic reform" and "liberalization," this rhetoric had already been used to open Eastern Europe to western capital. As recent history shows, the transition to market economies led to massive impoverishment and the transformation of one-party states into economic oligarchies that left ordinary people no more enfranchised than before. While economic "liberalization" was wedded to the rhetoric of "democracy" and "freedom" in Europe, in the Middle East ambitions were limited to "stability" and "prosperity" generally, and an end to the Israeli-Arab conflict in particular. The United States, the

101

jealous sponsor of the Middle East peace negotiations, was not about to contradict its decades-old policy of supporting undemocratic, pro-Western regimes in the Arab world.

Oslo architect, Labor Party stalwart, and former Prime Minister Shimon Peres, who assumed the post of Foreign Minister in Ariel Sharon's Likud Party–led coalition government after it assumed power in February 2001, has always been the chief spokesperson for this vision. Calling his post-war utopia "A New Middle East," Peres uses the language of economic integration to replace the search for a just peace, based on the withdrawal of Israeli military forces from Palestinian land, and the restoration of inalienable political rights denied to Palestinians since Israel was created in 1948. "A higher standard of living," wrote Peres in *The New Middle East* in 1993, "is a precondition for mitigating the tensions among Middle Eastern countries. As long as there is a gap between people's expectations and the opportunities within the sociopolitical system, there will be space for fundamentalism to develop." Hence, concludes Peres, "A cooperative regional organization that acts on an ultranational forum is the only answer to fundamentalism."

Unfortunately, such prescriptions for an elimination of the "real" sources of the Palestinian-Israeli conflict contradict the reality created by the peace agreements that Peres's own Oslo accords ended up imposing on the Palestinians. Providing legitimacy to Israel's continued military occupation of the West Bank, Gaza Strip, and East Jerusalem, while simultaneously creating a Palestinian Authority wholly subservient to Israel's "security needs," Oslo reestablished the basis for the conflict, and all of its logically fundamentalist pathologies. The colonization of Palestinian land, the dispossession of millions of refugees, and the maintenance of a brutal military occupation would continue indefinitely. But their alienated symptoms—radical Islamic movements which thrive as a reaction to the despair and the suffering brought on by continued Israeli military hegemony—would be explained by abstract economic "disparities" which exist outside any definable political context.

Never mind the additional responsibility for this situation shouldered by the broader political and economic architecture of the region, in which Israel and "moderate" Arab states maintain the status quo with the explicit backing of the United States. In this structure, Peres imagines an "innocent" Palestinian people who can be rescued from the grip of fundamentalism, not by viewing them as equals and agents in building their own future, but as objects of Israeli benevolence. While Peres was writing in 1993, at the beginning of the Oslo peace accords, he has continued to speak in the same language even as part of the Sharon government and even when as of mid-2002, Palestinians are, in the words of Israeli journalist Gideon Levy,

> in the worst situation they have been in since the Israeli occupation befell them. Their lack of freedom has reached a level they have never known before. Only a few peoples in the world still live under such dire conditions of occupation, and none of them have been subjected to occupation for such a lengthy period. The very limited freedom that the Palestinians enjoyed until this past year has disappeared as though it never was.

103

Nor can there be any doubt that the vastly increased impoverishment experienced by Palestinians in the occupied territories since the "peace process" began is not an unintended result, but one which flows logically from the increasingly complex structures of domination and exploitation put in place.

"The peace process," writes economist Sara Roy in an essay in *The New Intifada* (Verso, 2001), "not only failed to ameliorate, let alone end, Palestinian economic decline or the terms on which it is based; it accelerated that process by introducing into the Palestinian economy new dynamics that further attenuated an already diminished socioeconomic base."

The principal reason for Palestinian unemployment, which increased ninefold between 1992–96 from an average of three percent to twenty-eight percent, according to Roy (who cites figures from the World Bank), is the Israeli policy of military closure and isolation of Palestinian territory into hundreds of units separated from each other. Although there are grounds to believe that the World Bank figures consistently underestimate the true level of unemployment, the basic trend is clear. "Israel's continued domination of the Palestinian economy is not accidental," concludes Roy,

> [t]he continuation of pre-existing power relations between Israel and the Palestinians, and the structures that underlie them, is a characteristic feature of the Oslo agreements. Their agreements were designed not to alter the structures of occupation but to maintain them . . . In this way, the Oslo agreements, like the policies that preceded them, preclude the need for economic restructuring.

While Israel has deliberately undermined the institutional and social bases for a functional and civil society in a post-occupation Palestinian state, it has pointed to the disasterous results of this policy as evidence of Palestinian incompetence and unwillingness to seize golden opportunities to lay the groundwork for "peace." Nevertheless, Israel's increased repression of Palestinians, necessary to maintain the occupation and the construction of Jewish-only colonies in East Jerusalem, the West Bank, and Gaza, has rendered it increasingly difficult for Israel to draw on Palestinians as a source of cheap labor. And yet, despite the violence that is required to force Palestinians to integrate in the new regional economy on such unfair terms, for the time being, the "peace process" continues to open up new financial opportunities which conform well with Peres's vision.

The Jordan-Israel Relationship: The Shape of Things to Come?

The conclusion of the Oslo accords between Israel and the Palestine Liberation Organization in 1993 cleared the way for the 1994 peace treaty between Israel and its neighbor Jordan. In July 2001, the *Jerusalem Post* reported that yet another Israeli clothing manufacturer, Delta-Galit Industries Ltd., was to shut down its factory in northern Israel, costing 120 jobs. According to the company's spokesman, Dror Shavit, many of the dismissed workers "are believed to be Druse [Arab] women."

"While he would not confirm published reports that the sewing operations will be relocated to Jordan," the *Post* said, Shavit "did note that they would be positioned in a 'cheap labor country,' and that Egypt and Jordan are both possibly locales."

Such a move would save the company a great deal of money, according to the report, since Arab women are paid $800 per month in Israel, while wages for garment workers in other countries in the region, including Jordan, are often less than one-tenth as much.

This story is a good illustration for the wider picture of Jordanian-Israeli economic relations, as well as an example of how a wider Middle East settlement encompassing Syria and Lebanon may well be built on terms that will neither bring prosperity to them nor give them any stake in peace.

Beyond its regional implications, it is just one more example of how global "free trade" really means freedom for companies to move operations from one country to another seeking much lower wages in poorer countries, where workers rights are often less protected and environmental standards weaker. At the same time, workers have no similar freedom to migrate and seek better economic prospects on their own, and those from poor countries especially face very high barriers to international movement and migration. This combination of free movement of capital on the

105

one hand, and strict controls on human migration on the other, puts workers at the mercy of global corporations who essentially say, "If you don't want to take these jobs at the low wages we want to pay you, we can find poorer people in a poorer country who will."

In recent years, thousands of garment jobs have been transferred to Jordan, where wages and benefits are far lower than in Israel and far less costly for the Israeli industrialists. The vast majority of the jobs eliminated in Israel belonged to Palestinians with Israeli citizenship, especially women, but also to Palestinians from the occupied territories who are no longer permitted to enter Israel. In this dynamic, Palestinians in Israel are being turned into the economic adversaries of Jordanian and Egyptian workers, and Israeli companies are reaping ever greater profits at the expense of these workers.

Following the 1994 peace treaty with Israel, Jordan established so-called "Qualifying Industrial Zones" in certain parts of the country. Products manufactured in these areas are given special duty-free status by the United States, but only if they are the result of "joint ventures" with Israeli companies. This has certainly encouraged the transformation of well-paying jobs with insurance and benefits for Palestinians in Israel into extremely low-paid jobs with no benefits in Jordan. It is also one of the means through which the United States has attempted to force "normalization" between Israel and Jordan, despite the reluctance of many Jordanians to grant such normal relations while Israel refuses to end its brutal repression of the Palestinians and recognize their rights. The rights of Palestinians in the occupied territories are not an abstract concept in Jordan, but one which directly affects the families and interests of half the population who came to Jordan as Palestinian refugees in 1948 and 1967.

And if such low-wage jobs do little for the longterm development of Jordan's workforce or economy, or to address growing poverty and skyrocketing inequality in Jordan, the U.S.-Jordan Free

Trade Agreement passed by Congress in late 2001 does not promise much better.

Jordan is in a very small club of countries, with Mexico, Canada, and Israel, that have concluded such agreements with the United States. But combined with the present state of Jordan's economy, this agreement may simply accelerate the transformation of Jordan into a dumping ground for low-wage industries. The pact, which eliminates all tariffs on goods traded between the two countries, will likely have little benefit for Jordan's indigenous exporting industries. Jordan's exports to the United States amounted to a negligible $11 million in 1999, according to the U.S. government, and included mostly low value-added goods such as jewelry, precious metals, and garments. Meanwhile, Jordan imported $276 million of goods from the United States, including wheat and corn, aircraft parts, automobiles, and high-technology goods. A visitor to almost any Amman supermarket will find a huge and growing array of basic foods and goods imported from the United States, often selling at prices far higher than in the U.S. itself.

Under the new agreement, the United States has much more to gain, as its companies will have the ability to flood Jordan with ever more consumer goods at cheaper prices. At the same time, American companies—like the Israeli ones—will be able to move manufacturing operations to Jordan, exploiting the country's low-wage workers and exporting their products back to the United States without any tariffs.

The emergence of a "border economy" between Israel and Jordan underlines the fact that increased economic integration for capital does not translate into increased integration for people, in the sense of freedom of movement and the right to follow capital for exploited workers. Consider how the provisions for border passage for Israelis and Jordanians differ, and yet mirror closely that for U.S. citizens and Mexicans. Any Israeli citizen can show up at a Jordanian border crossing and enter Jordan by showing a passport and paying a

107

small fee. A Jordanian citizen wishing to enter Israel, by contrast, must apply for a visa at an Israeli consulate weeks or months in advance, face long delays, high expenses, and frequent rejections. Making this all the more galling is that most of those Jordanian citizens applying for "tourist" visas to Israel are in fact people of Palestinian origin trying to visit their own hometowns and families.

Because these economic developments took shape in the context of a much-celebrated (at least in the West) Jordanian-Israeli peace treaty, and were held up as a model for future bilateral relationships, it has been easy for Israel, Jordan, and the United States to paint those who oppose them as being "anti-peace," in much the same way that those who oppose economic liberalization in Eastern Europe are termed "anti-democratic." Indeed, the signing of the Jordanian-Israeli peace treaty heralded the beginning of the end of a brief period of political opening which began in 1989, when widespread protests against IMF-imposed austerity measures led to Jordan's most free parliamentary elections ever. Faced with the choice between a democracy in which the vast majority would likely reject a peace treaty which was at best premature (as long as Palestinians remained under occupation and in exile) or an autocratic government that could maintain the facade of a "warm peace," under pressure from the United States, the Jordanian regime chose the latter. Space for public expression and debate on the economic and political issues arising from Israeli-Arab peacemaking has now all but disappeared.

Inherent in all of these economic relationships is injustice and inequality. Rather than competing on the same terrain as U.S. and Israeli exporters, Jordanian workers are merely competing with other Arab workers in a race to the bottom of the wage scale. At a time when Israel is fighting a war against Palestinians in the occupied territories, and continuing to deny equal rights to Palestinian citizens of Israel, Arab countries should suspend trade arrangements which allow Israel to further punish Arab communities inside Israel by taking away their jobs and sending them to Jordan or Egypt.

Things might take a different, much more positive path, but the experience of Mexican workers following the 1994 free trade agreement with the United States, and other workers around the world, suggests this is by no means certain. Trade unions, political parties, and other forces that could lead opposition to such an economic order have suffered under decades of political repression throughout the Arab world, while the Islamic movements which have been the main channel of opposition are under severe attack. Although these movements have often articulated strong critiques of prevailing economic policies, and provided the kinds of social and educational services that help people survive them, they have not generated an appealing alternative that encompasses the vast political and religious diversity of the Middle East.

Yet Jordan and the occupied Palestinian territories are particularly ill-suited for transformation into low-wage assembly economies. People in both societies have placed an enormous stress on education as a route to economic improvement and both have very high literacy rates, and rates of university enrollment and graduation. Economic empowerment in these countries would take advantage of the high levels of skill, and the high quality of human capital. Until the 1990–91 Gulf War, Jordan's largest trading partners were Iraq and the Gulf states. Iraq imported manufactured goods, including prepared foods, textiles, and fertilizers from Jordan, while the Gulf states relied on highly skilled Jordanian and Palestinian labor to staff their schools and universities, banks, engineering firms, and other vital sectors. The ongoing UN embargo on Iraq has all but destroyed Jordan's trade with that country. Strained political relationships between Jordan and some of the Gulf states stemming from Jordan's refusal to back the 1991 "coalition" war against Iraq have prevented more than a handful of Jordanians from returning to those countries. Hundreds of thousands of Jordanian citizens were expelled by Gulf states such as Kuwait as punishment for Jordan's wartime position.

109

Conclusion

Jordan's traditional and hitherto most viable markets for manufactured goods, agriculture, and its well-trained workforce are not in
Israel or the United States, but in the now largely closed markets of
Iraq and the Gulf. Jordan could make huge and rapid economic
gains at all levels if it could return to them. Israeli and American
strategy has been not only to keep Jordan isolated from these markets by maintaining the embargo on Iraq, but to try to tie Jordan
into the economic orbit of Israel and the United States, where its
economic advantages disappear. Jordan's highly educated, but largely Arabic-speaking workers are of less value to the U.S. and Israel,
notwithstanding high barriers to migration which further diminish
the role of skilled labor, while Jordan's products, competitive in the
Arab world, are currently manufactured neither in sufficient volume nor quantity to appeal to Western tastes.

In the long run, there is no reason to assume that Israel will
not also be seen as a beneficial economic partner in the region. But
this is likely to happen only after a political settlement has been
reached with the Palestinians that removes completely the relationship of asymmetrical power that continues to exist and worsen
today. Peres's vision of a "New Middle East" is rhetorically appealing, but it fails in substance because it seeks "integration" without
addressing gross injustices, while promoting policies which exac-
erbate the disenfranchisement and vulnerability of those already at
the bottom. As long as Israel is a colonizing and occupying power,
and as long as the United States continues its unconditional support for Israeli policies, efforts to extend economic relationships
with both countries will be seen as a continuation of Israel's military war by other means. Popular refusal to "normalize" economic
relationships with Israel will thus be viewed as a necessary and
legitimate form of political resistance, despite the best efforts of the

United States and the governments allied with it to impose their own vision.

Visions of Leviathan
J.C. Myers

*A*las, poor Orwell: in life a snitch, and in death the victim of his own personal Room 101. As Frances Stonor Saunders's study of the CIA's cultural campaigns during the Cold War revealed, the ending to *1984* was a bit bleak for the Agency's tastes, and so, as the film version of the story was put into production in the mid-1950s, it was carefully re-written by some dutiful Winston Smith for the Psychological Strategy Board.[1] The broken man who could struggle no more and who now loved his iron-willed political masters was re-born defiant, crying, "Down with Big Brother!" as the camera left him to his fate. And while several generations of American schoolchildren were raised on Orwell's text with its grim ending intact, as the year 1984 rolled around, yet another rewriting of the story was publicly performed. Apple Computer, the ascendant golden child of the nascent New Economy purchased a minute or so of the most exclusive airtime available—halftime during the Superbowl—to show a lone man breaking from a herd of his cowed compatriots to destroy a huge telescreen image of what everyone knew was, and could only be, Big Brother. The message was clear: the hot, young corporation was not just a money-making venture; the personal computer was not just a tool or a toy—these were the implements of freedom with which we would resist the totalitarian impulses of politics, the state, and perhaps also Apple's main competitor, IBM.

Not all politicians, though, were collaborators in the Inner Party's conspiracy. 1984 was also the year in which Ronald Reagan reprised his campaign call, "Down with Big Government!" placing himself squarely in the middle of a long train of American candidates whose rhetoric centers on their denial of having any association with politics. Countless are the television ads during campaign season that identify their candidate as an outsider: "Not a politician, but a successful businessperson . . ." If the state stands for American culture as an object of fear and loathing, the market entrepreneur is held in the same image to be its natural antagonist. Contradictions, of course, abound. Market entrepreneurs require for their very existence certain types of law and regulation, just as they struggle mightily against others. The "anti-government" Reagan administration oversaw a massive buildup of American military forces and their associated bureaucracies, financed by taxation and deficit spending. Yet, the image of the state as looming Leviathan, opposed only by the valiant entrepreneur, emerged from the Cold War unscathed and victorious, both fueling and being fueled by the end of the welfare state. At the heart of this image lies a particular conception of the relationship between persons, states, and markets that overwhelmingly defines the ideological terrain of contemporary neo-liberal capitalism.

113

The Three Leviathans

Earlier thinkers pondered the ties that bound citizen to polis and subject to king, but it was Thomas Hobbes, in *Leviathan*, who first reflected on the relatively novel association formed between the state and the modern individual—the legal and political form born alongside modern capitalism that remains with us today. Yet, for Hobbes, the individual was not really a novelty at all. Remove society from the picture, he famously proposed, and what one would find was a world of radically subjective agents, all pursuing their independent desires by means of the roughly equivalent stock of talents and abilities endowed in them by their Creator.[2] Rather than having come into the world through bourgeois forms of law, the individual—atomized, desiring, and born free—had been there all along.

But the natural condition of radical individual freedom would be no blissful anarchist paradise. Without the law to define particular rights to property, Hobbes reasoned, everyone would lay claim to everything. Total freedom among equals would immediately mean total war between them. The only way to preserve ourselves in such a situation would be to give up our natural individual autonomy to some dominant sovereign power that would then see to the conditions for our well-being. We would trade freedom for existence; our birthright for the right to go on living. Which is to say that what Hobbes recognized in the individual's bargain with the sovereign ruler, contemporary libertarians saw in the citizen's bargain with the welfare state: an exchange of freedom for well-being. Hobbes's version of our deal with Leviathan, though, understood it to be essentially unavoidable and ultimately beneficial. For the libertarian critic of the welfare state, it was a bad deal from the beginning.

The popular version of the libertarian anti-statist case is easy enough to find: Take a seat in any small-town American bar-room and ask the person next to you to describe their feelings about taxation. Alongside the unfailing description of each and every candidate for political office as "an outsider," the most common and successful refrain in American electoral politics is the call for, or promise of, a tax cut. But the anti-statist critique has its more thoughtfully considered side as well. Isaiah Berlin's famous defense of the liberal concept of negative freedom, for example, argued persuasively that if what was special and unique about human beings was their ability to make autonomous, individual choices, then nothing could constitute a deeper violation of their humanity than to choose *for* them—even (or perhaps, especially) when we think we have their best interests in mind.[3]

This, of course, is exactly the sort of mischief liberals and libertarians charged the modern state with having been up to for most of the twentieth century. In the early '70s, as an unlikely collection of ultra-leftists and right-wing libertarians joined forces to condemn the erosion of individual freedom by a bloated and monstrous state, they chose to recall Hobbes, entitling their work *A New History of Leviathan*.[4] But if Hobbes's original had taken one giant step down from the glory of divine-right kings, revealing to us that its power was really nothing more than the amalgam of our own collective powers, the new Leviathan was sorrier looking still—a gigantic, nagging, nanny state: Mary Poppins in dominatrix gear.

The state feared by libertarian defenders of individual freedom was not so much the diabolical dictator as the over-eager do-gooder. As Berlin imagined the well-intentioned Big Brother to be thinking in his 1997 essay, "Two Concepts of Liberty":

> Nature I can, at least in principle, always mold by technical means, and shape to my will. But how am I to treat recalcitrant human beings? I must, if I can, impose my will on them, too, "mold" them to my pattern, cast parts for them in my play. But will this not mean that I alone am free, while they are slaves? They will be so if my plan has nothing to do with their wishes or values, only with my own. But if my plan is fully rational, it will allow for the full development of their "true" natures, the realization of their capacities for rational decisions, "for making the best of themselves"—as a part of the realization of my own "true" self. All true solutions to all genuine problems must be compatible: more than this, they must fit into a single whole: for this is what is meant by calling them all rational and the universe harmonious.[5]

115

Reason itself, as Horkheimer and Adorno had suggested in *The Dialectic of Enlightenment,* seemed to self-expand into an irresistible totalitarian urge. In similar fashion, for Foucault, the micro-level technologies of discipline—from the drilling of soldiers on the parade ground to the medical management of the body in clinics and hospitals—steadily worked their way into a vast, looming, yet unnamable presence. Equally present in the work of both the Frankfurt School and the postmoderns, but equally un-nameable, was the implied utopia of unblemished authenticity and unchallenged personal freedom. If the nightmare was the iron cage of reason, surely its antithesis was a kind of frolicking, anarchic madness.

Thus, a curious convergence had taken place between the intellectual avant-garde, whose heritage lay on the political left, and the gray-suited stockbrokers who once made up the ranks of their opponents. Both now believed that the best of all possible worlds would be a foundationless flowering of individual subjectivity—which is precisely what the radical liberals had always argued markets, and markets alone, could provide. Even the most hard-nosed bourgeois economist is liable to get a bit misty-eyed when making the case that the fundamental force behind any working market is the expression of personal preference. Markets disclose to us *what people want.* In choosing to trade their personal resources for one thing rather than another, people reveal what is important to them and what is not. Their baskets are not filled for them by some pseudo-omniscient state; their choices are their own. Market behavior, in this sense, could be seen as a revealing of the authentic self. And to this extent, the market society—deregulated to the fullest extent—would be the nearest achievable approximation of true utopian freedom.

Yet, the inflation here of a micro-level principle for decision-making into a macro-level principle for social organization runs the risk of a genetic mutation. My decisions in the supermarket aisle are, presumably, my own. True, I choose from within a given range of products—but free choice could never be infinitely free. True also that I may be influenced by the siren songs of advertising or the wails of an unhappy five-year-old—but these, too, the rational-choice theorists would say, express a preference that is ultimately mine: to look sexy rather than frumpy; to feel satisfaction in giving my child what he or she desires. Barring the unproven effects of subliminal communication, we can at least say that my decisions in the marketplace are *conscious* ones. I may not know precisely what I am getting—advertisers or salespeople may succeed in deceiving me—but I know what I am *trying* to get. The decisions made by market transactions at the level of social organization, however, are of a fundamentally different order, in that they are *unconscious* ones: *Sie wissen das nicht, aber sie tün es!* What the market decides is what none have consciously chosen. As a form of social organization—a way of determining how many hospitals we should have or how many people should be able to find work this month—the market is, in effect, a non-human governor, a planner without a plan, or as Fredric Jameson has suggested, Leviathan in sheep's clothing:

> Market ideology assures us that human beings make a mess of it when they try to control their destinies ("socialism is impossible") and that we are fortunate in possessing an interpersonal mechanism—the market—which can substitute for human *hubris* and planning, and replace human decisions altogether. We only need to keep it clean and well oiled, and it now—like the monarch so many centuries ago—will see to us and keep us in line.[6]

The market is, in the most real sense, a form of social power—yet, it is an illusory form of power. It appears to have no body, no location, no origin; it barely has a name. Above all, it is a non-political form of power, having no processes for debate or appeal. And in this it bears its strongest resemblance to Hobbes's mighty Leviathan: the ruler whose rule is unquestioned and unchallenged.

We often read *Leviathan* as a passionate argument for authoritarian rule, reading into this the Orwellian nightmare of a world in which all forms of freedom are surrendered to the state. But this

117

would be to neglect Hobbes's explicit conditions for a return of freedom by the sovereign power to its subjects. Like the liberals, for Hobbes, freedom is conceived of negatively. Freedom is freedom from opposition or compulsion, a vacant space in which our own agency is allowed to run unimpeded. To be sure, there can be no talk of political freedom for Hobbes, uncontested sovereignty being the only safeguard against civil war and social breakdown. Other types of freedom, though, are not only imaginable, they are expected:

> The Liberty of a Subject, lyeth therefore only in those things, which in regulating their actions, the Soveraign hath prætermitted: such as is the Liberty to buy, and sell, and otherwise contract with one another; to choose their own abode, their own diet, their own trade of life, and institute their children as they themselves think fit; and the like.[7]

Freedom, then, is the freedom of the marketplace and the home—a concept immediately recognizable to any member of a contemporary capitalist society. That freedom was not always conceived of in such terms is not only arguable, but revealed by Hobbes himself when he cautions against the subversive potential of ancient Greek and Roman thought.[8] To the student of Aristotle and Cicero, Hobbes warns, "This way sedition lies!" and here we can gain another insight into his vision of the hegemonic, sovereign state. The power of Leviathan flows not simply from the subjects' abdication of their individual political rights, but from the manifestation of their concrete, everyday, lived existence in a fundamentally non-political world: the world of the entrepreneur and the consumer, rather than that of the citizen. Thus, while Jameson is entirely correct to see in the market's invisible hand the scepter of a phantom monarch, its reign need not imply any sapping of the state's strength. On the contrary, the liberal's ideal state might be a bulky and well-armed night-watchman, indeed.

Nation of Lemonade Stands

How are we to judge the nature of the state? By its actions, surely. And while no historical state could be said to have wholly exempted itself from social welfare activities of some sort, the coining of the term "welfare state" was always meant to suggest something markedly different: the management of social well-being—and in particular, the mopping up of the market economy's excesses, insufficiencies, and dysfunctions—as the centerpiece of the state's *raison d'être*. To the extent, then, that this was an accurate characterization of the advanced capitalist state, the process of "welfare reform" (or, more accurately, welfare elimination) would seem to indicate a major shift in orientation, rather than just a minor readjustment of policy.

Although the assault on the American welfare state was begun under Reagan in the 1980s, the truly decisive turn came only in 1996 with the elimination of Aid to Families with Dependent Children (AFDC) and its replacement by the Personal Responsibility and Work Opportunity Reconciliation Act (PRA). In total, the PRA amounted to a dense condensation of conservative and anti-statist policy objectives, from the privatization of social services to the demonization of out-of-wedlock births. Two of its elements, however, were central to the shaping of a post–welfare state. First, the notion of a federally guaranteed minimum income for those in poverty was sharply curtailed. While state governments were required by the Act to develop programs to replace AFDC, the PRA contained no guarantee that a person falling below the poverty line would receive support. Further, regardless of their circumstances, those persons who did receive income support would now be limited to five cumulative years of assistance. Second, the role of work requirements—previously a minor component of poverty-alleviation programs—was massively expanded. The new state-level programs were mandated by the Act to require anyone receiving assistance to be working after no more than two years.[9]

119

The results of the new policy were swift and dramatic: a forty-four percent drop in the number of welfare recipients within two years of the PRA's passage into law.[10] All too predictably, however, those now being shed from the welfare rolls did not necessarily find themselves employed in good jobs, earning decent wages. One early study found that of 137 Iowa families dropped from AFDC, forty percent saw their monthly income rise by an average of $496. Forty-nine percent, though, lost an average of $384 per month.[11] A later study of former welfare recipients now making their way into the job market revealed that most had no health insurance. Many of those surveyed reported that they were often unable to pay rent and utility bills and sometimes skipped meals at the end of a month when the money ran out.[12] While the PRA demanded in strident and moralizing tones that the poor be made to work, it was curiously silent on the question of whether everyone who wanted to work could find a job, or whether the income earned at a minimum-wage position would be enough to bring an individual or a family above the poverty line.

Whether or not welfare reform could be considered a success, of course, depended on the definition of its objectives. Had the elimination or alleviation of poverty been marked out as its goal, the PRA's record would be a questionable one, at best. According to the U.S. Census Bureau, in 1998, just under thirteen percent of the population lived below the poverty level—a one-percent reduction from the number in 1995.[13] Taking into account the sustained economic expansion that occurred during the latter half of the 1990s, such a minor fluctuation could hardly be trumpeted as a major victory in the war against want. But such news was unlikely to trouble the members of Congress who drafted the new policy, or the state-level administrators who oversaw its implementation. In one sense, the new program repeatedly stressed the importance of work. Marking the shift in both policy and political valence, New York City's welfare offices, for example, were renamed "Job

Centers." But, whether or not people in need actually found jobs turned out to be of little or no importance. Instead, discouraging aid-seekers from applying for public assistance of any kind was a policy openly pursued as a key element in the new approach to social services. As the newsletter of the Queens Job Center described their strategy:

> No matter how you phrase it, the goal of the Financial Planner, Employment Planner, Social Service Planner, and Resource Staff is the same: Redirect the participant to another source other than Temporary Assistance.[14]

When asked whether placing people in jobs or simply diverting them from public social services was the more important goal, New York Mayor Rudolf Giuliani replied,

> Both are important. But if you ask me for the order of priority, the most important number is decreasing the numbers of people dependent on the government to support them—because, after all, that's really government's role.[15]

Why was striking people from the welfare rolls now a more pressing goal than lifting them out of poverty? In describing the work of government as the active minimization of people's dependence on it, Giuliani had hit upon a crucial touchstone of the post–welfare state's political vision: the people receiving government income supports were not truly in need of such assistance, they had simply been allowed to become dependent upon it. As Representative Ed Bryant of Tennessee argued before the House in March 1995 during a debate over the PRA,

> ... the original intent of the welfare system has been lost. What was intended to be a compassionate provision to help people has turned into a destructive and permanent fixture of dependency for many who are entrapped within it.[16]

Social welfare benefits, his colleague from Ohio, Deborah Pryce, added, did not alleviate poverty, they condemned people to it:

> For five million families, the average length of stay on welfare is thirteen years. The Democrats have coated the social safety net with glue and millions of Americans are crying for help to become unstuck . . . it is these same Democrats who are standing in the doors of the nation's ghettos, refusing to let people out.[17]

From this perspective, the ending of welfare could be understood as a type of emancipation in itself. The shrinkage of benefits was, in fact, a benefit—an idea that some in the private sector were not slow to pick up on. After passage of the PRA, in thirty-nine states and the District of Columbia, the distribution of what few temporary income supports now remained was shifted from paper checks to electronic debit cards, provided by a handful of large financial houses. But like wayward bank customers sanctioned for using a rival company's automatic teller machine, welfare recipients making withdrawals using the cards were charged a transaction fee, deductible from their benefits and payable to the financial firms operating the system. One might be excused for thinking that to a single parent struggling to survive in New York City on $448 per month, a $2.35 fee for each purchase of food or withdrawal of cash would represent a loss rather than a gain. Citigroup, the largest provider of electronic benefits transfer (EBT) services, saw it differently. "The most important benefit," the company's representatives told government regulators, "is that EBT allows low-income individuals a point of entry into the mainstream of electronic banking."[18] In other words, the important matter was not how much a person had to spend on things like food or shelter each month, but that they were as fully removed as possible from the world of public social services and incorporated instead into the world of private industry, commerce, and the market.

122

It was, of course, the persistent failure of the market economy to provide jobs and incomes for all that once led to the building of public social-welfare institutions. As cross-national studies of social-welfare regimes have consistently demonstrated, the levels of pre-transfer poverty produced by advanced capitalist societies are both high and unvarying. Before taxes are collected and government benefits distributed, the U.S., Canada, the UK, Sweden, the Netherlands, France, Italy, and Australia all generate approximately the same levels of relative poverty—around twenty percent of their populations.[19] The differences in post-transfer poverty rates, however, are dramatic. Over a ten-year period (1985-94), post-transfer poverty rates drop to around thirteen percent in the U.S., six percent in Germany, and less than one percent in the Netherlands.[20] It might be said, then, that the existence and extent of poverty in advanced industrial societies is the result of a choice made by political authorities, economic elites, and middle-class electorates. Yet, for the architects of "welfare reform" in the U.S., such as Representative Bryant, the problem to be solved had less to do with collective political choices than with individual economic ones:

> Sadly, many of these people have chosen to make their living for themselves and their families without working by choosing to take AFDC, food stamps, and countless other programs which cost over $300 billion annually. This is wrong and unfair for them and taxpayers, and it must stop. What the Personal Responsibility Act aims to do is to require individuals to look to themselves and their families and not to Washington in order to become productive members of society.[21]

123

What, exactly, would it mean for the poor to "look to themselves and their families" to make their living? Mayor Giuliani offered this advice: "If you can't get a job, start a small business. Start a little candy store. Start a little newspaper stand. Start a lemonade stand."[22]

In one sense, this sort of giddy market fundamentalism represented an almost dreamlike denial of reality. Candy stores require business licenses, inventories, display cases, cash registers, and—unless the proprietor is lucky enough to own a piece of prime commercial real estate—rented premises, entailing security deposits and favorable credit histories. Anyone eligible to receive government income assistance was highly unlikely to possess or have ready access to any of these. Giuliani's prosaic lemonade stand—the one business venture possibly within reach of those now being ejected from the social-welfare system—would be a bad bet to provide for anyone's needs in a city like New York. In another sense, however, the mayor's feverish Horatio Alger fantasy contained a coldly sober assessment of what the neo-liberal state now stood for.

Poverty reduction was clearly not one of the new state's goals, nor was ensuring that all adult members of society earned their living through work. Had work itself been the crucial issue at stake (as some, such as sociologist William Julius Wilson, suggested it was), the creation of large-scale public works projects on the model of the Depression-era Works Progress Administration would surely have been the order of the day. But while some states developed public "workfare" programs, these were both small in scale and temporary in duration, being tied to the same five-year limits as other forms of assistance. As the U.S. economy slid into recession in 2001, the first generation of post-welfare poor reached the end of their eligibility even for "workfare" with dimming hopes of finding employment in the private sector. Just as Giuliani had implied, though, employment, or the lack thereof, was of little concern to the neo-liberal state. Instead, its attention was now focused on a type of self-purification; a purging of the social-democratic elements that had crept into advanced capitalism over the course of the twentieth century. More than anything else, welfare reform announced a return of the capitalist state to its liberal fundamentals.

Like every other form of social and political organization, liberalism assembles its conceptual scaffolding and ideological imagery around the central figure of an ideal being. What the citizen is to a republic or the lord to a feudal fief, the entrepreneur is to the world of liberal capitalism: the one whose measurements all garments are cut to fit; the one for whom every foible of the law makes perfect and immediate sense. As an incarnation of liberal fundamentalism, then, what welfare reform sought to create was neither a world free from poverty, nor a world of work and contribution, but a world in which all persons would be treated as entrepreneurs: expected to live by their wits and their stock of personal property in the hostile environment of the free market.

On the one hand, such an expectation was patently unrealistic. An advanced economy of giant multinational firms could hardly be rolled back into an eighteenth-century colonial frontier society of family farmers and cottage industries, nor would any contemporary neo-liberal desire such a transformation. Even by its simplest economic logic, the profitability of any one capitalist demands that a much larger number of persons remain dependent on wage labor rather than entrepreneurial activity for their survival. On the other hand, though, unlike feudalism or even certain forms of republicanism, liberalism holds out the false promise that anyone might aspire to its ideal. Liberal forms of law, after all, claim no concern with the particular distribution of wealth and resources—let the chips fall where they may! The difference between a factory worker and a factory owner is marked not by the rights granted to each under the law, but by the simple accident of their possessing different amounts of property. Nothing other than self-interest prevents the factory owner from signing over his or her deed to some randomly-selected worker on the assembly line. More importantly, nothing in the law prevents the workers on the line from striking out on their own, opening candy stores and lemonade stands that may one day flourish into multinational titans.

This is neither a new nor an unfamiliar phenomenon. Just as each form of social organization configures itself around an ideal

125

image, the wrenching contradictions present in each form of class society give birth to unique dreams of salvation for the exploited, classifiable by their reversal of the terms of domination. The slave dreams always of violent rebellion. In the feudal society, the laboring majority dream of magical transformation or misplacements at birth that will one day be revealed. For the capitalist working class, only a happy entrepreneurial accident—the brilliant invention, the ingenious business plan, or the lucky stock purchase—can be hoped for to improve one's fortunes. Other escapes are, of course, possible. Yet, as bell hooks suggested in *Ain't I a Woman,* none seems so immediately intriguing for the oppressed as assuming the way of life of the oppressor.[23]

Speculators and Detectives

One way of describing the world of the entrepreneur would be to say that all of its objects exist only as expressions of pure exchange value.[24] The small business owner may harbor some emotional attachment to particular products or services or cling to some personal identification with a way of work and a way of life. But these are really lingering connections to pre-capitalist forms of production and craft. For the true entrepreneur, all such emotional encumbrances must be dispensed with. An object or an action, a product or a service is nothing more than what it can be sold for on the market. We can recognize the purest forms of entrepreneurialism, then, in the corporate conglomerate's acquisition and merger of various disparate businesses, or the stock market investor's assemblage of a portfolio from fragments of firms having nothing whatsoever to do with one another. In either case, the gritty details of production and service are now irrelevant. What matters is that at the end of the day, the investment should show a profit.

But if, for the entrepreneurial investor, all objects are transformed at a glance into their bare cash equivalents, in precisely the same way, each and every moment of time comes to be recognizable only as an opportunity to buy or to sell. In the game of buying low and selling high, profit can be made only by buying and selling at exactly the right instant. This morning's hot stock may plunge by afternoon. Did you get in before the rush? Did you get out before the collapse? There is, of course, a natural limit placed upon this frenzy to truck, barter, and exchange, but it is one set by the brute force of technology alone. In the 1920s, when stock and commodity prices were relayed to investors by telegraph and tickertape, the day remained laden with expansive pauses between transactions. In the 1990s, as Internet technology began to allow for nearly simultaneous order-execution and twenty-four-hour access to markets around the world, not a moment remained in which money could not be made or lost. At the turn of the century, advertisements—such as one in which a hip, young investor humiliates a colleague at work for losing five cents per share on an ill-timed Internet stock transaction—began to popularize the notion that vast fortunes lay within the grasp of anyone savvy enough to follow the minute-by-minute movements of The Market and click their mouse-button at exactly the right time.

For a brief moment it appeared as if, in the words of the Internet stock pimps themselves, "the rules had changed." It was no longer just heavily capitalized Wall Street arbitrageurs who could make money by buying and selling stock—anyone could do it. Ordinary people could simply quit their dead-end jobs and become day-traders, renting a cubicle and a computer connection to NASDAQ to chase the Next Big Thing with borrowed cash. The quick and the daring would retire at forty-five as their carefully crafted portfolios ballooned in value, while the slow and the timid would be left behind to staff the cash registers at Wal-Mart. Nothing, it was made to seem, separated the professional investment banker from the person in the street, except the fervent belief in capitalism's promise. The resulting psychosis was brought to light

127

in July 1999, when a day-trader in Atlanta, Georgia, deeply in debt from losses in the once-booming high-technology sector, walked into the offices of his investment firm, pulled out two handguns, and opened fire, killing nine people and wounding twelve. As Mark Barton began his homicidal rampage, he was overheard to say, "I hope this doesn't ruin your trading day." The killer fled in his family mini-van, only to be pulled over by police later that evening. Before he could be taken into custody, he shot and killed himself.[25]

In one way, of course, the Atlanta massacre was a perfect example of the Hobbesian state at work: The rules of social order had been violated and the arms of the sovereign state reached out to ensnare the perpetrator. Yet, in a slightly different way, the case of the day-trader-gone-mad would seem to expose a deficiency, an oversight, or even, possibly, a deception on the part of Hobbes and those liberals who also imagine the state in terms similar to his. Both Hobbes's mighty sovereign and the liberals' night watchman were charged with ending the war of all against all. Enforceable rights to private property were supposed to bring peace, order, and the benefits of commerce where otherwise only chaos and anarchy would have reigned. What Mark Barton's last words and deeds would seem to reveal, however, is that the war of all against all was never really ended, but merely exiled, contained within the walls of the capitalist economy. Civil society, in this sense, is unveiled as the world of anti-social behavior: Friends are stabbed in the back, colleagues are thrown to the sharks, and the basic needs of the ordinary person rank a poor second behind the most frivolous desires of the elite. The bottom line of the Hobbesian vision, though, remains the same: Only a strong-armed, ever-vigilant state could keep such a society from exploding in an apocalypse of self-consuming violence.

It is no surprise, then, that contemporary neo-liberal capitalism has brought with it a variety of distinguishable, albeit related, cravings for law and order. For the propertied, the end of the welfare state meant both new opportunities for profits to be made and new threats to be defended against. Hungry people, after all, are desperate people, and it is no coincidence that as the U.S. welfare state eroded, its prison population skyrocketed. In 1970, the average monthly benefit received by a family on AFDC was $676. By 1993, that amount (adjusted for inflation) had shrunk to $373.[26] During the same period, the prison population expanded from 200,000 in 1970 to nearly 1.1 million in 1995.[27] But for those both more numerous and less fortunate than the corporate elite, cloistered in their gated communities, law and order has also taken on a curious new appeal. Primetime television brims over with investigation and arrest, and what politician could possibly be criticized for offering more prisons and more police?

We could try to explain this latter phenomenon as a type of false consciousness; a misplaced sense of loyalty to the system on the part of the working class. Ernest Mandel, though, once proposed a more subtle and interesting possibility—Detective stories and the solution of mysteries might be particularly satisfying for those awash in the constant accidents of capitalism:

> Isn't the whole of bourgeois society operating like a big mystery, anyway? Here you are, slaving away at your job, obeying all the rules . . . and then you are still fired. Worse, you are unexpectedly hit by a recession, a long depression, even a war. Who is responsible for all this? You aren't. Nor are your neighbors or acquaintances. Some mysterious behind-the-scene conspirators must have something to do with it. Let at least some of the mysteries be cleared up, and you'll feel less alienated.[28]

129

Anti-capitalism, then, cannot be satisfied with a search for conspiracies and conspirators. When this week's corporate shadow-government collapses under the weight of its own fraudulent accounting schemes, another will quietly rise to take its place. Naming the names may fulfill the demands of history, but it will not move us any closer to a meaningfully different way of life.

That transformation would mean breaking down the artificial and illusory wall that liberalism and its contemporary variants seek to erect between the state and civil society. It would also mean, then, overcoming the fear of politics instilled in us not only by the capitalist right, but by the 1960s libertarian New Left. Political power brings with it risks that no anti-capitalist movement can dare to ignore. But it is also the only power with which capitalism can be opposed and a new society can be built. Marx and Engels, we might recall, wrote in the *Communist Manifesto* that the first task of the revolutionary working class was to win the battle for democracy.[29] This remains true today. But it is also worth adding that as the battle for democracy is won, the next and more important task is to use it.

Endnotes

1. Fances Stonor Saunders, *Who Paid the Piper?* London: Granta Books, 1999, p. 297.

2. Thomas Hobbes, *Leviathan*, London: Penguin Books, 1985.

3. Isaiah Berlin, "Two Concepts of Liberty," in Robert E. Goodin and Philip Pettit (eds.), *Contemporary Political Philosophy*, Oxford: Blackwell, 1997, p. 399–400.

4. Ronald Radosh and Murray Rothbard (eds.), *A New History of Leviathan*, New York: Dutton, 1972.

5. Berlin, p. 404.

6. Fredric Jameson, "Postmodernism and the Market," in Slavoj Zizek (ed.), *Mapping Ideology*, London: Verso, 1994, p. 290.

7. Hobbes, p. 264.

8. *Ibid.,* p. 267.

9. Personal Responsibility and Work Opportunity Reconciliation Act of 1996 (P.L. 104-193).

10. U.S. Department of Health and Human Services—Administration for Children and Families, *Change in Welfare Caseloads*, January 1999, www.acf.dhhs.gov/news/stats/caseload.htm, April 12, 1999.

11. *New York Times*, June 30, 1997.

12. *Washington Post*, August 3, 1999.

13. U.S. Census Bureau, *Statistical Abstract of the United States*, (Table) 759, "Persons Below Poverty Level by State: 1980 to 1998," 2000.

14. Quoted in Jason DeParle, "What Welfare-to-Work Really Means," *New York Times Magazine*, December 20, 1998, p. 55.

15. *Ibid.*, p. 56.

16. Rep. Bryant (TN), "Modern Welfare System has Not Worked," *Congressional Record*, March 23, 1995, v. 141, n. 54, H3717.

17. Rep. Pryce (OH), "Help—I've Fallen and I Can't Get Up," *Congressional Record*, March 23, 1995, v. 141, n. 54, H3578.

18. *New York Times*, August 16, 1999.

19. Lane Kenworthy, "Do Social-Welfare Policies Reduce Poverty? A Cross-National Assessment," Working Paper No. 188, Luxemburg Income Study, 1998.

20. Robert E. Goodin, Bruce Headey, Ruud Muffels, and Henk-Jan Dirven, *The Real Worlds of Welfare Capitalism*, Cambridge: Cambridge University Press, 1999, p. 276.

21. Rep. Bryant (TN), "Modern Welfare System has Not Worked," H3717.

22. Quoted in DeParle, p. 89.

23. bell hooks, *Ain't I a Woman*, Boston: South End Press, 1981, p. 156.

24. "This boundless drive for enrichment, this passionate chase after value, is common to the capitalist and the miser; but while the miser is merely a capitalist gone mad, the capitalist is a rational miser." Karl Marx, *Capital*, vol. 1, New York: Vintage, 1977, p. 254.

25. *Washington Post*, July 30, 1999.

26. Mary Ellen Hombs, *Welfare Reform*, Santa Barbara: ABC-CLIO, 1996, p. 52.

27. U.S. Census Bureau, *Statistical Abstract of the United States*, (Figure) 5.2. "Federal and State Prisoners: 1970 to 1996," 1998.

28. Ernest Mandel, *Delightful Murder*, Minneapolis: University of Minnesota Press, 1984, p. 72.

29. Karl Marx and Frederick Engels, *The Communist Manifesto*, London: Verso, 1998, p. 60.

131

Interruptions in the Empire, the Power of the Exodus: Interview with Toni Negri
Giuseppe Cocco & Maurizio Lazzarato

*A*t the beginning of Israeli director Amos Gitai's 2000 film *Kippur,* two twenty-something Israel Defense Force (IDF) reservists find themselves speeding towards the Golan Heights in a well-worn European sedan during the first days of the 1973 war. Eager to join up with their unit at the front, the soldier in the passenger seat expresses displeasure with the state of the car. Annoyed, the driver asks whether his passenger has ever read Herbert Marcuse, and proceeds to engage in a critique of modern consumerism, explaining why it's more morally correct to purchase used cars.

Fast-forward thirty years from today, and imagine a similarly like-minded anti-war film recasting the same scene featuring two techno-loving Israeli software engineers heading to join their unit prior to the onset of Operation Defensive Shield. If such reservists were to have any conversation resembling the one between their scruffy baby-boomer predecessors, in all likelihood the driver would invoke the name of Antonio Negri in place of that of Marcuse. This is not meant to suggest that Negri is regularly read by turn-of-the-century Israeli reservists—though undoubtedly he is read by some of them. Nor does the political transformation of

Israeli society since the advent of the Al-Aksa Intifada provide one with much hope that leftist intellectuals like Negri are having the kind of influence on participants in contemporary colonial struggles that they ought to.

The point in proposing such a potential scenario is that it's not altogether unreasonable given the overwhelming reception accorded to Negri and Michael Hardt's best-selling 2000 publication, *Empire*, a remarkable 500-page volume that, as *Guardian* commentator Ed Vulliamy wrote in July 2001, provides an optimistic prognosis for the future of traditional progressivism—in particular, the notion that history remains oriented toward humankind's inevitable overcoming of exploitation, and that economic globalization presents the best opportunities for communist revolution.

"[*Empire*] rehabilitates the C-word, 'communism,'" states Vulliamy, "not despite the fall of the Berlin Wall but because of it—along the corridors of respectable academe and on to the streets of Genoa . . . It is a matter of Zeitgeist."

Indeed, this is where the analogy with Marcuse forcefully comes to bear. Like the former Frankfurt School thinker's 1964 treatise on the diminishing possibilities for revolutionary action in an advanced industrial society, *One Dimensional Man,* Negri and Hardt's analysis of contemporary imperialism was a cultural event that defined the new terrain of the left's revolutionary potential during an era of radical economic and technological globalization.

The most important Marxist intellectual to emerge in Italy since the death in prison of Antonio Gramsci in 1937, Toni Negri first rose to prominence in the early 1970s as a leading theorist of Italy's New Left, in particular the Potere Operaio and later the Autonomia movements. In April 1979, as a lecturer in Political Science at the University of Padua, Negri was arrested and accused of anti-statist, insurrectionist activities, along with five thousand other members of the Autonomist workers movement. Negri was also accused of leadership in the left-wing terrorist group respon-

133

sible for the 1978 kidnapping and murder of Christian Democratic Party president Aldo Moro, the Red Brigades.

After Negri was acquitted on all charges four years later, the Italian government then voted to send Negri back to prison. Negri proceeded to flee to France, where he taught at the Université de Paris for nearly fourteen years. During this period, Negri authored numerous influential works, including *The Politics of Subversion: A Manifesto for the 21st Century* (Polity Press, 1989) and *Communists Like Us: New Spaces of Liberty, New Lines of Alliance* (Semiotexte, 1990, with Felix Guattari).

Negri voluntarily returned to Italy in 1996 in order to serve out the remainder of his prison sentence, hoping to help spark a resolution to a situation in which hundreds of Italian leftsts remained imprisoned for their politial activities during the 1970s. An inmate of Rome's Rebibia prison since 2001, Negri spends his days outside Rebibia's walls on parole, rebuilding and reviving the intellectual resources of the left.

October 27, 2001

GC/ML: At the beginning of the '90s, just after the fall of the Berlin Wall, we were together in the streets of Paris to demonstrate against the bombing of Baghdad. International intervention in the Gulf, under the aegis of the U.S., seemed to launch an expansive phase of imperial management of international relations. In regard to this phase, do the attacks on the World Trade Center in New York on September 11 constitute an interruption, or are they milestones in its continuation? Have the New York events put an end to a phase begun with the fall of the Berlin Wall? Or should one rather consider that it had already ended with the adoption by the U.S. of a unilateral position on the Palestinian question, the biological-weapon non-proliferation treaties, Kyoto, and finally Durban?

TN: At the beginning of the '90s, we were really too small a group

134

to demonstrate. Today there are many more of us, at least here in Italy. This is already a fact to reckon with. But it is also true in the United States, I think. Over and above this significant factor, the events in New York certainly pose an interruption. A disruption of imperial management, and one which happens inside the continuing process of constructing an imperial network shored up by collective capital. This construction had its origin, no doubt, in the early '90s, with the end of the Cold War. We are talking about a genuine interruption, because it's something which comes from outside, or, more specifically, from outside this process, without, nonetheless, coming from outside the imperial network. By that I mean that there was a process of forming the imperial constitution, in other words, the expansion of the sovereignty of capital throughout the weave of international relations, thus a major displacement of sovereignty in which international diplomacy was supplanted by imperial sovereignty.

It was at this moment that a suspension, a break, occurred: the attack on the United States. The interruption thus came from outside the process, but at the same time occurred inside the Empire. What occurred was a glitch in the process, a setback, a blockage— something that has been imposed. Before this braking action, there was, without doubt, an American initiative to unilaterally appropriate the direction of the process. But now they must cope with severe difficulties. To clarify, it's better to employ an abstraction. In my opinion, three crises are unfolding. I say three to simplify, but in fact there are multiple crises. These three crises involve the definition of imperial sovereignty.

The first revolves around the military aspect. This crisis has to do with the fact that the sovereignty, the enormity of the power which the Americans have amassed, the bomb, and, as a result, that capacity for absolute hegemony which exists, is confronted now with something which it must address: kamikazes, suicidal acts. If sovereignty was in the past the power over life and death, pushed to the extreme

135

of nuclear power extended worldwide, today this power no longer exists. Thousands of people are now prepared to oppose it with their voluntary deaths. It's the principle of the razor: What we have is a contradiction which we must resolve, one way or another.

The other contradiction, the next crisis, is that of currency. Sovereignty is also the power to impact the currency. The great crisis stems from the fact that the impact on currency has been managed within the thematic context of neo-liberalism, that is to say by the *"lex mercatoria"* (law of the marketplace), in short, by way of the private sector's ability to harvest value from misery. The state has abrogated its regulatory power; eighty percent of all regulatory function has been ceded directly to the private sector. Now, with the impact of this bomb arises a problem of trust. Who can guarantee the private process? They want to keep government out, but that is not possible: it is not possible to marginalize a standard of measurement which has general application.

The third crisis is that of communication; it is a crisis linked to the delivery of content, dizzying in its complexity and seeming almost to lose meaning. It's an interesting phenomenon but also a highly dramatic one. The crisis of communication is catastrophic. The complexity of meaning, once we find ourselves in the situation we've been in since September 11, has worsened to the point that the crisis has become unmanageable: there are factors which definitively challenge the framework of communication as usual. The question thus arises in terms of a manifold crisis. I said that at the beginning of the '90s that there were fewer of us, and that there are more of us nowadays. There are more people who realize this crisis, a crisis at the heart of the foundations of Empire and by way of which we have touched on three fundamental limits: the three interruptions which I've just cited. What must be underlined is that the Americans have attempted to duck the Palestinian question, the biological-weapon non-proliferation agreements, the ecological issues at Kyoto, the issues of racism at Durban. Now, they've been thrust brutally into these escalating contradictions, into this three-fold crisis.

GC/ML: After New York, the greatest world power, the imperial pole, declares war on "one man." What significance do you attribute to this new rhetoric of war and its political, military, and diplomatic expressions? What kind of war will this be? Does the alteration of the idea of sovereignty imply a change in the concept of war?

TN: The press seems baffled by one sole question: Who can tell us that this is not going to be an open-ended war? That it means fighting with technology, certainly, and even waging it in the Afghan valleys and mountains, we know, at the risk of a guerilla war which goes on forever—in other words, a risk of "Vietnamization" of the conflict. The concept of war has changed. The reaction to this crisis seems to be based on a strategy which entails, in an absolutely direct manner, war as a central tenet of maintaining discipline. When the violence is no longer "outside," when the language no longer carries meaning, when the standard becomes obscure, clearly one has to impose them with extreme force and violence.

We are passing through the problem of sovereignty. I am convinced that sovereignty, as a concept, is a smokescreen, that there is no sovereignty which is not at the same time a connection, a relationship. The concept of sovereignty, as Luciano Ferrari-Bravo put it so aptly, always has a double face. It is a sort of hegemony which integrates, paradoxically, something which it is unable to subsume. In the concept of state, of the political, it is impossible to exclude one of these two terms. The powers of Empire, by contrast, are constrained to exclude one; they are required to believe that war is the institutionalized basis of the new order. Which means precisely to advocate violence, measurement, language: the norms of violence, the standard of measurement, linguistic significance. They want to transform sovereignty into an operating system.

137

GC/ML: Empire is not a place. All the same, is a battle for primacy over this non-place possible? Aren't we experiencing this exact battle now? How do we define the rapport between Empire and the United States—a rapport which has spawned so much misunderstanding around the concept of Empire—in light of the events in New York? How do you read the establishment of the Euro in the center of this process?

TN: I can't say that the worldwide capitalist leadership is American. For those accustomed to extending the rules of power to those of exploitation, it's only in the second instance that you can, strictly speaking, begin to talk about a people. That was still possible when imperial powers existed. What does imperialism mean? It's the opportunity to elevate the theme of exploitation to the international level. If today all that is over—or partly over, or rather, if all that is tending toward the point of being over—it is no longer possible to speak of "American Imperialism." There are only groups, elites who hold the keys to exploitation and thus the keys to waging war, and who strive to impose their sway at the world level. Of course, this process is very contradictory and will continue to be, of necessity, for a long time to come.

138   For now, it is primarily North American bosses who are maintaining this dominion. Just behind them are the Europeans, Russians, Chinese: they are there to shore them up, or to disrupt them, or again to be ready to carry out a shift of centrality—but this shift will stay superficial because in the end what works is again and always capital, collective capital. If you view this from a political-science standpoint, you might think that the ones who stand to gain the most from the Americans are the Russians, whereas the Europeans stand to lose the most. Since the beginning of the '70s, each time that Europe—I'm not speaking of big European capitalism, which is always in harmony with its American counterpart, but the European ruling classes—tries to build up its institutions, its monetary tools, or even its militaries,

and it sometimes succeeds, a great international crisis systematically sweeps Europe along.

GC/ML: You think, then, that there is really a hegemony of capital?

TN: There is a hegemony which operates in the same way as American capitalism, but I am convinced that Italian capitalism, German capitalism, or French capitalism are equally involved in this operation.

GC/ML: With the destruction of the Twin Towers, men and women of the most cosmopolitan backgrounds in the world were slaughtered: not only top managers or leaders of large financial concerns, but also immaterial laborers and immigrants of every nationality. Can we think about the suicide attack on the city as an attack on cosmopolitanism, against the might of liberty and exodus?

TN: Your question is very intriguing because it helps us to understand this war. In effect, this confrontation is a means of determining who will be directed by Empire, and who will direct. From this point of view one can affirm that terrorism is the double of Empire. The enemy of Bush and Bin Laden is the multitude. I don't think we can say that we are all Americans. I think that on the other hand, we are all New Yorkers. That strikes me as highly significant. If we are New Yorkers, this is not because we embrace the American culture, but because we accept the culture of New York, the mongrel culture, the big wormy apple.

GC/ML: Before G-8 you spoke of alternative forms, Roman and Byzantine, Empire could take. How is the Byzantine form of Empire taking shape?

TN: It's quite evident that the prediction of a Byzantine empire is entirely based on the hypothesis advanced by the Bush camp: sort of a spatial shield that is again and always the discourse about war

139

as the constituent machine, a machine grafted in actuality onto what was a sort of technological innovation pushed to extremes. The already ancient design which aimed to afford an automatic defense and which sought also to give a post-Fordist form to military buildup itself. What are its tenets? First of all, the automatic nature of the response of the spatial shield. It involves on one side an enormous amassment of fixed capital, on the other extreme adaptability of the military arts, of ways of making war. This is known as RMA, Reform of Military Affairs, substantially put in place in the '90s, and founded on two pillars. We're talking about a post-Fordist military organization.

Today, the events of September 11 have seized this mechanism, to the point of turning it upside down. This reform continues to develop principally for the utilization of armies as international police—which is what the Americans are actually up to in Afghanistan—but at the same time, the barrier of the spatial shield which had divided the capitalist elites of different world regions—in particular, the rift between Americans and Russians—has evaporated. The American right-wing ruling class sacrificed the spatial shield to deepen the alliance, this "grand alliance," for the creation of single world power. In this regard, a new form is in the process of emerging.

140

GC/ML: The United States appears to have definitively ended a period of neo-liberalism. American initiatives to support the economy and finance have been defined as "Keynesian." But how is Keynesianism possible when Fordism no longer exists? Increasingly, we persist in talking about the return of the state and of politics, but are constrained by the logic of war. But war, as you reminded us recently, has always been the foundation of the state. What, then, would be the politics of the multitude? To avoid war?

TN: The United States is engaged once more in centralizing the organizational forces of war, in the war-structuring of the world according to a sort of authoritarian neo-liberalism, as opposed to Keynesian methods. It's true that the state has once more become a central figure in this intervention, but this question takes us back to the discourse on sovereignty. The state intervenes as one of the supporting poles of sovereignty, and not as the force behind unitary recomposition of social processes in the political arena. I might say that this authoritarian neo-liberalism has an open mind and a broad conception of sovereignty, along the same lines as the rapport which linked, for example, Stalinism and socialism. It's that aspect which is particularly disquieting.

GC/ML: How has the movement of Italian multitudes reacted to the events in New York? How can the multitude movement pry apart the deadly scissors squeezing them? Who will call today for the exodus? Are multitudes, to stay with the metaphor, Christians or barbarians?

TN: I will be cautious on these questions. My feeling is that the movement's reaction is without doubt very sound but still very fragile. And this second element is certainly negative. The renewal of a cycle of struggles envisioned since Seattle and Porto Alegre, and as far as Genoa, has been thwarted. Since the end of the '70s, unfortunately, we've gotten used to this disruption of cycles. In *Empire,* we describe the struggles—those of Los Angeles, those of Chiapas, that of Tiananmen—but also those which led to the fall of the Berlin Wall. We're talking about real struggles, but struggles whose connecting thread is absolutely impossible to identify. But after Seattle, on the other hand, we have arrived at putting our finger on a genuine cycle of struggles. There is no doubt: at that level, there is today a halt.

141

The problem does not inhere in the fact that there might not be any more new places to demonstrate. There exists an actual difficulty in interpreting the future (whatever the future watchwords are, how will it be possible to relate these discourses on a global scale?). But it is not any less true that *"quod factum infectum fieri nequit,"* what is done cannot be undone. This movement had established a true plan of ontological consistency; today there is a blockage of all that, there is an obstacle. It is like water flowing down a mountain: you can try to stop it, but if at the earliest point the flow goes around the obstacle, it will ultimately carve out a new path. We are in a similar situation, we are in a situation where there is a blockage which we must circumvent before we can revert to our course.

Let's analyze, then, the reactions of the Italian movement. These reactions are very interesting. In the first place, the movement tried to maintain its hold, no matter the cost, on what it had erected. We must notably consider the Catholics, very important in Italy: the theme of civil disobedience plays an important role in this context. The same thing, moreover—the attempt to keep erect what has been built—happens in the United States, or in other countries where political life is very open.

A second extremely important element: keep the networks open and continue to enlarge them. What is happening today in factories, in schools, in universities is crucial because that fosters the consolidation of alliances which now become alliances of identification, of planned struggles, of movements, of inclination, which were previously inconceivable. Which is not to say we must forget the difficulties which we face today, in bringing a half million people to the streets, as was the case in Genoa, nor that it has to be done in the same manner as in Genoa. This is a phase which is still potent, and I underline that word, "potent," because for me, this actually means "full of possibility."

Another thing which strikes me as absolutely fundamental: people understood. They understood from that point on that subjectivity produces, and that all activities become places of production once there is no longer a "place of production." When there is this sort of consciousness, always bigger, always deeper, those who take part in pacifist movements blend with workers' movements, tangible as well as intangible, which in turn will unite with women's movements and youth from social centers. Really, as long as that consciousness spreads and deepens in as powerful a manner as we're seeing today, certain watchwords begin to have weight, such as "desertion." And when we speak of "desertion," we are not calling on a negative watchword! It's negative as long as desertion defines itself simply in terms of strike. When capital alone has all the means of production at its disposal, then a strike, desertion, can only be passive.

Today, if one deserts, if one opposes the power alliance or the capital linkage, the power alliance or the knowledge linkage, the power alliance or the language linkage, one does that from a position of power, producing at the same time one is refusing. With this production, not only of subjectivity but also of intangible goods, desertion becomes a formidable material tool in the struggle. We need to examine closely the hacker's world to find a model of this sort. We speak of models where the construction of a network operates in the same space as an escape; that is, in the same moment we are recoiling from, refusing, escaping the capitalist organization of production, the capitalist production of power.

MGC/ML: It's thus in this context we must understand the discourse on desertion, of exodus? But for desertion to be effective today, here and now, wouldn't that entail the problem of transmuting values?

TN: It's clear that desertion—exodus—ought to be understood as a political laboratory. But it is true also that we face a fundamental alteration of values. The problem is to understand that *private* and *public* no longer signify anything, that they have no value anymore, that what is important is to construct a "commons" and that all production, all expression, must be given in common terms. So the main problem is that a transformation of values must take place and that it must spark a decision. Meanwhile, neither the decision nor the objective can be identified in a void. It springs from the very heart of the material transformation process of the multitude, or else nothing at all is happening and we are advancing to the rear. A cycle of struggle had been detonated and it allowed us to begin ourselves to build our little engines of war, very Deleuzian engines.

It is clear that today we are lagging behind, because there was a foreshadowing of this process which expresses itself by way of this hiatus. Or this hiatus, if it is well understood and mastered, could paradoxically be a very powerful moment. The most serious error would be, as some suggest, to revert to the national electorate, that is, to the methods of traditional political representation, which would mean to re-territorialize action. We must not therefore commit the error of retracing our steps, all the more since we risk getting stuck in the process. The fundamental concept is this: At the level of bio-power, at the level of a situation of power like ours, it is not possible to avoid rapport with the *other*, particularly rapport with the other who produces, rapport with the other who thinks. And the other whom they seek to destroy, contrary to what they try to argue, is not Bin Laden and terrorism, but the multitude. This passage is absolutely fundamental. The capitalist attempt to present this war as total destruction of the other is a big hoax . . . for them, most of all.

This interview originally appeared in Multitudes. *English translation by Kathleen Devereaux.*

Globalization and Trickle-Down Human Rights
Joe Lockard

Rights of capital have long prevailed over human rights. This ideology lies intrinsic within capitalism, which establishes itself upon the guardianship of property and processes of accumulation. That protective "riding shotgun" duty is the primary function of contemporary Western legal systems. Classic liberal human rights theory was born and continues to live a dependent existence in the shadow of capital's relation to labor, affordable to those classes with means to pay for the privilege. Poor and disenfranchised people have regarded human rights advocacy with due skepticism, fully aware that a disadvantage in resources means probable inability to assert such rights when confronted by state authority.

145

Normative human rights discourse, the language of global capitalism, continues to emphasize non-economic rights despite their intrinsic dependence on economic capacity. Indeed, the very normativity and acceptability of this discourse derives from its inability to alter established economic hierarchies. This partial and incomplete anti-economism has informed mainstream human rights discussions for generations. A holistic concept of human rights integrates economic and labor rights, emphasizing their dominant centrality rather than leaving them as a supplement to the discussion.

Without a radical recognition of labor, economic conditions, and egalitarian concepts of equal protection and due process, then the corpus of human rights remains incomplete.

Absent such recognition of their necessary foundation within economic justice, liberal human rights—free speech, free movement, free association—can become little more than market commodities. That commodification establishes human rights as only one more nation-product, more available and warranted in upper-tier global economies than in poorer economies where market discipline keeps citizens on shorter leashes. Under the terms of such commodification regimes, richer countries produce and consume more human rights and poorer countries have fewer available rights distributed to fewer citizens. Under liberal constitutionalism, human rights are a trickle-down product that works as well as the rest of trickle-down economics.

From the perspective of First World political orthodoxies in the United States and the EU, human rights become the promise of prosperity achieved. That these rights include a challenge to the prerogatives of transnational capital is unacceptable and economically self-defeating. From the perspective of Second World economies (China, Singapore, Gulf states), human rights are the subject of intense public management in order to achieve economic success. Anti–liberal state bureaucrats conceive of limited human rights as necessary only for the instrumentalization of their economic plans, and regard the excess production of such rights as a positive social danger and source of instability. It is under such rights-repressive governments that the Internet, now necessary to ensure economic growth but simultaneously a threatening field of free expression, provokes such inventive censorship. And across vast swaths of the globe, illiteracy inhibits and poverty prohibits realization of U.S.-style human rights, as limited as these may seem to many Americans. Whether in the conditioned submission of Indian *dalits* or the enforced silence of indigenous Guatemalans,

146

the global poor know from bitter experience that human rights are a luxury item.

Exporting Liberal Constitutionalism

The legal order of human rights in the United States relies on a massive disestablishment of human rights outside its national borders. Domestic constitutional protections, the limited legal basis for a selective list of human rights, seldom achieve realization outside the U.S. Although the U.S. constitution has served as a model for various countries—the Philippines and Japan, for example—the effectiveness of its transplantation has been linked to adherence to capitalist economic formations (i.e., greater income disparity, less access to legal protections).

Liberal constitutionalism has synchronized itself with the culture of capitalism on a global scale. Instruments of government have been organized to parallel commercial instruments; indeed, this is precisely the case for entry into the European Community, a procedure that requires national ratification of a series of pan-European law titles. That synchronization of economic organization with legal culture becomes the central expression of democracy, not a synchronization of economic and human rights. The distortion entailed underlies the operating philosophies of the major globalist organizations, beginning with the IMF and World Bank. 147

If capitalist culture emphasizes cheap labor, resource exploitation, and high profits, liberal consitutionalism can endorse these goals as compatible with its promotion of human rights, regardless of flagrant disregard for democracy. After decades of effectively unlinking national finances from democracy, the IMF—an institution that cannot conceive itself as separate from liberal constitutionalism—threatened to remove its aid from Pakistan after the 1999 army coup. "Democracy is in retreat, and when democracy retreats, countries are in danger" stated the IMF's managing director. With such words, the

IMF leadership sought to tie their vision of integrative exchange and no-barrier global marketplaces to a preservation of democratic values, whereas basic economic law remained unchanged post-coup. The IMF, which had no previous problems dealing with military governments in Pakistan and other nations, voiced a new-found allegiance to the cultural *symbolism* of liberal constitutionalism rather than its actual practice.

Yet the attendant liberal models of human rights invest a misplaced faith in the protections of constitutionalism as guarantors of those rights. There is barely a constitution written that does not nominally specify preservation of human rights as a central purpose of that document. Part of this faith comes from mythification of some successful defenses of rights in the United States constitution and British constitutional law, but it is a mythification that relies on an exclusionary legal historiography. Complimentary appreciation of U.S. constitutionalism rarely mentions the Alien and Sedition Acts, Indian removal cases, Dred Scott, or *Plessy v. Ferguson.*

Imitation of a legal system is an imitation of power, not of human rights achievements. An American-style constitution and legal system provide no greater intrinsic protection of human rights than hand-me-down traditions of British constitutionalism did in post-colonial anglophone Africa. The colonial Emergency Regulations survived in former British colonies, even though they had been targets of intense anti-colonial execration for rights violations, because their legal conveniences proved too great for authoritarian post-colonial governments to resist. Former colonial subjects adopted the means of imperial governance as reiterations of learned models of relations between rulers and ruled, without incorporating any fundamental respect for civil rights.

In a similar manner, governments that submit to the ideological banners of Euro-American capitalism promulgate legal memoranda of concern for local human rights. It's not the principle; it's

148

BORDERS
BOOKS AND MUSIC

8701 Germantown Avenue
Philadelphia PA 19118
(215) 248-1213

STORE: 0082   REG: 03/71   TRAN#: 7635
SALE   02/07/2003 EMP: 00041

ANTI CAPITALISM READER
      6832456   QP T   16.95
PERIODICAL
   725274813797 56 PR T   6.95

            Subtotal   23.90
            PENNS 7%   1.68
   2 Items Total   25.58
            CASH   40.00
            Change Due   14.42

        02/07/2003 11:04PM

   THANK YOU FOR SHOPPING AT BORDERS
PLEASE ASK ABOUT OUR SPECIAL EVENTS

Visit our website @ www.borders.com!

exchanged for replacement copies of the original
items only.
- Periodicals and newspapers may not be returned.
- All other refunds will be granted in the form of the
original payment.

BORDERS®

- Returns must be accompanied by the original receipt.
- Returns must be completed within 30 days.
- Merchandise must be in salable condition.
- Opened videos, discs and cassettes may be
exchanged for replacement copies of the original
items only.
- Periodicals and newspapers may not be returned.
- All other refunds will be granted in the form of the
original payment.

BORDERS®

- Returns must be accompanied by the original receipt.
- Returns must be completed within 30 days.
- Merchandise must be in salable condition.
- Opened videos, discs and cassettes may be
exchanged for replacement copies of the original
items only.
- Periodicals and newspapers may not be returned.
- All other refunds will be granted in the form of the
original payment.

the money. Governments antagonistic to any expression of democratic opposition embrace Western human rights ideology because it's good for business. Where the imperium of capital subtly suggests that improvements in the human rights climate would help the business climate, mildly ameliorative changes may occur. A fine balance exists between apparent human rights improvement and social risks caused by liberalization, and the history of the late twentieth century is scattered with the bleaching political bones of governments caught off balance.

Liberal constitutionalism enables the realization of human rights to the degree that these do not challenge the basic tenets of capitalism. In the United States especially, this has created a politics of constitutional expansionism, a progressive rhetoric that argues for the legal reinterpretation of constitutional clauses and phrases for the benefit of disempowered racial, gender, and sexual classes. This rhetoric co-exists with the economic enabling functions of that constitutionalism and has only rarely succeeded in altering capital's terms of privilege. Effective bifurcation of rights of capital and select human rights, with primacy to capital, is the current export model of liberal constitutionalism.

Commodifying Rights

149

Constitutionalism always needs its framers, interpreters, and practitioners. Before liberal constitutionalism provides human rights to anyone, it provides an income to a lawyer. In many countries, including Europe and much of the Americas, entry into the legal profession is class-bound, influenced by family connections and heavily restricted by professional organizations. Outside the United States and several other countries, the ratio of legal practitioners per thousand in population drops precipitously. For most of the world's population, the realization of constitutional guarantees through legal representation is a practical impossibility. Human rights become legal products, commodities that can be translated from abstract assertions into real protections for a price.

Disparate national legal systems, which often emerged from local culture and culture-bound concepts of justice, integrate into a Euro-American international law system that necessitates development of an high-priced transnational class of legal professionals. A rapidly expanding set of multinational law firms, with strategically-distributed offices in dozens of cosmopolitan cities, operate out of and profit from this legal environment that has emerged in tandem with economic globalization. The ideological principles of liberal constitutionalism support international law as a profit center, though the human rights of the disenfranchised have nothing to do with profitability.

This integrative merger of legal systems and capital flows, the leading characteristic of late twentieth-century international law and global trade agreements, works to promote orderly capital relations and disadvantage any concept of human or labor-based rights. Skilled international law professionals are integral to investment and production decisions, and have located themselves as agents of capital rather than intellectual protectors of constitutional rights guaranteed to individual citizens. As a form of legal globalization that nominally seeks to achieve protections for individuals, the ideals of constitutional liberalism entail legal labor that offers no profit opportunities, turning those protections into bottom-market commodities or work for idealistic non-governmental organizations. To hope for any significant alteration in the legal profession's overall alignment with capital rather than working people is an extravagance of political self-delusion. Stewart Alsop once observed half-facetiously that unemployed lawyers have been the leading historic cause of revolution. If there is any truth to Alsop's observation, contemporary capitalism has annulled that possibility by assuring that even the worst of economic times means a good income for lawyers.

The commodification of human rights as legal products available only through law professionals has been immensely detrimental to the achievement of those rights. To understand and pursue human rights as non-commodities would require radical reorganization of presently prevailing concepts of equal protection, access to legal assistance, and due process. It would require community-based justice systems and legal advocates with a specific charge to prevent inequalities of wealth from translating into unequal justice. In a most basic sense, a social change from current available-for-payment *legal* rights would require re-conceptualization of *human* rights as a proactive legal intervention into relations between capital and labor.

Labor-Based Human Rights

An irremediable antagonism exists between human rights and capital. Capital formation proceeds by any means necessary, within limits prescribed by legal systems expressly created to protect capital. Property rights are near-inviolate, whereas labor rights are contingent and conditional.

When Condorcet, who among French philosophers of the Enlightenment epitomized faith in social rationalism, wrote, "Our hopes for the future condition of the human race can be subsumed under three important heads: the abolition of inequality between nations, the progress of equality within each nation, and the true perfection of mankind," he inherently synthesized early mercantilism with a just and equal international and domestic order. No contradiction existed between human self-amelioration and a progressive European economic order; they were complementary objectives. However, European capital in the eighteenth century was deeply engaged in the pursuit of putative civilizational progress through enslavement and exploitation of laborers in Africa, Asia, and the Americas. Capitalism involves a central belief that the protection and advancement of capital represents the source of human progress. Since this is one of the most demonstrable of historical

151

falsehoods, in normative Western economic discourse, this belief lies in the realm of religious faith rather than empirical holding.

Human rights discourse disturbs this comfortable faith because it employs some of liberal constitutionalism's philosophic elements—particularly an insistence on individual freedom and self-determination—as a counter to capitalism's assaults against personal freedom and autonomy. A robust concept of human rights emphasizes, at a minimum, co-equality between labor and capital in either individual or collective economic decision-making. A viable labor-based concept of human rights demands the primacy of labor over capital, and argues that organized labor guarantees individual and democratic rights.

But since the Industrial Revolution, the "rights of capital" have expanded as an ideological and social parasite upon human rights ideology. For example, the conversion of the U.S. constitution's fourteenth-amendment equal-protection and due-process clauses from guarantees of human rights into property rights protections in the aftermath of the 1873 *Slaughter-House* decision by the Supreme Court illustrates how capitalism historically has endowed human rights upon corporations and inanimate objects of capital accumulation. Corporations and capital acquired the legal attributes of personhood, and thus benefited from the extension of human rights.

152

The constant enhancement of the rights of capital, which never received quite the historical setback in the twentieth century that some progressive historians would like to believe, has characterized the development of Western legal systems. Even the creation of labor-law protections can be viewed as a stabilization of labor costs to benefit capital formation and achieve cost predictability. Thus, some of the most beneficial developments toward protecting worker rights (e.g., workmen's compensation in the United States, national health and pension schemes in Europe) were driven by business needs rather than labor's right to health, safety, and income security.

However, the domestic cost of providing such rights to European and U.S. workers has diminished profitability. Profit maximization implicitly regards labor cost as a production necessity subject to search for the cheapest available labor source. This drive toward profit maximization has set the terms of daily existence for over a half-million Mexican *maquiladora* workers as much as for Indonesian shoe-factory workers. The global self-reproduction of capital relies on cheap labor producing goods and services for consumption by wealthy economies, without cognizance of the damage done to lesser-valued human lives. At most, capitalism treats such damage as a production cost.

From a labor-based perspective, this damage represents true human rights abuse. Third World wages, set at the minimum level necessary for survival in local economies, emerge from coercive socio-economic regimes that deny education and operate through gender discrimination, and which depend on state authorities that routinely violate human rights. The same liberal constitutionalism that nominally promotes social rights of free expression, operates by turning an economic blind eye toward labor conditions, their means of enforcement, and the disastrous effect on the unprotected classes. In this preference for blindness toward labor rights, contemporary globalization ideologies share much with their predecessor, eighteenth-century European mercantilism, that promoted domestic social reform while endorsing overseas colonialism as economic opportunity and civilizational progress.

That contradiction between domestic advocacy of limited social rights and the institution of policies depriving foreign subjects of the same rights has been a central piece of liberal Euro-American human rights ideology since the eighteenth century. Thomas Carlyle, who as an avatar of classic British mercantilism passionately advocated for the civil freedom of British subjects, could still argue in *The Nigger Question* (1849) for re-enslavement of emancipated Caribbean blacks who refused to work in British-owned sugarcane

153

fields and preferred to raise vegetables for self-support. Where international trade and the autonomy of native labor clashed, Euro-American liberalism had no problem choosing sides.

Corporate formations of capital, organized under recognizably neo-liberal legal tenets, scour the world for production conditions suitable for high profits. Governments anxious to integrate themselves into this global economic order adopt the necessary legal structures for foreign investment, with guarantees of human rights serving as either public relations sideshows or arenas of contest. The inextricable intertwining of economic and human rights would mean the end of a liberal charade of legal distinctions, for these rights can only be completely inseparable.

Interview with Doug Henwood
Charlie Bertsch

Although he can reel off numbers with the best of them, Doug Henwood is not your typical economist. Despite his mastery of financial data, he is an outsider to the profession. An unapologetically pro-government leftist swimming in a sea full of free-market sharks, Henwood directs his talents not to building portfolios, but to exposing the inequalities perpetuated in the pursuit of wealth. His labor of love is the *Left Business Observer*, the newsletter he has been publishing since 1986. Henwood is best known for his boldly titled 1997 book *Wall Street*, which has been encouragingly successful. His follow-up, *The New Economy*, applies the general insights of its predecessor to the absurd—and absurdly costly—boom of the late 1990s. Henwood is also the author of *The State of the USA Atlas*, an eye-opening work that has found its way into many college geography courses.

155

Interview conducted in two parts: September 1999, March 2002

CB: What exactly is the *Left Business Observer*?

DH: The *LBO* is a newsletter on economics and politics that intends to come out monthly but never quite makes it. It covers macro-economic issues such as trade, development, income distribution, poverty levels, and fiscal policy. In other words, it's "big picture" stuff. It doesn't report on plucky little companies.

CB: How does the *LBO* make ends meet?

DH: By getting some 3,500 people to subscribe to it. The basic subscription is $22. I ask for $50 from high-income people and institutions. By 1991, after putting the *LBO* out for five years, I had a subscription base of around 1,000.

CB: So basically the *LBO* is a longterm project that you've developed through word-of-mouth.

DH:Yes. I advertise in *The Nation* now and then. Our website actually pulls in a lot of subscriptions.

CB: How did you get started in independent publishing?

DH: I just got the idea one day. I was reading *Rock and Roll Confidential*, actually. I thought, "Hey, I can do a newsletter like this!" I took the plunge without thinking about it too much. How I got to that point is a story in itself. As I explain in a piece I wrote for the political zine *Bad Subjects: Political Education for Everyday Life*, I was a teenage right-winger. And during my freshman year in college I was planning to be an economics major and make a lot of money. But I'd always been interested in literature and culture, too, so I was wavering. When I gave up the right-wing politics early in my sophomore year, I decided to give up the economics as well and became an English major. I went on to graduate school in English and even toyed with the idea of writing a dissertation.

But then, as I was doing research for the dissertation, I started reading about economics again. I got the idea of tying the evolution of American poetry to changes in political economy. And when I gave up the dissertation, I kept reading the political economy. I went to work at a medical publisher for a couple years and then my wife and I started doing freelance work making book indexes. I figured out once that we'd done close to a thousand of them over the course of about ten years. It gave me enough flexibility to start writing the newsletter.

CB: I'm intrigued by the fact that *Rock and Roll Confidential* was the newsletter that started the ball rolling. For people who don't know this, in the world of economic advising there are lots of newsletters, many of them with very high pricetags. Didn't they inspire you, too?

DH: I got some of the ideas about how to present material from them, the way they used graphics and so on. But the idea for the format and the belief that I could pull it off came to me while reading *Rock and Roll Confidential.*

CB: In radical circles, people tend to take it for granted that independent production and distribution are good things, particularly in this era of corporate consolidation. People think, "If I can't avoid buying things, I might as well by them from the small, independent merchant who is resisting the corporate monoliths." You have a strong critique of this mindset. Can you explain why it's a bad idea to think that being "independent" is good in and of itself?

157

DH: In a practical sense, a lot of independent operations screw their employees and customers as much as anybody else does. You could say that there's often something other than the logic of profit maximization at work in independent operations, but you can't be sure of that. There are lots of scumbags and frauds everywhere, including independent publishers and music labels. Another point to consider is that the independent model can only be applied in certain contexts. You can't universalize it. You can't have "independent" computer companies or locomotive manufacturers or things like that. You have to think about what kind of arrangements make for large-scale operations, unless you want to give up on industrial civilization. I don't think most people seriously want to do that, even if they might fantasize about it. Once you start trying to conceive of some larger-scale, more cooperative way of doing things, you have to get beyond the fetish of independence.

I find the anti-corporate attitude nostalgic and hair-shirtish. I just can't stand the whole *Adbusters* approach to life. And there's always a risk of radical politics devolving into that kind of thing. I like McDonald's. I can't endorse a protest that consists of blowing the roof off a McDonald's.

CB: Somebody blew up one in Tucson, Arizona right before September 11. It was blamed on radical environmentalists.

DH: *[Laughs]* I'd rather see McDonald's workers better paid and their food produced under more sustainable circumstances. But this whole war against modern consumerism gives me the creeps.

CB: Why do you think that the fetishization of being independent is such a key part of the cultural left in the United States?

DH: That's American individualism at work. We don't think of political action, but what we can do for ourselves. An extreme example is people who blame themselves for being unemployed and take a resumé-writing course instead of thinking about why so many people are unemployed. There's this fantasy that you can opt out of the system. Then again, I've actually done that to a certain degree! But everybody couldn't do that. So if you want to think about politics, you have to think about some way of doing things collectively that's not exploitative and hierarchical.

CB: What about those people like yourself—and I realize you have probably been more successful than most—who have managed to opt out of the system and still make a comfortable living? Do they have something which other people lack?

DH: It's a combination of being good at it, finding a niche, and luck. I guess it also takes a certain kind of personality. And I also think you need what the economist John Maynard Keynes called "animal spirits." You don't really think about what you're doing. Instead of doing market research, you just plunge into it.

CB: One of the biggest problems with the contemporary left is its fragmentation. For example, although there's a left-wing music community, it doesn't necessarily have a lot of contact with other leftist circles. And this leads to a lot of redundant effort, with different sectors of the American left repeatedly reinventing the wheel instead of pooling their resources and knowledge. In fact, when I met you I was surprised to find out how interested you were in music, specifically punk music, because it's hard to find leftists who move comfortably beyond their field of specialization. What can we do to bring leftists together?

DH: That's a tough one. The most important thing is to create a sense of resistance and community and maybe some sense of a possible future while you're at it. The problem you're talking about is so widespread. I'd like to be part of a broader magazine covering a lot of culture and politics in addition to the economy, where all these people who don't normally talk to each other would do so.

159

CB: *The Baffler* falls into that category to a certain extent.

DH: It does. I should put in a good word for *The Baffler*, because I definitely feel an affinity for what they're up to. They're serious about being old-farty, which is a pretty hard thing to do. *[Laughs]* The temptation for so many leftish periodicals is to soften their message in order to broaden their audience. And they end up with a lot of pablum as a result.

CB: The fragmentation of the left frequently leads to a debilitating near-sightedness. People spend so much time worrying about their scene's internal politics that they forget what they have in common. At worst, this can result in a *Lord of the Flies* situation, in which leftists turn on their neighbors instead of focusing their energy on the real problems. The situation has improved somewhat since the anti-globalization movement took off, but fragmentation remains a huge problem.

DH: You could make a long list of that sort of thing—identity politics vs. class, cultural politics vs. "real" politics, Marxism vs. Postmodernism—and it's all tedious camp-building, an exchange of volleys that's really a sign of weakness and defeat and a recipe for more weakness and defeat. It's really kind of sad.

CB: Your website is a compendium of different resources, not just for leftists, but for anyone who's interested in questioning the status quo in the United States and throughout the so-called First World. What other stuff do you do that may be less obvious to someone who doesn't know you well?

DH: The *LBO* sponsors an Internet mailing list, too. The founding manifesto emphasized the importance of speaking across all these divides. It's not always as successful as I'd like it to be, but that's my ambition for it. It'd be nice to see more publications trying to bring people together personally.

CB: I recall you saying, on your book tour for *Wall Street* a few years back, that you had a pre-established audience of *LBO* subscribers who turned out in force. Did you find that having those people together in the same room led to more personal exchanges between them, as opposed to just being subscribers united by a common interest in what the *LBO* does?

DH: Unfortunately not, people just come and go.

CB: You were in Seattle for the demonstration against the World

Trade Organization. There was a real sense of excitement on the left afterwards. But the landscape has changed radically since then. Does the anti-globalization movement still have momentum?

DH: First, I want to emphasize the sense of something being born in Seattle, kind of by surprise. There was an exuberance there. We all knew that something was going to happen, but didn't know exactly what and certainly didn't know it was going to be of that scale and importance. I was struck there by both the organizational model of anarchism, which combined incredible flexibility with great discipline, and the spirit of it, which combined great seriousness and fun. It was much wittier and—I hesitate to use the word—*erotic* than any protest I'd attended before.

CB: Out of curiosity, what was your perspective on anarchism prior to the Battle of Seattle?

DH: I've always been sympathetic to it. It's a wonderful idea. I think it often tends to be juvenile in practice. A lot of it is an infantile "No!" translated into a political philosophy. But, on the other hand, I can find it very charming and engaging. One of the reasons why I like Toni Negri's style of autonomous Marxism is that it combines that anti-statist, anti-authoritarian, anti-hierarchical spirit with a more rigorous analysis. An awful lot of the anarchists one meets don't read or think very much, partly because they believe that action is more important than thought. That's true of many activists, of course. The anarchists don't have a monopoly on that attitude. But I do think that it grows naturally out of their philosophy, which emphasizes spontaneity and self-expression.

161

CB: But you think the so-called "organized left" could learn a thing or two from the way in which the protest in Seattle was organized?

DH: Exactly. When I got back from Seattle, I gave a report to the local Labor Party chapter. I was still in the glow of the moment. And some grim, old Leninist gets up—he's not that old, actually—and says, "What you describe sounds like carnival," and goes into this long diatribe about imperialism using all the Leninist jargon. And I was thinking, "Yeah, it was carnival. So what?"

CB: Flash forward to Genoa in 2001. Were you still feeling as hopeful about the anti-globalization movement?

DH: I was still quite optimistic. The first shock, really, was that the Swedes shot three people. That just seemed so un-Swedish. The brutality in Italy was less surprising since they have a very violent history. And if the guy really was trying to throw a fire extinguisher through the window of a cop car, that's kind of a dumb thing to do. He didn't deserve to die for it, but it didn't make much sense as a street strategy. As far as the big picture goes, you can't sustain that Seattle magic for very long, that moment of self-discovery. It was a unique moment that couldn't be repeated. And part of the reason is that the cops in Seattle were taken off-guard. In subsequent protests they knew exactly what to expect and were well prepared for it. But, in any case, you can only go so far throwing street parties. It gets much more difficult when you start thinking about what your agenda is and what your longterm mode of organization will be.

CB: And there's the danger that the protests will become nothing more than an empty ritual. You want to avoid the sort of demonstration where nobody is listening, not even the people who are talking.

DH: The good thing is that the bourgeoisie was getting very nervous. You could see these anguished articles asking, "What's going on?"

CB: Not to mention that Toni Negri and Michael Hardt had that op-ed in the *New York Times*.

162

DH: That was an amazing moment. One of the reasons that their book *Empire* had the success it did was that it offered some attempt at a theoretical explanation of what was going on, what was new about the capitalist world today, but also what kind of opposition it might inspire. There's a big hunger for that.

CB: Now let's talk about what's happened in the past few months. It's difficult to project into the future from the time of this conversation. But regardless of what happens, it's clear that there is a great deal more uncertainty on the world stage now. In a recent piece in *The Nation*, you made the point that anti-globalization activists can't proceed as they did prior to September 11. You wrote about a conference you attended in which "there was little serious acknowledgment of the fact that we were attacked and some U.S. response was inevitable and even justified." Where do you see things right now?

DH: I caught a lot of shit for that line. It's hard to reconcile the acknowledgment that smashing airplanes into buildings is a horrible, violent, evil thing to do with the sense that the world is also a deeply unjust place and the United States is responsible for a good bit of that. Mixing those two messages is very hard if you want to talk to an audience larger than the already converted. What struck me at this conference—and I think this is broadly true of a lot of people on the left—is that most people can only do one thing or the other. Either they go into this raving patriotic mode or they just denounce U.S. imperialism.

CB: Noam Chomsky.

DH: Yes. As much as I admire Noam—and I admire him a lot—he seems to have a hard time talking about anything that isn't the result of U.S. imperialism. There are no bad forces in the world except those that are inspired by Washington. God knows, the United

163

States is deeply guilty of many things. I don't want to deny that. But, on the other hand, we have a much worse class of enemy than we used to. I mean, these people are really vile. Look at the series of enemies the United States has had over the last ten years. They really are bad people. It's not like we're dealing with the Viet Cong, or the Cuban Revolution, or the Sandanistas anymore. And it's hard to talk about a conflict in which there are no good guys.

CB: You mentioned that there are lots of activists who don't really read. This illustrates a larger problem facing the left: the lack of people with expert knowledge. The irony is that, despite all the years Marx spent in the reading room at the British Museum, leftists tend to be particularly clueless where the economy is concerned.

DH: There's a tremendous amount of mystification about economics. Its practitioners like to treat it almost like physics, as if it were a natural science. I think a lot of people whose instincts are oppositional nonetheless get taken in by that mystique—the pretension to science, the sense that the economy is this independent mechanism impervious to human influence. So I try to demystify it. I tell people who's really got the money and how things are distributed. This is part of a broader project to show how power works economically and politically, because I think a lot of people who have this gut instinct that things are pretty fucked up don't know exactly how or why. I try to fill in those blanks.

164

CB: A good example of this would be your tireless work exposing the mythology of the New Economy. A few years back, everyone was talking about taking control of their investments. People were leaving good jobs to become day-traders. That path is a lot less attractive in 2002. But it's perfectly possible that we will see a resurgence of interest in playing the stock market when the economy improves. What's wrong with the dream of getting rich overnight?

DH: These wondrous stories are targeted to a youngish age group.

Yet younger workers are actually worse off relative to the averages than older workers were in their youth. But that's not the image you'd get from reading the papers, even in the middle of the present recession. I think the boom of the late 1990s, which was dependent on people in the stock market feeding money to technology firms, created an illusion among people that things were a lot better. But it also fed this sense among them that there was something wrong with them if they weren't participating, that they were somehow defective if they were missing this great boat. In fact, that situation was extremely unusual from an historical standpoint. And it involved so few. It was really only people whose incomes were in the top one or two percent that made out like bandits in the great boom. Everybody else was just barely getting by.

CB: So you're saying that even before the decline of the stock market in 2001, the economy wasn't doing nearly as well as people imagined.

DH: That's right. People forget about the recession during the first Bush administration. It wasn't until the height of the boom in 1999 that average incomes regained their pre-1989 levels.

CB: Why do you think that this particular brand of entrepreneurial ideology was so successful at saturating the culture beyond the world of the business section? Looking back at times when Americans were not supposed to question what was going on, it's hard to find much that compares with the celebration of the free market we witnessed in the past decade. Even at the height of the Cold War, the superiority of Western countries was usually explained in terms of the freedoms they permitted: speech, conscience, and association. Free enterprise was just another item on the list.

DH: There's a big difference between what was going in the 1950s and what's been happening lately. From the 1950s into the 1960s, there were very broad income gains throughout the working population. The overall income distribution was actually getting slightly less unequal and kept doing so until about 1967 or 1968. So there was this sense of broad prosperity. Certainly a lot of people were excluded from it. People romanticize that period of our history. It was nowhere near as stable as nostalgia would have us believe. But it had its good side for the American worker. The situation in the past decade was not at all similar. What we have now is a fragmentation of economic and social life. Old hierarchies have come undone and people feel responsible for themselves.

CB: That supports the whole entrepreneurial myth.

DH: Yes. The fact is that some people were getting very rich during the boom. And it did excite myth-making. But there's a long tradition of that in American history. People have been coming here to get rich for a very long time. I think it's just a matter of degrees. But the era of the so-called New Economy presented one of the more extreme examples. We've had several moments like this—in the late 1920s, the late 1960s and early 1970s, and now—in which the stock market mentality has infected the whole culture. Because people have been convinced that Social Security is going under, they feel that they have to trade their way to retirement security. And this is true despite the fact that the death of Social Security is a complete fabrication, and the fact that most people are not going to be able to trade their way to retirement security anyway.

166

CB: There's a flipside to the belief that it's impossible to intervene in the economy. These days, people can play the stock market without any of the economic knowledge that would have been necessary at other times in American history. What do you think of the people who do this without necessarily knowing what they're doing?

DH: I think most of them will end up losing their shirts. We don't really know for sure, but there have been preliminary studies—conducted before the fall of the stock market, mind you—showing that seventy percent or more of the people involved in day-trading lose money. Even very educated people don't understand the basics of finance. They don't understand the arithmetic of interest rates or anything like that. Asking them to manage their retirement plan is really a lot. Even professional portfolio managers consistently underperform. And most people, except maybe those in the top twenty percent of income, are not going to be able to save very much money in their lifetimes. They have to rely on a generous and secure public pension check, possibly supplemented by a private pension fund of some sort. Because they're not going to be able to take care of their own retirement, they better spend their time preventing Wall Street from privatizing Social Security. That would be a much better expenditure of energy than trying to beat the market.

CB: Trying to prevent the privatization of Social Security is not something that has the aura of excitement that other forms of political activism have.

DH: No, it certainly doesn't! Fiscal policy is pretty boring. I think that's the great ruling-class advantage. These areas are native terrain. And most lay people feel completely out of their depth. They defer to experts, and all sorts of scams get perpetrated as a result.

167

CB: In discussing ways that we might try to win more control over large corporations, you write in *Wall Street* that, "the Japanese structure, with its cross-holding and monitoring mechanisms, seems like a promising model for a more socialized mode of ownership of larger firms." There was a time when everybody was looking to Japan for answers. Yet now the economy of Japan is being held up as a model for how *not* to do things. Do you still see Japan as a viable model?

DH: Yes. I'm looking for things that are *not* dynamic in a capitalist system, things that are more sustainable. And so I think the fact that the Japanese model does restrict competition, that it does create more cooperative structures, is good. These are virtues. But it's hard to make that argument these days, because everybody is pushing capitalist dynamism as the true aspiration for all humankind.

CB: And in that context, it's hard even for an economy as strong as Japan's was—or maybe still is—to sustain itself.

DH: It was a great strategy for catch-up, serving them very well from 1950 to 1989. But now it's clear that the American hyper-competitive model is in the ascendancy. It's very ugly, very damaging, but also very powerful. On its own terms, it's pretty successful.

CB: If I've read you correctly over the years, you've been a pretty strong advocate for state intervention in the economy in a self-conscious way. Now, of course, we're in a situation in the United States where we're getting a much stronger sense of state control as a result of the semi-wartime that we're in, with the return of deficit spending. But I don't imagine that this is the kind of state intervention that you or any other leftist really wants. What's your position on the state these days?

DH: That's a real tough one. I was evoking my fondness for anarchism and autonomism earlier, both of which are explicitly anti-statist. And they have a great appeal for me. But, on the other hand, we live in this world of powerful states. I think a lot of anarchists and autonomists have been pushing the end of the nation-state argument because they *want* it to be true. But I don't think it is. Certain states are weak, like Zambia or Jamaica. However, the governments of the G-7 countries are very powerful. And we also have entities, like the IMF, which are essentially state bodies. They're not weakening.

CB: Is it the case, then, that these powerful nation-states make themselves look a lot weaker than they really are because they're servicing only a small percentage of the population?

DH: Yes. The state has been returning to its roots as a coercive entity doing the work of capital.

CB: As Marx described it.

DH: Yes. We're back to the model of primitive accumulation, in which the state does nothing but criminalize poverty and vagrancy, and privatize property. Over the last twenty years, all of the more benign roles of the state have been cut back, but its more punitive roles have been increased. And that sucks! As a leftist, I'm looking for anything that's going to reduce the power of competition on people's lives. Welfare states do that. They take the sting out of unemployment and reduce the power of the boss. By contrast, punitive states increase the power of the boss. You're more likely to go to jail, more likely to be surveyed. So I'm all for jacking up the better functions of the state. And if you're talking about the poorer places of the world, they clearly need a state that's going to foster some planning and development scheme. A poor country can't get less poor without an honest and competent government doing serious work for it. I'm trying to reconcile my anti-statist aspirations and my statist residency in the real world. One of the things I like about the recent activism spearheaded by the anti-globalization movement is that it's not focused on lobbying the state. It's trying to build networks of solidarity among people outside national lines. And that's very exciting.

169

Today it is claimed that the bourgeois ideals of Freedom, Equality, and Justice have proven themselves to be poor ones; however, it is not the ideals of the bourgeoisie, but conditions which do not correspond to them, which have shown their untenability. The battle cries of the Enlightenment and of the French Revolution are valid now more than ever. The dialectical critique of the world, which is borne along by them, consists precisely in the demonstration that they have retained their actuality rather than lost it on the basis of reality.

—Max Horkheimer, "Materialism and Morality"

Open Up The Iron Gate

How Parallel Economies Are Working Against Global Capitalism
Megan Shaw Prelinger

As 2001 drew to a close, the promise of global economic integration became clear. With networks of capital linked worldwide across increasingly porous borders, the downturn of the United States' economy was pulling the world down with it. The global supply funnel that pours First World "development" capital into countries such as Taiwan, Mexico, Singapore, and Argentina has left those countries in deep recession as the U.S. economy retracts. At the same time, those countries that have lagged behind globalization are suffering less.

The phenomenon of globalization has created a new economic geography as capital accumulates in new patterns of centralization that no longer fit state-based economic patterns. While most accounts of anti-globalization initiatives tend to focus on anti-capitalist protests and debt-relief movements, little focus has been placed on an entirely different set of responses to globalization that emphasize the creation of alternative modes of commerce. Around the world, new mechanisms of exchange are being developed such as trade and barter associations, mutual credit associations, and local currencies. These exchange mechanisms are redefining how wealth is created and distributed in small-scale economies. This essay will

175

examine how capital is being reconceived at the local level world-wide, and how local economies are operating in parallel to the global economy.

Parallel currencies and community-level economies are not new. Historically, people have used a wide assortment of value units and trade groups as media of exchange. In the United States, local currencies flourished in colonial times and currencies were backed by a variety of goods such as corn and timber. Independent coinage was not outlawed until 1864, and the centralized banking system was not established until 1913. Even after the national currency was federalized, it was rarely the only operating currency in the country. Local scrip was used widely during the 1930s to allow goods to be traded in the face of extremely scarce federal currency. And in the early 1970s an experiment by the decentralist Ralph Borsodi established a new currency called the Constant in Massachusetts that was designed to operate independent of the raging inflation of that era. That experiment didn't last, but it started a new era of interest in local currency and other decentralist strategies that gathered momentum throughout the 1970s and '80s. Then globalization raised the stakes.

The passage of NAFTA in 1993, the Uruguay round of GATT in 1994, and the creation of the WTO in 1995 together redrew the flow of capital worldwide. The dismantling of the Soviet Union has allowed capitalism to attain a level of global hegemony that was unimagined before 1990. At the same time, the high-speed computer networks that became ubiquitous in the mid-1990s facilitated the development of what has been termed the "casino economy." As a result of this new economic geography of the 1990s, parallel economies have taken on heightened significance. They have become important experiments in defying global capitalism by creating working economic alternatives that have direct impact on people's livelihoods.

What Are Parallel Economies?

In Ithaca, New York, a local currency called Ithaca HOURS is circulating widely. It has transacted more than $1.5 million of business in the late 1990s. HOURS are accepted at local hospitals, can be deposited at local banks, and are accepted at 280 businesses within the town. At the other end of the Americas, in Argentina, thousands of people are feeding themselves and using each others' products and services through trading and barter exchanges that are operating independent of the collapsing national economy. In 2001, over five hundred trading clubs and local currency systems were busily operating independently of the generalized national economic depression. The Argentinian system, RGT (Global Exchange Network), circulates the equivalent of several million U.S. dollars every year. Both of these economic systems were devised at the local level and are in healthy operation, parallel to their macro-economies.

These examples illustrate two main types of parallel economies: *local currencies* and *non-monetary systems* such as local employment and trading systems (LETS), also known as local exchange trading systems. In local currency systems, the unit of exchange is usually linked to the U.S. dollar or other national currency, but with the valuation moderated by a calculation of the value of time, or of real goods and services. HOURS currency systems base the currency unit on the value of an hour of time, in terms of U.S. dollars. HOURS systems are the most common kind of local currency system.

In Ithaca, where the HOURS system was invented in 1991 by Paul Glover, the currency is valued at the price of one hour of semi-skilled labor, or ten U.S. dollars. This varies across HOURS systems; in Berkeley, California, where wages are higher, the BREAD unit of currency is valued at twelve dollars. In Mexico City, the local currency system is called Tianguis Tlaloc and the unit of exchange is the Tlaloc. Tlalocs are similarly valued in denominations of hours of time, with one Tlaloc being valued (in 1996) at

177

twenty-five pesos or three U.S. dollars. HOURS systems are overseen by a local HOURS association which issues the money and keeps track of its flow and volume. HOURS are traded just as regular U.S. dollars among whoever elects to trade them.

The proliferation of LETS systems worldwide has resulted in heterogeneity across those systems; but in general they can be described as clearinghouses where goods or services are traded on account among participating members. The accounts track the amounts that are exchanged in terms of a unit of value that is agreed upon by participating members, and no interest is charged or paid. Although trading clubs are as old as civilization, the LETS system as it is currently understood was developed in British Columbia in the early 1980s by Michael Linton. He devised the first LETS system as a member-operated nonprofit barter system that caters to individual traders, as opposed to commercial barter systems which cater to businesses and charge fees on transactions.

LETS systems provide an organized network for people to exchange labor, goods, or services on a small scale, as small as person-to-person. In the United Kingdom, over one hundred LETS systems are currently organized, averaging seventy-two member traders per system. LETS systems, like HOURS systems, started in "First World" countries but soon were taken up in much poorer countries where the need for economic alternatives is much greater. As in Argentina, the Tlingis Tlaloc system of Mexico City is actually a hybrid HOURS/LETS system. The system includes both a printed currency used as a medium for public exchange and a mutual credit system in which members accept the currency in exchange for goods and services.

How Parallel Economies Work Against Global Capitalism

In our current federal currency system, money is created in banks by the push of a button as credit, and interest is charged for the "loan" of that "money." The privilege of our banking system to charge a fee for something they have created out of thin air amounts to usury. The accrual of "wealth" that has no backing and demands a service fee creates inflation. This money system malfunctions in three important ways, as characterized by Thomas H. Greco, Jr. in *New Money for Healthy Communities* (1994): it is valued based on scarcity; the interest system pumps the flow of money from the poor to the rich; and it is misallocated at its source (banks).

The project of establishing parallel currency systems attempts to combat all three of these misdeeds. Local currencies represent a real alternative to the usury inherent to our system. The money in local currencies is an exchange medium, not a savings medium. Interest is not charged on it, and there is no value that accumulates without a one-to-one match of contributed labor, goods, or services. LETS systems are organized as mutual credit systems, but the sense of credit in this case is very different from the imaginary money that our traditional banking system charges us for. In a mutual credit system, all value existing within the credit system is backed by either labor, goods, or services. Mutual credit cooperatives track accounts as value moves into them and out of them. If an account is above zero, it is in credit; below zero, it is in debit. In such a system, being in debit only means that you have temporarily purchased more goods than you have traded. Account balances fluctuate above and below zero without penalty.

179

Capital is therefore never abstracted from labor or real goods, nor does it accumulate without having been earned. Money itself is not allowed to become a commodity. Although business continues as usual for individual small enterprises, and capital still accumulates in the standard currency as the volume of business increases as a result of the use of local currency, the flow of money is directed toward other participants in the local economy. The money system itself is cooperatized. As the money supply is expanded, more people have more money to do more things. Also, there is no incentive to hoard credit or currency in a parallel currency system. Because the local money does not accumulate interest, it is of little value sitting in the bank. Its only use is in circulation, so it encourages economic activity. And because most currency transactions involve a combination of federal currency with local currency, the federal currency "piggy-backs" on the tradeability of the local money. Therefore the scope of the local economy increases independent of whether the macro-economy is growing, insulating the local economy to some degree from national and worldwide economic fluctuations.

There are two specific ways that parallel economies can operate to insulate local economies from the mood of the macro-economy, depending on whether or not their unit of exchange is linked to the units of the macro-economy. Where the local currency is pegged to the U.S. dollar (or Mexican peso, etc.), the currency allows for general economic expansion by creating a parallel money supply that counteracts any constricting trends that the macro-economy dictates. Where the local currency is valued according to a standard agreed upon by the trading community, it operates independent of the parallel national currency.

How Parallel Economies Redefine the Economic Landscape

The purpose of establishing a "local" in "local currencies" is not to draw lines of exclusion, nor to create spaces where the benefits of local currencies are prohibited. People living in between different local currency regions can form their own trading groups, to the extent that groups can be organized among people given the distance that separates them. The line that is drawn between participants and non-participants in the exchange community is self-determined by those electing to participate, and only the practical accessibility of trading partners to one another determines the limits of the physical geography of "local."

Within the limits of practical accessibility that define the space occupied by a parallel economy, the capital resources of a region are encouraged by the economic system to remain within that region. Those who choose to join the parallel system are selecting themselves to be part of a new economic geography. They have begun to de-couple their economic life from the global exchange system and its inherent problems.

A core characteristic of the global exchange system is that it redirects the flow of wealth: as the "free" trade of globalization engenders the hyper-mobility of capital and jobs, new corridors of wealth are opening up worldwide. Yet just as the forces of globalization redraw the geography of wealth, they simultaneously redraw the geography of poverty and underdevelopment.

One key to this problem is the issue of accountability for the trade system. As capital leaves the aegis of nation-states, the regulatory functions of those polities (such as they exist) decline in their power and significance. The decline of the nation-state as a site of concentrated economic power would be constructive if that power was being dissipated and redistributed. But the current decline is only pulling in the opposite direction, toward the hyper-concentration of resources. The WTO's governance rooms in Geneva currently house a power center that has the potential to regulate the environmental and trade policies of all 143 member nations. Combating this concentration then becomes a challenge to reclaim the governance and accountability of economic systems.

In *Globalization and its Discontents* (The New Press, 1998), Saskia Sassen looks to the emerging transnational urban cores—such as Geneva, Tokyo, London, New York, and Singapore—as sites for the implementation of mechanisms for governance and accountability in the global economy. Her theory may predict the future evolution of the world economy, and she is quite correct to recommend the evolution of economic accountability systems into site-specific realms. In the opposite direction, a parallel set of forces is drawing the economies of smaller population hubs, and regions of sparse

181

population, into smaller economic and political units. By redefining the place of communities within the economic landscape, local trade systems and currencies ensure a level of accountability that is absent from large-scale, especially global, economic set-ups.

There are several ways that accountability is ingrained in locally operated economic systems. Most obviously, in a trade system with only three hundred members it is likely that over time all the members will come to know one another. Secondly, the governance mechanisms of parallel economic systems are generally transparent to their members. The governance is either elected, or the system is governed by default, by whichever members show up regularly for the governance meetings or whichever members are free to donate time to the oversight group. At the same time, the very nature of the capital being controlled is dissuasive to abuse. As I have already remarked, it is useless if transported out of the community, and almost equally useless when hoarded.

Parallel Economies and Anti-Capitalism

Local currencies and nonprofit trade and barter networks are not necessarily consistent with radical politics. They are embraced by the "green business" community, which takes note that parallel economies do not stop capital (as expressed by national currency) from accumulating, yet they do address many concerns of the progressive conscience.

Although parallel economies do not seek to eliminate the national currencies beside which they operate, they do increase the money supply in their regions. The profit motive is not prevented from operating within a local currency system, but it does behave very differently. It responds to local concerns, it is accountable to local currency holders, and the benefits it bestows on profit holders are more likely to be transferred to other members of the community.

Although parallel currencies are still best established in developed countries, their potential is greatest in debt-ridden countries where the money supply of entire nations is held hostage by the World Bank. Again, the problems of globalization are at the core of the new relevance of parallel economies. The recent hyper-concentration of wealth is a geographic concentration, and this has changed some of the considerations for the redistribution of that wealth.

Parallel economies do have one tremendous advantage as projects of radical economic reform: they are actually happening. And internationally, they are growing rapidly. As described by economist Stephen DeMeulenaere, in the past five years, local currency systems have been established in Dakar, and in Thailand, Japan, and Indonesia, in response to the Asian economic crisis of 1998–1999. Local currency systems are now operating in more than thirty-five countries worldwide, and in Mexico, Australia, and England, the systems are actively supported by the national governments.

Conclusion

It will be interesting to see how parallel economies find a place within the discourse of American political alternatives. From community supported agriculture cooperatives to regional statehood movements, people are working to re-scale the socioeconomic pieces of their world. And decentralization has immense popular appeal in the cultural sphere. In North America, private communities are increasingly normal, both in suburban hells where inhabitants are prohibited from installing lawn decor, and in green communities open exclusively to dwellers of self-contained Earthships.

183

But whether a new economic geography can take root and make a difference within our culture remains to be seen. It is arguable that the scale on which the liberatory potential of local currency is actualized is too small to be statistically significant in the face of the scope of globalization. Rural America is being hit very hard by glob-alization, as communities that rely entirely on exports of extractive resources can no longer compete in the global marketplace. It will be the great challenge to decentralist economics to solve the problems of these communities with no central economic activity apart from being a node in the global economic superstructure.

Like private communities, local currencies answer questions posed to society by both radicals and conservatives. They create new sites for the formation of wealth, and they also echo some of the discourse of traditional American conservatism. Much of the language around local currencies emphasizes their power to help communities become more "self-reliant." There is an old-fash-ioned and conservative impulse to keep jobs in the community that drives some of the effort behind local currencies. But that does not contradict the potential for economic liberation that par-allel currencies present. They offer structure for communities that are working to meet their needs from within and uncouple from the global capitalist system. The BREAD Hours local currency in Berkeley goes so far as to state its aims to promote economic jus-tice, ecological sustainability, community building, food security, and diversity. One might only hope that a single initiative could aim so high.

It is yet unclear how our economic lives will proceed after the global exchange system attains its critical mass and begins to fold inward. The transition that conventional money is making toward greater and greater abstraction is unsupportable. Money as we generally understand it has ceased to represent any value other than that assigned to it by the shared imagination of its holders. Eventually this shared vision will falter, and capital holders will experience the self-fulfilling prophecy of devaluation. We saw this happen in the Silicon Valley bubble of the late 1990s, and there is no reason to suspect that the world economy is less vulnerable. For this reason especially, it is of interest to track the progress of parallel currency systems. The success of local currencies as an alternative system for the creation and distribution of wealth has implications for the future of many yet-unanticipated political projects.

From Bunny Rabbits to Barricades: Strategies of Anti-Capitalist Resistance
Scott Schaffer

. . . the very differentiation of the economic and the political in capitalism
. . . is precisely what makes the unity of economic and political struggles
essential, and what ought to make socialism and democracy synonymous.
—Ellen Meiksins Wood, *Democracy Against Capitalism*

*A*pril 2001, Los Angeles. I'm watching CNN International's coverage of the Summit of the Americas protests in Quebec, Canada. The footage is familiar, as I'd seen it with the Seattle and Los Angeles protests: angry young people lined up at a chain-link fence surrounding *l'haute ville*, chanting slogans and yelling at police. The remains of tear gas canisters litter the ground, and smoke wafts through the air. Then, I see it—a pink bunny rabbit, launched from a catapult by twenty-nine-year-old Montreal activist Jaggi Singh, flying through the air over the fence into the "red zone." Sureté Quebec is furious. They start firing tear gas at the crowds, who surprisingly enough don't flinch or flee.

Just before this moment, though, something gloriously unfamiliar happened. The protesters were allowed to speak, live—as if given five minutes to state their best case against global capitalism.

And they did—eloquently, simply, so that Bob Jones in Oklahoma could understand why thousands were in the streets, risking injury and potentially their lives, in the name of something as nebulous as "globalization." Since Quebec, though, only the "peaceful demonstrations" at the 2002 World Economic Forum in New York have seen anti-capitalist resisters able to give their reasons for acting.

Anti-capitalist protests, from Seattle in 1999 to New York in 2002, have generally been portrayed in two ways—either as aesthetic displays of political disagreement, or as the actions of people yet to be defined as "terrorists," bent on destroying property and causing trouble. Yet, there is much more to this phase of anti-capitalism than its discrediting by law-enforcement authorities and the media would lead you to believe. We need to understand why it is that people struggle against market-driven systems of political authority, and how such struggles can include people who are sympathetic to their concerns, but don't want to be subject to police violence. Beyond this, though, we should address more fundamental questions about the ways in which anti-capitalist movements organize themselves and act against the structures of exploitation indigenous to the contemporary marketplace. Our concerns need to be with not only gains and losses, but with understanding how anti-market activism can increase democracy and serve as a defense mechanism that helps people protect themselves against uncontrolled economic forces in the post–welfare state era.

In order to do this, we need to come to a clear understanding of the theoretical and practical tensions involved in late twentieth and early twenty-first-century anti-capitalist resistance, particularly those surrounding the organization of movements, their tactical issues, and how activists relate their concerns to the general public. The last two issues are particularly crucial for the future of anti-market social-justice advocacy. Given the hostility of the post–September 11 political climate to leftist criticisms of such abstractions as "our way of life," there is an urgent need for anti-capitalist movements to make a greater case for the good that they serve in helping reinforce pre-existing democratic political traditions. Especially given the kinds of stresses that war inevitably places on civil liberties, the toleration of difference, due process, and ideological pluralism.

"Freedom of Speech" and the Issue of Protest

Marx's analysis of the capitalist social order highlights a key problem when trying to develop a program of resistance—namely, the separation of political society, civil society, and the economy. One of the primary factors in anti-capitalist resistance—the economy—is structurally separated from both political society and civil society, so that control over the economy is privatized. People's ability to earn money, expropriate other people's labor, and amass capital falls completely outside of the government's ability to control it or to legislate a new way of organizing the economy. This structural separation ensures that control over capital cannot fall into the hands of the people as a whole, ensuring that wealth stays in the hands of the few. Parallel to this is the fact that the rights and liberties granted to people living in market societies are not political rights—we're not granted the absolute right to participate in political decision-making processes. Rather, we're granted civil *liberties*—the latitude to hold and express our opinions, to assemble peacefully with others, and to publicize our grievances. These rights only really exist in our individual and social realms; we're allowed to voice our opinions and to try to convince others of the rightness of those opinions. But we do not have the right to compel those in power to listen to us or act in accordance with those opinions.

What this means is that protests, whether they be against the World Trade Organization or the persistence of sweatshops in the United States, are moments at which the liberties of civil society are used to struggle against the imperatives of political society. The economy is left out of the struggle. We can speak and endeavor to be heard, but there is no rule saying that those in political power have to listen. Accountability, especially in the U.S., is not built into the Constitution. There is no right of recall against elected representatives, so we have no way to enforce our opinion upon those who are supposed to represent our desires and interests. The only mode we feel that we have, at least now, to try to make our voices heard is through popular protest—through the mass expression of dissent at particular moments, in particular places.

This blocking-out of popular influence is intentional. Scholars who have analyzed the American and Canadian constitutions have shown the ways in which they're designed to create an oligarchy, a system in which a few, generally wealthy, rule under the guise of "democracy," taking the form of an occasional vote to validate policies. And, as a Republican senator said during the 2000 presidential election debacle, "The U.S. isn't a democracy; it's a republic." So we're left believing in the "right to free speech," thinking that if we just raise our voices loudly enough, we can have an impact, and continue to believe that public expressions of disagreement can compel changes in how our society conducts its affairs.

This has been the way in which anti-capitalist resistance has most prominently manifested itself. People have collected themselves in ostensibly democratic nations—the U.S., Canada, Sweden, Italy—to exercise their free speech rights and say to decision-makers at economic summits and gatherings of world leaders, "We will no longer tolerate this." And in spite of the increasingly repressive measures taken by states to insulate business elites and statesmen from demonstrators—such as those which transpired in Gothenburg and Genoa in 2001—people continue to get together to publically express their discontent with abstract economic phenomena such as "global capital."

The aftermath of September 11 will have a drastic impact on this tool of political expression. In particular, North Americans will

189

increasingly find that they have even less of an ability to effect some kind of policy change through mass rallies and acts of street protest. Most G-7 countries passed legislation severely limiting the ability of people to congregate and protest international meetings, going as far as potentially defining these protests as "terrorist acts" since, as Canada's 2001 Bill C-35 says, participants in international monetary organization meetings are now "protected persons." Now, it seems, the respect for "free speech rights" has become capricious, granted or withdrawn at the whim of government officials who are willing to encourage consensual agreement with their policies, but not dissent.

So what are we left with? Democracies are structured so that the political system and the economy—objects of legitimate contestation in nominally free states—are insulated from the expression of public opinion on the basis of constitutionally guaranteed civil liberties. The political system has essentially detached itself from the people it purportedly serves, meaning that maintaining an impartial commitment to freedom of speech and protest is the best insurance we have against anti-democratic impulses inherent in market-driven societies.

In the wake of the "war on terrorism," these impulses and their influence on an already quasi-democratic political culture have been enhanced by legislative initiatives designed to combat terrorism, by widening the definition of "terrorist" to anyone suspected of actively working against, for example, American foreign policy. This leaves the formulation of anti-capitalist protest strategies stuck between states' need to legitimate themselves as "protectors of democracy" and their need to ensure that the economic basis of the societies they rule remains intact. Taking advantage of and protecting what liberty remains in such scenarios—that is, expressing dissent through freedom of speech—means that it is important to remain mindful of the tensions between the state's conflicting responsibilities, and highlight how they contradict one another.

Through the promotion of such ideas, protest movements which concern themselves with the market help create a discursive space for themselves where they are better able to problematize the market's antipathy toward democracy, and thus, make a more convincing claim about their right to be heard.

Problems for Anti-Capitalist Resistance: "The Impotent State"

Given the difficult nature of political liberty in market-driven societies, it might appear that anyone protesting something like "global capitalism" or "economic injustice" always does so for naught. In part, this gives rise to the sense that the battle against these forces has to be taken to the highest levels—to the international monetary organizations whose policies foster this injustice—thereby skipping the nation-state. The notion, often false, of "the impotence of the state," draws from and reinforces this notion, leaving "anti-capitalist resistance" to be something that only happens in televised locales during highly touted meetings. Yet generations of activists in the U.S. and elsewhere, who have achieved everything from the shortening of the workweek to environmental protections, have shown that the state is still an important piece of the struggle for social justice.   191

Prior to the 1970s, it seemed that the nation-state was the main player in the market, and that much of the work to be done in fixing or eliminating the economy's injustices ought to be focused there. However, the separation of politics and the economy meant that anti-market politics could not be effective if it worked strictly through the state—or, rather, that the democratic institutions were for the most part impotent to deal with the control of wealth by the few. The "new social movements" that arose in the 1970s and 1980s tried to work around this by mobilizing people to make their claim directly to the public at large. But in the 1980s, as the globalization process picked up steam, activism at the national level appeared to no longer work. With the development of transnational proto-state entities like the WTO and IMF, people felt themselves increasingly alienated from the state. It always felt somewhat out of reach, but now its hybrid abstraction into the form of world economic policy-making bodies made it feel that much harder to identify, leaving activists less sure about what institutions ought to be the objects of their struggles, and how and to what ends people could be mobilized.

What this shows is that activists have traditionally worked with only two ideas about making concrete social change: either one goes to the ballot box, or one goes to the streets. And with the increasing sense that international economic organizations and multinational corporations are the most significant players in international politics, people began leaving the voting booth behind and, with Seattle, moving to protest against the "real players." But forgetting the importance of the state as a player in the global economy, as it appears has happened, leaves out the institutions that enact the policies garnering so much attention on protest days— and the institutions we can access through already-institutionalized means. International monetary organizations depend on countries for their power and the implementation of their policies, yet leave no way for citizens to access them. Nation-states have elections and rely on public opinion for their legitimacy and policies; the WTO, IMF, and other international organizations have no need for the public except as consumers.

Because of this dependence, an important strategy is revealed, one that appears to have been neglected in this newest phase of anti-market struggles—focus more locally, more consistently. In addition to the protests against international economic organizations for not addressing the inequities in the world, it is important to develop a "practical politics," one that has the possibility of ensuring increased democratic participation in all spheres of our lives. By developing this practical politics, bringing an anti-capitalist program to state institutions and building the everyday basis for that agenda, we can make the call to change the economic and political orders a more frequent and effective one.

A Practical Anti-Capitalist Politics

The aesthetic critique of the oligarchic and unjust global market economy—ranging from the street theater at anti-market protests since Seattle to the American party conventions during the 2000 election campaign—highlights one important element of anti-capitalist resistance. It showcases the role that supposedly transparent institutions play in the expansion of global capitalism and its resulting ills. However, there are elements missing if this is to be an overall anti-capitalist strategy. While these protests make for a strong display of people's dissatisfaction and suggest a great deal of creativity in people's thinking about the state and the market, they cannot be expected to be the only tools for political change.

What is required is an expansion and channeling of this remarkable dissatisfaction into the political sphere, where people can be effective—in local, state, provincial, national, or, as the anti-globalization movement of the past several years suggests, in international politics. All of the ideologies and political philosophies floating around the anti-market movements of recent years must begin to inform the conduct of mainstream political discourse and activity. They must inspire greater participation in electoral affairs, and help spur the creation of new parties with their own distinct philosophies. The anti-globalization movement's strong concerns about democracy need to inspire voters to participate in the electoral system, so that they take advantage of those opportunities that voting still offers people to exercise control over the state and the economy. All such things are required to change that way that economic and political policies are formulated and enacted such that politics and economics are not exclusive of one another; such that politics can dominate economics and not vice versa.

193

The state may be set in its ways, but it's not so rationally over-determined by its historical role as an agent of the wealthy that it cannot be transformed and made to work on behalf of everyone. Which is why we have to overcome those feelings of alienation and apathy that our distance from it inspires, and recognize that our perception of the state reinforces its sense that it can function without concern for all of its citizens. Encouraging people to creatively participate in electoral affairs is one of the most effective ways to ensure that elected officials, dependent on "public opinion," begin to address more than just the concerns of business. If people become more engaged in the national debate, and encourage and mobilize participation in those channels open to them, then it is entirely probable that state policies and personnel can change, and government can be a true agent of public welfare.

But what is included in this vision of society? What would a society characterized by full democratic participation and accountability look like? In closing, I pose the following questions and ideas as points for future discussion about the development of such a practical politics.

Intention and sphere of concern: Most political programs that work for social justice take either reform or revolution as the goals for their struggle—either adjust the current economic and political order so that it operates in a more equitable manner, or overturn it and create a new system. Yet these two intentions cannot be separated. If we sacrifice improving the present for the sake of a future we won't likely see, no one will join any hypothetical struggle. Focusing only on tinkering with an unjust system to make it more palatable without a vision of a "better way" means essentially accepting the permanent inequalities inscribed by market economies. Anti-capitalist activists should look for ways in which both of these time frames and goals can be achieved. That is, anti-market activists need to focus on current forms of exploitation (through labor mobilizations, the establishment of pay-equity laws,

194

and the creation of global standards for working conditions) so that the future creation of a new system becomes easier.

Inclusiveness in issues and membership: Questions about who can participate in anti-capitalist work and what issues will be dealt with in this struggle need to be addressed as well. To date, one of the stinging criticisms of anti-capitalist organizations has been about the personnel—the preponderance of white, middle-class, moralistic-sounding young adults. Yet people who aren't able or don't want to march in the streets are just as affected by the expansion of the market economy as those participating in demonstrations. Activists need to figure out ways to ensure that everyone is able to participate in their respective movements, not only in protesting the system but also in deciding what to do about it.

Anti-market activists also need to decide what issues "count" as "anti-capitalist." Are racism, sexism, heterosexism, and other forms of domination part of capitalism? Or are they extra-economic, only occasionally impacting on people's standard of living and capacity for participating in social life? Linkages need to be built between all parties harmed by the market—women, homosexuals, people of color, indigenous peoples, elderly persons, the disabled, and immigrants—between their shared experiences of domination and exploitation, and what they have in common with the stereotypically "normal" and well-adjusted, white middle class.

195

Locus and tactics of resistance: Anti-capitalist activists need to figure out appropriate tactics to convey their messages in order to mobilize the widest possible public support without alienating anyone.

Measure of success: The injustice of capitalism is related to two requirements it places on those who do not control wealth or the tools of production—the stunting of our human (intellectual and social) capacities in favor of our productive (economic) capacities, and the emphasis on *having* over *being*. While the improvement of our standard of living and the distribution of wealth among all people is certainly a necessary goal, it cannot be the only one.

Anti-capitalists need to discuss the more utopian aspect of anti-market resistance, the end-state they wish to bring about. While many activists see utopian thought as misguided or delusional, without a direction or goal, they sometimes forget why we should bother to struggle at all. Determining the characteristics of what French sociologist Henri Lefebvre once called "the impossible-possible," a vision of a seemingly impossible future that we make possible through our actions now, needs to be a critical organizing principle for any progressive social movement seeking to actually effect change.

Secularization and Its Discontents: Critical Theory and The Critique of Religion
Joel Schalit

*W*hen trying to comprehend the character of political resistance in First World nations since the 1960s, social theorists working out of the Marxian tradition have concentrated on the so-called New Social Movements that rose from the ashes of the New Left: movements oriented around feminism, environmentalism, and similar concerns that have sought to make revisions in fundamentally sound constitutional democracies. But they have paid relatively little attention to social movements that have emerged from what cultural theorist Raymond Williams called "residual formations." The post-'60s era has witnessed a remarkable resurgence of religious movements, not only in the developing world, but also in nations with a relatively developed infrastructure and intelligentsia. However far removed these religious movements may be from the program of the New Left, they still exhibit striking similarities to progressive social movements. Both the religious right in the United States and the pagan revival in Europe are examples of this trend.

These developments must be taken as a clear sign that reports of religion's demise have always been greatly exaggerated.

Modernity may have rid the world of many species, but it will never rid the world of religion. Marxian theory must come to terms with this realization. To be sure, leftists have been rethinking their position on religion since the American civil rights movement and analogous struggles revealed the subversive potential in some religious institutions. Liberation theology marked an important step toward a possible reconciliation of Marxism and religion. And the crisis of values besetting the disintegrating welfare state has inspired some prominent left-leaning intellectuals to call for citizens to rediscover their religious roots; or, in the case of Palestinian-independence advocates from outside the region, to adopt the language and symbolism of the Islamic resistance— donning kaffiyehs, calling Palestinians killed by Israeli forces "martyrs" (an English translation of the Arabic term "shaheed," used to describe suicide bombers)—in order to demonstrate their sympathy.

In some respects, this willingness to grapple with religion is laudable. It's better to acknowledge religion's continuing influence than to pretend that it's no longer important. Unfortunately, however, this rediscovery of religion has not coincided with a rediscovery of the critique of religion. While the rise of far-right movements in the last decade has prompted some leftists to start monitoring fundamentalism, they have tended to prefer denunciations to dialectics. In either case, the result is an interest in religion that stops short of understanding it relationally. In a sense, leftists who have rediscovered the significance of religion are not much different from their opponents on the right. They see what is lacking in modern society and imagine that religion can help fill the gap. But as any Marxist worth her or his salt knows, to turn to religion in this manner is to reify it.

Intellectuals working in the Marxian tradition ought to reconsider religion in order to comprehend its complex relationship with modernity. In order to do this, they must realize not only that religion isn't going away any time soon, but that it is inextricably bound up with the forces of modernization that once seemed to herald its doom. In order to inspire such a move, I offer the following thoughts on Marxism and religion by examining its treatment in Frankfurt School critical theory and the orthodoxy it was reacting against. It should also be made clear that this is a strong reading of the tradition without the caveats and qualifications that make strong readings easier to defend. Finally, it should be noted that for anyone familiar with the relationship between Marxism and religion, much of what is said here will seem to be restating the obvious. But sometimes the obvious deserves another look.

Without exception, traditional Marxist critiques of religion are founded on two premises: 1) existing modernity cannot be understood apart from capitalism; 2) secularization is an inevitable consequence of modernization. These premises' most famous formulation appears in the *Communist Manifesto*, in which Marx and Engels argue that "all fixed, fast-frozen relations, with their train of ancient and venerable prejudices and opinions, are swept away" by the modernizing impulse of capitalism. Because "the bourgeoisie has stripped of its halo every occupation hitherto honored and looked up to with reverent awe. It has converted the physician, the lawyer, the priest, the poet, the man of science, into its paid wage-laborers." Religious awe gives way to real-world calculation. In "On Some Motifs in Baudelaire," Walter Benjamin makes a great deal out of a short prose piece in which a poet loses his halo crossing a busy street, but decides that it is better to be alive and profane than dead and holy. This tale concisely relates the demise of religion in allegorical form. It is mirrored in Marx and Engels's words: "All that is solid melts into air, all that is holy is profaned."

199

While there are a number of different secularization theses sharing the premise that modernity undoes tradition, Max Weber's is both the most famous and the most easily adapted to the Marxist critique of capitalism. In Weber's account, modernity is defined by "the increasing intellectualization and rationalization" of the world, which "does not mean an increasing general knowledge of the requirements of life," but rather, "the knowledge or belief that a person, if she or he only wanted to, could at any time learn." As their world becomes modern, people start to believe that it works according to plans that can, with proper training and effort, be deciphered and understood. This rationalization of the world thus implies that "there are no incalculable powers full of secrets that enter into play, that, instead, a person could, in principle, master all things through calculation." This means that, unlike "the savage for whom such powers did exist," a person need no longer "grasp at magical means in order to master or appease the spirits. Rather, the technical means and calculation manage this." What all this adds up to is "intellectualization as such" or the "disenchantment of the world."

Weber's claim that modernity brings about the progressive "disenchantment of the world" has been a powerful influence on Western Marxism because it resonates with Marx's insights about the modern world, while avoiding his doctrinaire followers' tendency to ignore subtleties in the "superstructure" of society. In Weber's day, most orthodox Marxists were content to argue that secularization was an inevitable byproduct of progress. This doesn't mean that turn-of-the-century Marxism lacked a critique of religion. Rather, the focus of the critique of religion in early Marxism concentrated on demonstrating how materialism logically superseded idealism in all its forms.

Today, Marxists usually dismiss such naïvete out of hand. But something strange seems to happen when today's Marxists discuss religion. It's almost like they've been teleported a hundred years back, to a time when science was science and religion was its enemy. The orthodox critique of religion still merits examination, because it lives on in today's Marxists, however "post" they otherwise seem. German socialist Joseph Dietzgen, for whom the critique of religion was of paramount significance, epitomized this

200

evolutionary account of secularism in arguing that socialism is an objective science of politics that "sticks to the facts," because "socialists live in the real world, not in 'spiritualist regions.'" Socialism, Dietzgen contends, represents the pinnacle of the secularization process because it represents the logical culmination of religion's own attempt to overcome itself, beginning with the emergence of philosophy, whose task is to reconcile the ideal and the real in the name of science. This historical process reaches its apotheosis in the writings of Feuerbach and Marx, who liberated philosophy from the tyranny of religion by replacing dogma with material facts.

The problem with this kind of materialist epistemology is that it uncritically identifies secularization with progress in scientific knowledge and capitalist development. In a series of essays concerning toleration of religion within the German Social Democratic Party, Franz Mehring exemplifies this equation when he argues against the right of party members to maintain their faith commitments privately because religion is the sign of a deficiency that originates from a collective set of delusions related to historically "given cultural development," delusions which are inconsistent with the ideal of emancipation embraced by socialism. Religious ideologies, Mehring argues, represent an imperfect knowledge of nature and industry that appear increasingly irrational in the light of modernization. He takes it for granted that, as social relations of production continue to be rationalized, there will be less and less reason for people to communicate "with supernatural forces through prayer and sacrifice."

201

Obviously Mehring is no Pangloss. He is not arguing that we live in the best of all possible worlds thus far. But what he is suggesting is that capitalist development, insofar as it opens up possibilities for socialist revolution, has potentially demythologized the one ideology which has always bound the working class to its masters, by making reality, as Lukács put it in his famous essay on reification, "something man cannot change." The danger inherent in such crude materialist critiques of religion, to go back to Lukács again, is to ignore how ideology constitutes reality in such a way that it appears so "sacrosanct that it is immaterial."

This is the paradox that the critique of religion in orthodox Marxism finds itself in: On the one hand, it wants to take religion seriously; on the other, it assumes that ideology takes only one narrative form, a religious one. This is a dangerous conclusion, because it leaves open the possibility that, as Lukács forcefully argues in *History and Class Consciousness*, other forms of ideology which lack the anachronistic, feudal narratives of medieval Christianity will take religion's place by creating an even more unchangeable sense of reality.

Mehring's teleological view of secularization is based on the presupposition that a profound and irreconcilable contradiction exists between the working class and religion. The working class is hostile to religion because class consciousness is inherently secularized. According to Mehring's account, class consciousness is the socialist equivalent of the understanding of enlightenment that Jürgen Habermas extrapolates from Kant, a kind of philosophical self-consciousness of autonomous, collective intersubjectivity which arises from increasing knowledge and control of the capitalist process of production. The more enlightened the working class becomes about its own situation, "the more it will be liberated from religion." This process of rationalization, of achieving self-consciousness of one's own role in the productive process, is Mehring's materialist reading of the process of Enlightenment.

Marxism inherits the Enlightenment project of demythologization by radicalizing the Enlightenment critique of religion. The class struggle is conceived of as means of illuminating the dark spaces in the production process by, as Mehring puts it, "shining the light of economic knowledge on the proletariat," in order to expose the material basis for the only true ideology. Even though the cri-

tique of religion emerged long before the rise of industrial capitalism, it was industrialization that created the material preconditions
for the elimination of ritual observance. The demand for more efficient production led to the development of a public culture in
which more than-perfunctory attention to religion was discour-
aged as a waste of time. Looked at from this perspective, the rise of
Protestantism appeared to have paved the way for industrialism by
promoting a doctrine of grace that took the work out of religion.

The difference between this account of secularization and the
one that underpins the Marxism of a Benjamin or Adorno is that it
takes disenchantment to be a monological, totalizing process.
Although the late Weber of *Economy and Society* is an extremely
sophisticated thinker in many respects, he frequently falls prey to
the same belief in the inevitability of total disenchantment. Marxists
who assimilate Weber's later work uncritically run the risk of making the same mistake. Although the turn to Weber has often dove-
tailed with a turn against Marxist orthodoxy, it by no means guarantees a more complex account of the status of religion in modernity. This is why it is of paramount importance that Marxists who
turn to Weber look to the early Weber as well, as exemplified in *The
Protestant Ethic and The Spirit of Capitalism*. As this seminal text
makes clear, the weakening of tradition results in the strengthening
of the form of religion best suited to the new mode of production:
Protestantism.

To run through Weber's famous argument in brief, he advances
the thesis that otherworldliness, asceticism, and ecclesiastical piety
have an intimate and mutually reinforcing relationship with capitalist acquisition. This is why it is no surprise that the most pious
Christians spring from capitalist circles. By giving birth to capitalism, tradition is actually able to revive itself. It just has to take a new
form. The link between Protestant doctrines and transformations in
the nature of work suggests that the economic order is a reflection
of the religious order. Weber's insights point to a troubling conclu-

203

sion. The apparent eclipse of tradition in modernity blinds us to the rise of something that functions exactly like tradition. To the extent that we believe tradition to be a thing of the past, we make it that much easier for this post-traditional tradition to secure unprecedented dominance over everyday life in the present.

It is exactly this understanding of modernity that underpins Marx's analysis of commodity fetishism. We'll forego a detailed reading of the famous passage in *Kapital* that discusses the seemingly "magical" commodity in terms of enchantment. Suffice it to say that because the disenchantment of the world does not mean the disalienation of the world, people still project powers that are rightfully their own onto objects that they have created. And they do so without realizing that they are doing it. Far from being exterminated, irrationality becomes harder to destroy. People are duped into believing themselves beyond duping.

This thesis is of crucial importance for the project of critical theory. More specifically, it forms the basis of its critique of religion. In *Dialectic of Enlightenment* and many of their individual writings, Adorno and Horkheimer combine Marx's analysis of commodity fetishism with Weber's early insights about the advent of a post-traditional tradition. The disenchantment of the world produces a world enchanted by commodities. As the notion of worship implicit in commodity fetishism suggests, religion is suddenly everywhere. It is this theorization of reenchantment that serves as a springboard for their most intriguing thoughts on the religion of modernity.

Most readings of Adorno and Horkheimer's *Dialectic of Enlightenment* concentrate on their version of a Weberian secularization thesis. Modernity brings about the reduction of the many to the one. Diversity gives way to singularity. But there is a flipside to this process that has received less critical attention. The totalizing logic of capitalism drains the world of differences, but produces new deities in the process. As the world becomes more monologic, it also becomes more polytheistic.

The work of Walter Benjamin was a crucial influence on this idea, particularly in *The Origins of German Tragic Drama* (The *Trauerspiel*). In that text, Benjamin adopts a seemingly counterintuitive approach to modernity. He locates the origins of modernity not in the Reformation as orthodox Marxists and Weber do, but in the counter-Reformation. In this era of the Baroque, the suppressed traditions that helped influence early Christianity find new expression. Whereas the Reformation tried to strip religion of its "too solid flesh" in order to get to its bare bones beneath, the counter-Reformation promoted a proliferation of folds, both of flesh and the finery in which that flesh was clothed. The Reformation rejected superfluity, it rendered religion more abstract. The counter-Reformation, on the other hand, incorporated everything it could and returned to a form of religion grounded in the materiality of ritual. For Benjamin, the initial move marked by the Reformation does not become fully realized until the counter-Reformation, because he believes modernity is no mere break with the past, but a new and more powerful way of revivifying past forms of life in the present.

Adorno and Horkheimer return again and again to this idea of an assimilative modernity. But they also advance an apparently contradictory thesis in which religion represents the initial social expression of an impulse toward the homogenization of all forms of political, cultural, and historical identity. Modernity makes room for the many forms of spirituality that had once been suppressed in order to reinforce the one true religion's dominance. But it is the era in which capitalism reduces the individual properties of both people and things to the least common denominator.

To the extent that modernity is able to integrate past forms of life into the supposedly disenchanted present, it could be said to promote a polytheism that permits pagan religious traditions to exist alongside Christianity. This point is made clear in analyses of the religious dimension of fascism, which explicitly invoked religious traditions inimical to monotheism. Of course, by fore-grounding the pagan dimensions to modernity, this argument that modernity is fundamentally polytheistic brings out a counter-secularization thesis already latent in the sociology of modernity. To give a particularly striking example, Durkheim counterbalances his account of secularization with the argument that modern societies are "constantly creating sacred things out of ordinary ones." He powerfully reinforces this point by noting that the French Revolution, which signaled the inception of the modern era, was also a time in which the "aptitude of society for setting itself up as a god or for creating gods was never more apparent."

The universal equivalence for which the market is responsible leads to a new form of monotheism, all the more dangerous for its not being perceived theologically. We are reminded here of a statement Marx makes in "On the Jewish Question": "The monotheism of the Jews is, therefore, in reality, a polytheism of the numerous needs of man, a polytheism which makes even the lavatory an object of divine regulation." We need another term if we wish to express accurately the double-sidedness of Adorno and Horkheimer's point about the status of religion in modernity.

There is a theological term adequate to this task: henotheism. Societies like the one exemplified in Hesiod's *Theogeny,* or in the rich religious narratives underlying Hinduism, have many gods. But these many gods are fixed within a rigid hierarchy in which one god rules supreme. In other words, henotheism describes the imbrication of polytheism and monotheism. And it is precisely this imbrication that Adorno and Horkheimer view to be the secret truth of a modernity that passes itself off as the product of secularization.

Returning to Marx's analysis of commodity fetishism, we can show how this henotheism plays itself out. The realm of commodities is otherworldly. People believe in the special powers of commodities, as surely as they once believed in the special powers of the gods. Commodities form a new and potentially infinite pantheon, for the totalizing logic of capital penetrates into every corner of the world. And, of course, like the Greek gods of old, these commodities "converse" with one another while humankind looks on. But the ruler of this pantheon cannot be any specific commodity-as-god. The supreme ruler is the rule that measures all. This "ruler" can have no positive content. It merely marks the intangible site of universal measurement. In the henotheism of modernity, the omnipotent one is a null; it is the void that reigns supreme.

We're now a long way from the total disenchantment envisioned in orthodox Marxism. The vision of a henotheistic modernity is infinitely more pessimistic, but it allows us to come to terms with the persistence of religion in modernity. The question now is how we can use it as we turn to the concrete historical problems facing the contemporary left. Cornel West suggests that many people are turning to fundamentalism these days because they seek redress for the injuries of the market. The failure of leftists to construct a credible secular alternative to capitalism leaves these people with nowhere to turn but religion. In a sense, we can read the turn to fundamentalism as an attempt to resist the henotheism of modernity. This doesn't mean we should condone it. But we have to do more than dismiss it out-of-hand by labelling it as false consciousness, pure and simple. And we have to think far more radically about tradition than the unreconstructed belief in secularization will allow.

207

Interview with Wendy Brown
Charlie Bertsch

*W*alking the halls of university political science departments, it can be hard to imagine a world much different from our own. The professors who take large grants to collect data on the electorate, the graduate students who are steered into the most conservative projects because they are desperate for jobs, and the undergraduates who join their fraternity and sorority friends as "Poli-Sci" majors because it's good preparation for law school—all contribute to an overwhelming sense that the action for true radicals lies elsewhere. But there are exceptions to this institutional blandness. Wendy Brown provides one of them.

208

A traditionally educated political theorist who can quote the classics with the best of them, Brown still manages to disturb the self-satisfaction of the academy without losing sight of its strong points. She also has a remarkable gift for leading those of us to the left of Bill Clinton to reflect on what our politics usually takes for granted. You need only read the discussion of human rights in her landmark 1995 book, *States of Injury,* to recognize that Brown refuses to play it safe. For all of its conceptual intricacy, her work is a wake-up call for a left that has forgotten how to think for itself. I talked with her not long after the publication of her new book, *Politics Out of History*.

January 2002

CB: What are you working on right now?

WB: My project is a critique of contemporary tolerance discourse. It's not treating capitalism explicitly. But I do have an analysis of the ways in which certain aspects of late modern capitalism have formed that discourse. Capitalism is always there as a conditioning context. My approach is to look at the way in which the recent embrace of tolerance involves a retreat from larger justice projects on the part of liberals and leftists, on the one hand, and a consideration of tolerance as a dimension of what Foucault called "governmentality," on the other. Tolerance as a primary political virtue involves a very thin notion of citizenship, a very passive notion of co-existence. More importantly, it casts differences as given—not as products of inequality or domination, but as intrinsic and something we have to bear in the social and political world; also as something we would rather not bear—you only tolerate that which you wish you didn't have to.

Tolerance is also part of a complex shell game that liberalism plays with equality and difference—tolerance is extended by the state whenever equality is refused or attenuated. Finally, tolerance is importantly a civilizational discourse, something that is used to distinguish good Western liberal democracies from bad fundamentalist regimes and transnational movements—as the rhetoric justifying America's current war makes clear. A lot of what I'm doing involves sorting out the protean character of tolerance discourse over the course of modernity, and also trying to understand how the relatively liberatory dimensions of tolerance at its origins serve to legitimate its troubling contemporary deployments.

CB: Where do you see our present-day discourse of tolerance beginning?

WB: I focus on two periods. I go back to the emergence of tolerance discourse during the Reformation. Tolerance had antecedents, but that's the place where it really takes shape for liberalism. When this discourse emerged, it was specified as something that was about religious dissent, difference in belief. It was a religious problem that later became a more general problem of conscience. But there's a transmogrification that happens in the nineteenth century in which the object of tolerance is no longer just belief, but what we today call "identity." That's the second period I'm focusing on. It is at that point that the discourse becomes attached to physiological attributes and other aspects of persons understood to be ontological rather than subjective. Thus, tolerance of the Jews as a "race," rather than as religious believers, is what's at issue in the late nineteenth century.

This use of tolerance really gathers steam over the next century, and becomes ubiquitous in our time: today we speak more often of tolerating differences in race, ethnicity, or sexuality, than of tolerating differences in religious belief. And this means that tolerance is now addressed to domains of social inequality, not simply dissenting faith. That's when it gets really troubling as a discourse, precisely because it treats subjects of inequality as if they were merely subjects of difference, as if nature rather than power were at issue.

210

CB: Can you say more about your project's contemporary aspect?

WB: The very recent resurgence of tolerance is a different story from the one I'm chronicling through modernity. Here's the question: Why, at the point in an Enlightenment narrative where you would expect a discourse of tolerance to disappear, has it instead returned full force? That narrative, remember, is about tolerating outsiders to a universal, and as the universal has gotten bigger and bigger—as more and more outsiders have been let in—you'd expect tolerance to be less and less of an issue. So I'm asking, "Why now?" And, as I've said, one answer to this question has to do with a very severe retreat from justice projects in which egalitarianism and the elimination of domination seem possible. That's where it converges with contemporary anti-capitalist projects.

CB: The call for tolerance signals a kind of fatalism, in other words.

WB: Precisely. Universal tolerance as the vision of multicultural justice doesn't hold out much hope for transforming the conditions making tolerance seem necessary in the first place.

CB: In the United States, the beginning of the last century is referred to as the Progressive Era. The world has changed a great deal since President Theodore Roosevelt was doing battle with the trusts, and reform movements were forcing politicians to greatly expand the role of government. We're entering the fourth decade of reaction to the supposed excesses of the 1960s. Nobody seems to believe in the power of government to improve everyday life through bureaucracy. But left-leaning Americans still call themselves "progressives." In your most recent book, *Politics Out of History*, you provide the tools for critiquing this reflex.

WB: At this particular point in history, it is important to be mindful of the ways in which an Enlightenment narrative of progress inflects not only the way that most of us understand history, but also the way in which we understand our political projects. And that's harder than it may seem. It's one thing to say that progressivism was just as religious a discourse as any other and that history doesn't have a linear course, let alone a project—like freedom or equality or reason—that guides its unfolding. We may have big disagreements on what does move history, whether it's still something we would frame primarily in materialist, idealist, or genealogical terms. But it's easy enough to come to some kind of accord about the giving-up of the myth of a purely progressive movement of history. I actually think that the difficulty here is that Marx was our most fabulous, brilliant, incisive, progressive political thinker.

CB: So you see a rift between the recognition that history isn't moving toward a clearly defined goal and the use of Marx, who argued that it was?

WB: More than argued—Marx premised so much of his theoretical, economic, and historical analyses on this idea. And our understanding of capitalism on the left is so hitched to a Marxist progressive historiography that even if we conclude that capital doesn't seem to be moving in a progressive direction, we still cling to the notion that its phases, its stages, its developments *do*. We still believe that there's progress, even if we don't want to give it a positive valence. That is, we still believe that capitalism itself continues to progress, even if we don't like its fruits and can't find the inherent redemption that Marx found at the end of the history of capitalism. It's very hard to detach from that line of thinking. I'm not sure that I fully *want* to detach from that.

I think capitalism does have certain forces that drive it in certain directions, and that also continuously free it from its previous forms. But that's a different formulation from one that's purely progressive. Now, even if we leave a little bit of the progressivism in place in our understanding of capital, arguing as I did a second ago that it continues to shed its previous forms and continues to have to invent new ones, then the question is how to free ourselves from the Marxist account of the inevitability of its collapse and the inevitability of mass opposition to it. Perhaps most difficult of all, how do we free ourselves from the progressivist notion that what comes after capitalism will be a higher form of life? I think that's the real catch these days for the left: Trying to think outside a progressive frame in opposition to capital requires that we say, not that we have some higher, more advanced, more humanly developed form of life to which we think the world ought to conform, but rather, that we wish to mount a political critique, advance a political analysis, cast a political judgement, and that all of these are contestable.

212

CB: So the trick is to remember that you're engaged in an argument?

WB: Yes. Look, I think capitalism is not just inegalitarian, not just full of maldistributions of wealth, not just wasteful of certain kinds of human energies and natural resources, not just producing for profit rather than human need, but also that it's a form of political economy that is fundamentally undemocratic, that it is full of forms of domination which prevent us from being able to organize the possibilities of our own lives. But that's a *political* critique of capitalism, not a scientific conclusion drawn from a set of contradictions in capitalism, not a result that comes out of an imagined dialectical movement of history. It's not, as Marx would have, the inner truth ultimately produced by capitalism. Rather, it's a political claim that will be contested radically by others. And the contest that ensues is a fight, a battle, a struggle, in which god and truth are on no one's side, even if power is.

I think there are many people in anti-capitalist movements right now—I'm conscious of it because a bunch of them are showing up in New York today—who actually can do that, who can say, "What we're doing is arguing for a different kind of world. Go ahead, argue back. We'll be in this argument with you." But I think there's still a tendency on the left, one that's strong on the European left and on the old left and the old "New Left" in this country, to see truth as being on the side of the anti-capitalist forces, truth as being on the side of the left, rather than understanding a left position as a political argument that one wants to prevail in a moral-epistemological universe where no one has the Truth.

CB: I'm wary of using the word "morality." But it would seem that one of the things that it would be good for people on the left to realize is that their resistance to capitalism proceeds from a judgment with an ethical quality rather than a simple assertion of fact. If this is the case, however, we're confronted once more with a question of foundations. On what might such a judgment be based?

Would it still require some form of truth, as when leftists state that "It is *true* that capitalism distributes things unequally"? Does it need that certainty as a foundation? Or does it rest on a presumption that equality is something that all humans should have?

WB: I'm nervous, as you are, about calling the arguments I have in mind "moral." Let's stay on the terrain of political analysis, which would allow leftists to say *not*, "Here's a position that's ethically superior," but rather, "Here's a devastating political analysis of capitalism as a life form and here's a picture of some viable alternatives to that life form." The question is whether we undertake that analysis and draw that picture without certain claims to foundational truth. I think that inevitably, strategically, certain foundationalist kinds of claims will emerge, but I think we need to know the difference between our strategic use of such claims and whether they are really viable politically or intellectually. Let's take the example of freedom, which I believe remains one of the most commonly contested term for leftists and liberals, with "liberals" used here in the old-fashioned sense. The liberal says, "Freedom means doing what you want as long as you don't hurt anybody, and free enterprise is part of that." The leftist says, or at least *this* leftist says, "No, freedom means freedom from being dominated by a social system such as capitalism that is outside of human control. It is the freedom to make a world with others." Now, those are deeply contesting definitions of freedom. I don't think one can finally be made true. I think they can only be argued for.

CB: Of course, they already have been argued for, and at great length. But you don't think that the debate has been exhausted?

WB: No. I think that these different notions of freedom really have to be taken seriously as arguments that are old, in the history of political and economic thinking, but that are with us still and must also take on new dimensions in the late modern and especially

214

post-communist era. We have to be willing to make and develop these arguments, and to make them in a rhetorically powerful way. We have to be willing to argue for a notion of freedom that is other than liberal, individual, bourgeois freedom, and do it persuasively. And I don't think, finally, that will happen through a reach for foundations. I don't think it will happen, as it could for Marx, by saying that it's human nature to be free together in collectivity. I loved that moment in leftist history, where you could reach for those foundations philosophically and prove them through a dialectically materialist reading of world history. It was beautiful. It was compelling. It was metaphysically and cosmologically perfect. I would love to return to it. But I don't think it's available to us.

CB: In making the sort of broad arguments you're talking about, it is very difficult to avoid giving directives, such as "People should do *x* or *y*." It almost seems that a "should" is built into the structure of political argument. My question is whether we should worry about the basis of that "should." Or do we just take it as a given that there's going to be an implicit "should" in any argument, and move on? The mere fact that I can't manage to ask my questions without recourse to a "should" of my own indicates what's at stake here.

WB: I actually think there is a way to avoid that "should," and I don't think it's just an academic trick. In my book *States of Injury,* I made an argument that one way to get away from certain kinds of conservative identity claims without rejecting everything about the importance of what we call "subject position" these days was to shift our language of political demands from "I am" to "I want this for us." That is, to replace, "I am a (fill in the identity position), therefore I demand . . ." to "I want this for all of us. This is how I think things should go in the world from the place in which I stand." Now, what if we used that same kind of linguistic shift to think about how we might get away from that "should" you were talking about? We can move from stating, "Freedom should be freedom with one another in which there is collective ownership and control and in which all human beings participate," to "The vision of human freedom that I am arguing for is one in which these things are featured and here's why."

I don't think the difference here is slight, because the first one does have a moral and therefore implicitly foundational claim. When I say, for example, "We must value basic human needs and care for the earth over corporate profits," I could do it in a way that makes this claim a moral truth, but I think it will actually be more compelling as a political claim. I think leftists today will be more compelling and also more honest if we accept that what we're engaged in is a rhetorical battle for a vision of human life and a vision of how it can best be organized. By "rhetorical," I don't mean something slight or cheap. I mean that what we need to be producing as a left is a vision that compels people, a vision of a world in which they actually want to live. And that's not a "should"! It's not saying, "You *should* live this way," but "Don't you want to? Doesn't this capture you? Incite you? Isn't it better than what we've got? Doesn't it make what we've got appear absurd, ridiculous, misbegotten?"

CB: So our task as leftists is to make the best possible case for freedom?

WB: Right. We say, "This is what it would be like to be free of domination. Are you compelled?" And if the answer is "No," then we say, "Let's argue." I think we've exhausted moral exhortation on the left. It hasn't been exhausted on the right, interestingly enough. One reason that it's exhausted on the left is that the "shoulds" persisted long past the point when what we used to call "actually existing socialism" could back them up. So our "shoulds" had what sounded *only* like a moral force, or worse—the moralizing force of mere critique, complaint, reproach, with no viable vision. They had no reality, no promise—let alone guarantee—that what we thought the world should look like could actually be brought into being.

And that really doesn't work politically. The right, by contrast, was able to exploit a certain kind of moral exhortation by reaching back into the past for images of what it imagined were better times: families were intact, the Third World wasn't rising up, kids were safe, and life was sweet. That's an utterly idealized picture of mid-twentieth-century life even for the few, of course. But the moral exhortation worked because it reached back to something of which people at least had a ghostly memory, an image if not an experience. Perfect Benjaminian political strategy!

CB: The right has seemed more comfortable doing what you've advocated here. Its ideologues are happy to do battle. And they aren't particularly worried about being consistent.

WB: You know, Stuart Hall wrote beautifully on this point in his analyses of Thatcherism. He recognized that what had made Thatcherism and Reaganism possible was a high level of tolerance for internal incoherence in the relationship of theory to practice, and also a deep appreciation of the purely rhetorical work of politics.

CB: Reading work by people like yourself, Stuart Hall, and Ernesto Laclau and Chantal Mouffe, who wish to move beyond the constraints of traditional Marxist thinking about history, one still comes across sentences that take the form of "More and more under capitalism, we see evidence of x." Or, "As technocratic ideals penetrate all aspects of everyday life, we see evidence of y." So, despite the firm insistence on the need to not think about capitalism in terms of stages, there's still a tendency to frame arguments in terms that imply progress. Is there a danger that these formulations might let progressive thought in through the back door?

217

WB: Capital comes closer to undermining an anti-progressive analysis than any other force on earth. Yet I think we can make a distinction between a developmental frame and a progressive frame. It seems to me that what was really incisive in Marx's own analysis is the theory of history in which capitalism not only seems to be going through stages, but to be going through stages in which, on the one hand, more and more wealth could be amassed more and more efficiently and, on the other hand, more and more inegalitarianism could be distributed over more and more parts of the earth. And it was that contradiction between the amassing of wealth and the impoverishment of the many that gave way to the idea of the inevitability of capitalism's overthrow. But what we have to face today, I think, is the fact that capitalism still develops—certain phases of capitalism give way to others, certain modes and objects of production give way to others—without moving toward its own demise. I would argue that even though the maldistributions of wealth under capitalism are still extraordinary, capitalism has become steadily less odious and more pleasurable for the majority of the population in the First World, if not elsewhere. Scenes of the masses in First World countries laboring at starvation wages for the wealth of the few are gone. They are present in the Third World, but they are not the dominant picture of capitalism in the First World.

Something else Marx never could have predicted: capitalist commodity production is increasingly oriented to the pleasures of the middle-class consumer. And the middle class is ever more oriented by its pleasures. On top of that, First World capitalism has developed an ethical face. It recycles, it conserves, it labels, it divests itself of GMOs and MSG, it caters to vegetarian and heart-healthy diets, it renounces testing on animals, it sponsors Gay Pride and the Special Olympics, and it provides educational supplements for the underprivileged. So are there still sweatshops? Of course. They're in the Third World. And occasionally we find out about them in L.A. and New York City. They're around. But does capital itself get horrified at this fact? Yes. Does the Enron scandal remind us that capitalism is still a robber-baron operation? Sure. But capitalists themselves claim to be scandalized by the scandal. So there is a quality to capitalism today that can no longer be characterized as simply the massive concentration of wealth in and for the few, and the starvation and impoverishment of the many. Now, that is not in any way to misunderstand or ignore the devastation of globalization for the most vulnerable. But I think we need to recognize that capitalism is neither progressing in a more and more horrific way, nor is it progressing in some better, moral, ethical, egalitarian way. It's clever and it's complex in its moves. And, politically, there is a whole set of possibilities for capital that exceed the imperative of profit and the needs of capital that Marx analyzed as pretty much operating on their own, independent of political intervention.

I think the important thing is for us to realize that capitalism has imperatives and needs. And it will develop responses to those. We can call that aspect "developmental." Indeed, late twentieth-century and early twenty-first-century capitalism doesn't look anything like nineteenth-century capitalism. It has phases that look, in some sense, like advances over earlier phases. But it also has ways of morphing that aren't simply about progress or development. This is one of the things that's so hard for the left. We have to make an argument against capitalism as a life form to other folks who are living well, yet are not at the top. That's why I think it's so crucial for us to break from the progressive narrative, because part of the progressive narrative from a Marxist point of view is that things will get worse and worse for the many. In quantitative terms, they haven't. But are there other ways in which capitalism's organization of human life is unbearable, or at least strongly impeachable? Here we inevitably return to Marcuse, who understood half a decade ago that capitalism could no longer be fought on grounds of exploitation or even inegalitarianism, but only on grounds of quality of life, broadly and radically understood.

CB: Reflecting on the last few years of the anti-globalization movement, starting with the demonstrations at the WTO meeting in Seattle, do you think that part of the problem for the left today is that by looking at those places in the world that are still succumb-

219

ing to an earlier phase of capitalist development, we lose sight of those people who may not be as happy as they would like to be but nevertheless are a lot better off than Marx imagined they would be?

WB: It's not that it doesn't matter what capital is doing in Latin America or the Philippines or any other place recently decimated by certain aspects of what we've come to call globalization. But, unfortunately, those unsympathetic to the globalization protesters have an easy rejoinder: "They were so bad off before. They may be having a rough time now. But they will be so much better off in the future." This is how progressive thinking continues to work in the service of capitalism. "Hey, it's a little rough-and-tumble when you're first getting incorporated into the capitalist order. The nineteenth century had that quality for Europe. Look at Europe today." That argument doesn't always get made expressly, but it's there in the background.

Another part of the problem is that an anti-capitalist position focused tightly on the Third World won't compel people living modestly well within the First World—or at least imagining that they are—whose motivation for living in some other kind of social, economic, and political order would have to be something besides wealth. That's not to say that most folks don't have stupid, meaningless, boring jobs and are paid too little to live decently in cities with astronomical costs of living. But these folks are not going to be compelled by an argument that defines capital as the sole reason for their dissatisfaction. As I said before, you actually have to make an argument about ways of life. You have to incite an interest that has been pounded out of us, an interest in shaping our own lives and the larger orders we live in . . . You have to incite an interest in what we have been talking about today: freedom.

220

A society cannot be reduced to its economic base or social structures. It includes superstructures as well. It requires not only institutions but also "values" and ideas, bodies of knowledge, ethics and (a)esthetics. These terms are not found in Marx and their meaning is perhaps not quite precise. They nonetheless convey the fact that for Marx every society is a totality.

—Henri Lefebvre, *The Explosion: Marxism and the French Upheaval*

Culture and the Angels of History

Mama Cash:
Buying and Selling Genders
Charles Anders

*W*hen transvestites talk about "bingeing and purging," we don't mean bulimia.

Instead, we're referring to a common pattern among men who dress—often furtively—as women. They buy nice dresses, skirts and lingerie, then trash or burn them. A mixture of guilt and the fear of discovery by a spouse usually drives this sartorial Stalinism.

The Internet is full of sad stories of binges and purges, genetic males whom remorse drives to destroy what they've built again and again. More often than not, the purgers are working class or poor, and the expense of replacing their finery endangers the rent and bills. The online narratives come to resemble addiction tales, with the hero unable to break the cycle that ruins his/her life.

But what people don't usually discuss about these stories is the starring role consumerism plays in them. The binge/purge victim always consumes, and never owns. One reason for purging is the idea that ownership of women's clothes is a woman's sole privilege.

But another reason is that buying is most of the fun. Crossdressers who make themselves start from scratch over and over have boiled their pursuit down to its purest rush—the thrill of acquisition.

227

It has become a cliché to talk about the commodification of gender, how people buy and sell masculinity and femininity in the form of pretty things or toys.

The recent movie *What Women Want* dramatized the idea of gender as a commodity. Mel Gibson gains empathy with women through a freak telepathy accident involving a hair dryer, and this allows him to sell them things! It turns out that all women really want is a man who can feed their need to be understood and to shop until they plotz. Running shoes have a starring role, as Gibson lends the full power of his newly simpatico persona to putting together a Nike ad.

These days, people don't buy just clothes and accessories, but body parts. Men increasingly have cosmetic surgery on their abs just as women have nipped and tucked their way to beauty for years. In *The Beauty Myth*, Naomi Wolf discusses how women are coerced into enduring the "violence" of cosmetic surgery. Their family bonds, social standing, and employment all depend on getting svelte throats and airbag breasts.

The binge-and-purge cycle discussed above is just a more extreme form of the experience all men and women share: gender is confirmed and renewed through consumption.

228

But transgender people have a unique perspective on the relationship between gender and money. We've had to use capital accrued in one gender to buy our way into another. We understand more than anyone the high cost of gender, having adopted identities as adult neophytes.

That experience also qualifies us uniquely to imagine how people could construct gender in a world without capitalism. And, conversely, how freeing gender from money's baggage could help dismantle the social scaffolding that holds capitalism up.

Why would transgender people, in particular, want to imagine gender without capitalism? Perhaps because we, more than most, have suffered alienation under the current system. Trying to navigate gender in a mature economy often seems like trying to buy underwear at a convenience store designed by Terry Gilliam.

Gender and money both manifest in our relations with others. Tom Hanks, marooned on his desert island in *Castaway*, has no need for either, which doesn't stop him from becoming *so* butch!

So for TGs especially, money is about being in the world. When we try to imagine alternatives to capitalism, it's from the perspective of the self-made man or woman. We start with a heightened awareness of the artificiality of the social roles which money both confirms and constricts.

But if gender is a kind of consumption, it's also a form of labor. People often work harder than they think to maintain the boy/girl behaviors expected of them. You may have learned through painful trial-and-error not to use certain phrases, or to walk a certain way. After a while, learned gender behavior becomes almost second nature, like compensating for a weak eye.

Most of us have, as an unspoken part of our employment agreements, a requirement to present as our assigned gender. Transsexuals increasingly have had success in convincing human resources departments to change their assigned genders, after which they must carefully project the image of their revised gender, perhaps even going "stealth."

Again, transgender people are just experiencing what everyone goes through. No matter where you work or how you present yourself, part of your paycheck rewards you for dressing and acting to match the letter on your birth certificate. You end up regarding your male or female identity as a part of your work uniform.

A man who risks losing a promotion if he swishes too much or doesn't follow pro football copes with this issue, as does a woman with a buzzcut who loses her job. I know a dyke, leaning toward becoming a man, whose ambiguous gender made it impossible for her to find a job.

The business manual, *Put Your Best Foot Forward,* published in

2000 by authors Jo-Ellan Dimitrius, Ph.D. and Mark Mazzarella, offers a revealing look at the economic value of gender presentation. The gurus cite research demonstrating that attractive women are twenty percent more likely to be hired by women, and three hundred percent more likely to be hired by men.

Women who don't wear makeup often suffer discrimination in the workplace. But makeup shouldn't be "dramatic," and women shouldn't wear high-heels inappropriately for fear of sexualizing their appearance, Dimitrius and Mazzarella warn. At the same time, facial hair on a woman, or unshaved body hair, raises questions about their character.

Dimitrius and Mazzarella also tell the story of Bob, a successful attorney sporting short hair and conservative suits. After a divorce and mid-life crisis, Bob decided he had "paid his dues" and it was time to cut loose.

"What he settled on left him almost unrecognizable," Dimitrius and Mazzarella write. "His hair crept down well below his collar," and he got an earring and wore more colorful clothes. People began to question whether Bob remained "committed to the practice of law and his clients."

Later, they warn that long hair on a man connotes irresponsibility and "loose morals." And men who style their hair, beyond just washing and combing it, are "egotistical." Interestingly, Dimitrius and Mazzarella also warn against being an "ethnic poster child" by wearing too many signifiers if you belong to a minority group.

It's not just whacko business-guru wannabes like Dimitrius and Mazzarella who are trying to equate traditional masculine/feminine divides with competence or professionalism. Noted intellectual Jacques Barzun has made waves recently by decrying the lapse of formal (read: gender-conformist) clothing in law firms and other professional establishments.

Meanwhile, other theorists have worked to turn gender into a workplace issue. Georgetown University linguistics professor Deborah Tannen has written a series of "men and women talking" books, among them the double-colon-wielding *Talking from 9 to 5: Women and Men in the Workplace: Language, Sex and Power.*

Tannen tends to treat male and female behaviors as immutable constants which must be negotiated. Gender roles are largely an immutable feature of the social topography of the office. But even if you believe gender comes naturally, as Tannen appears to, it's up to both sexes, especially men, to become aware of these issues.

In *You Just Don't Understand*, Tannen explains that women are naturally collaborational and non-confrontational. To women, "disagreement carries a metamessage of threat to intimacy." But Tannen preaches that women should learn that "a little conflict won't kill them." However, the overwhelming impression her work leaves is that the most you can hope for is to moderate the extremes.

Tannen spends a lot of time in *You Just Don't Understand* writing about men dominating office meetings, examining the fact that a meeting involving both men and women will proceed along much the same lines as one involving only men. But when only women are present, the meeting will run very differently. "Male-female conversations are more like men's conversations than they are like women's," she writes.

Tannen doesn't seem to want to redefine gender roles, just tweak them to make them function in the workplace. She wants to move the goalposts for the two teams at work a little, and curb the worst abuses. Men must stop belittling and sexualizing women, but that doesn't mean they should lose sight of the differences between the sexes.

By showing how women's contributions in mixed-gender discussions often fall through the cracks, Tannen hints at a workplace status quo in which women's jobs are construed as being more feminine or "supportive."

231

In other words, gender designations also facilitate a division of labor. Men tend to dominate as mathematicians, while women have a corner on the exciting fields of medical billing and bikini waxing.

As Donald Lowe points out in *The Body in Late-Capitalist USA*, society regards women as best suited to "supportive services, e.g., nursing rather than doctoring, secretarial work rather than executive management, public school teaching rather than college teaching." Even when women have entered traditionally male fields, they're expected to make more "nurturing" authority figures than men.

In their book *Familiar Exploitation*, Christine Delphy and Diana Leonard argue for a paradigm of "delegation" in the home. Tasks performed by women in the home are actually delegated by the "head of the family," who would otherwise have to perform those tasks himself. Meanwhile, women have "subordinate consumption" of the goods they produce in the home, like food.

A number of commentators, including Barbara Ehrenreich, have argued on behalf of assigning economic value to women's traditional tasks. Ehrenreich argues that women's work should be defined as labor. If people were being paid to do traditional housewife tasks, we could begin to see the economic significance of that work, even if it were undervalued massively.

Meanwhile, there's an emotional division of labor in which men and women each only feel a portion of the emotional spectrum. Men are allowed to be angry, defiant, competitive, and lugubrious. Women positively must emote on all cylinders when it comes to "softer" emotions like grief or weltschmertz. It makes you feel like one of the smurfs or seven dwarves, forever labeled with one characteristic: Stoic Smurf, perhaps.

The recent nostalgia for the 1940s and the "Greatest Generation" feels like a call for emotional demarcation as well. In war movie after brain-crushing war movie, we're reminded that back in the '40s men were men and women were women. Men gritted their teeth and did what had to be done, while women cried a lot.

It's easy to satirize movements toward giving men more of an equal share of the emotional tasks. Bruce in Christopher Durang's *Beyond Therapy*, who cries at the drop of a hat, is only an extreme caricature of the stereotype of the "sensitive new-age guy." But just as it wouldn't kill women to express more anger, it wouldn't kill men to shoulder some of the chore of weeping.

Finally, gender often serves as a proxy for class in our society. Among men, effeminacy is frequently portrayed as one of the main signs of membership in the upper classes—look at the difference between Martin and Niles on *Frasier*. Meanwhile, stereotypes of working-class men always emphasize their Tom-of-Finland toughness.

Among women, femininity can connote privilege both by its absence and its presence. The media presents stereotypes of rich women as unbelievably pampered and therefore feminine. But it also warns that too much money and success will turn women into men, like "iron lady" Margaret Thatcher.

Two movies make a compelling argument for a link between femininity and lack of power. In *Working Girl*, the deserving Melanie Griffith is denied career advancement because her hair is too big. She learns to emulate Sigourney Weaver, whose femininity fits neatly into a businesslike package. Gone are the mane, the flouncy outfits, and the heavy makeup. The newly executive Griffith wins the heart of Weaver's boyfriend, played by Harrison Ford.

In *Legally Blonde*, Reese Witherspoon totes a foofy pink wardrobe and tiny dog to Harvard law school, only to find nobody takes her seriously. Unlike Griffith in *Working Girl*, Witherspoon's character comes from a wealthy background. But the uptight Boston Brahmins snub her and her only ally turns out to be her manicurist. The film broadcasts its message clearly: the ultra-feminine Witherspoon has more in common with her trailer-dwelling manicurist than with the masculinized female law students. In the end, Witherspoon shows the value of girly knowledge and wins over her classmates, but the film's linkage of femininity and disempowerment remains similar to *Working Girl's*.

So we're really left with two separate but related issues. First, how can we imagine gender free from all the baggage we've identified above? Secondly, how does that help us build a more egalitarian society?

If we eliminate all the extraneous stuff, genders will become much less rigidly defined. If your masculinity isn't what you own or what you do, it's much harder to put a finger on. And it's much easier to migrate from one piece of real estate to another in boygirl land.

Beyond that, it's hard to say. Some believe that eventually we'll all download our consciousnesses into cyberspace and leave our bodies, thereby escaping gender altogether. Or we'll become cyborgs with identities based on how many prime numbers we can generate in the time it takes to say "Toffler."

I have a hard time believing in utopias. I don't have enough faith in people. I always imagine that somehow the screenwriters of *Ernest Goes to Afghanistan* will end up running the world.

When I think of a classless society, my brain gets stuck on images of a "Free to Be You and Me" horrorscope, where everybody wears too much corduroy. Or I imagine a tyrannical order in which we crack down on Hello Kitty T-shirts in the name of destroying privilege.

In my worst nightmare, I end up living on a commune where we pool all our resources, and all my pantyhose ends up being used to line the chicken coops. As an Asian studies major, I read way too many first-hand accounts of China's Great Leap Forward for my own good.

So I'm skeptical about utopian predictions. But I do believe we're going to treat each other with more respect in future. The ultimate evil in the gender/money axis is its reliance on hierarchies, and once we root that out, we can build a fairer system.

Feminism has done a lot to expose the phallogocentrism in our culture. We've begun to collectively unravel how homophobia protects traditional economic arrangements based on gender and sexuality, chief among them marriage.

Now we need to take it to the next level. We need to expose the ways in which *all* gender stereotypes are reflections of the market.

That means moving past feminism and GLBT rights toward a broader-based movement to dismantle all forms of privilege and hierarchy that rationalize sexual identities for their own economic purposes. That doesn't mean seeking a better place in existing hierarchies or expanding privilege to include us. It means that wherever we see the man/woman thing being used to prop up a one-up, one-down system, we need to slash and burn.

Recognize that gender subversion is a profoundly political act. Sponsor a "crossdress at work" day, and make sure all your coworkers participate. Paint lipstick on the Marlboro Man's mouth. Buy videos like *Bend Over Boyfriend*, an instruction manual on how to use a strap-on heterosexually that brings a whole new meaning to the phrase "stick it to the man."

235

Most of all, look at how your consumption and work patterns reinforce the "old economy."

As international capitalism grows ever more sophisticated, it relies on demographics and pigeonholes to sell ever more specific items to ever more tightly defined groups. Cookies on the Internet and shopping "club" cards are just two ways the machine strives to herd consumers. Corporations target ads at "gay men" or "straight women in their thirties."

Instead of buying the items the system selects for you, trade clothes with your friends. Change your behavior at work, subtly, and see if anyone notices. Make it harder for marketers, your boss, and even your loved ones to pin you down.

Peace, Love, Linux: When the Open Source Movement Got in Bed with Capitalism
Annalee Newitz

A walk through the vacated warehouses of San Francisco's South-of-Market and Mission districts in early 2002 reveals signs of the dead dot-com revolution everywhere. Former dot-com lofts and shops stand empty, or have been filled by nonprofits, galleries, and artists. A large warehouse built before World War II for industrial production is vacant, while the painted sign for "Spinner.com" is still bright on its old smokestacks.

But the paint is beginning to fade on a series of "wild" ads that IBM paid some marketing company to spraypaint on the sidewalks in this formerly technocash-rich area. The ads are three simple icons: a peace sign, a heart shape, and a cartoon penguin. During the Internet boom, it would have been a rebus any geek or dot-com marketing droid could recognize. Peace. Love. Linux.

Linux, whose chubby penguin mascot is the only new part of this bohemian equation, is a computer operating system, a piece of software that provides an interface between computer hardware and the applications or devices it runs. If you want lots of people to be able to use the same devices and software applications, it's helpful if lots of people are running the same operating systems. Large corporations like Microsoft, whose Windows operating system is installed on ninety percent of PCs, dominate the market in OSes.

And yet Linux managed to take a bite out of Microsoft's share of the OS market by doing something completely counter-intuitive and anti-capitalist. Linux was available for free, and it was collaboratively written by many people working together who seemed motivated by nothing more than their burning love for publicly available, functional software.

Linux is the most visible product of a much larger open source movement in the high-tech industry during the 1990s tech bubble. This movement, whose origins can be traced back to the radical free software movement, was a powerful force in the construction of the early public Internet and World Wide Web. Most of the free software available on the Internet is a result of the free and open source software movements. Open source ideals are responsible for everything from the celebrated and widely implemented Apache server (www.apache.org) and indispensable openssh (www.openssh.org), to the smallest hobby project hosted on open source community development site Source Forge (www.sorceforge.org).

As the well-received Linux began to make inroads into a market dominated by Microsoft, the proverbial Biggest Corporation in the World, people began to wonder if the end of capitalism was nigh. What would happen if lots of people produced and consumed products that were free? How would the market handle it? And moreover, how would our notions of private property fare in a system where all software code was freely available for you to use, modify, and distribute as you liked? For a while, it seemed as if progressive forces in the open source movement might force the market to take on more humanistic, socially constructive values.

But just when a genuine alternative to capitalist production seemed about to hit the big time, Linux's popularity suddenly soared on Wall Street, peaking with several crazed Linux-related corporate IPOs in late 1999 and early 2000. By the time open source companies like VALinux, LinuxCare, and Andover.net were tanking, open source had become just a silver wrapping around yet another free market, high-tech commodity. In a few short years, open source had been co-opted.

And yet there were parts of the open source movement that had a lasting, progressive impact on capitalist culture. Certainly, the free market hadn't been reigned in, but many high-tech workers had experimented with anti-capitalist forms of production—forms of production that remain strong in the software world to this day. Moreover, there was another side to the open source movement that was rarely covered in the media or at high-tech conferences. This was the cultural side of open source, the "peace and love" part. Many people involved in the open source community espoused countercultural values, especially sexually subversive ones. Just as 1960s anti-war activism was tied to sexual liberation in the public mind, 1990s open source evangelism was tied to open sexuality.

In high-tech bohemian cities like San Francisco, the open source movement seemed to merge almost seamlessly with the queer and polyamorous communities. What open source left in its wake were not only a batch of powerful, useful open source projects to inflame the anti-capitalist imagination, but also a new techno-sexual counterculture.

239

The policies of many high-tech companies (not just ones involved in open source) reflect this countercultural influence. Major tech employers like Microsoft and Sun have "domestic partner" insurance policies that allow employees to share insurance with a partner of the same sex or a live-in partner. Large tech corporations also have non-discrimination policies which include trans-sexuals and homosexuals along with other, traditional protected categories. When bellweather companies like Microsoft make tolerance for homosexuality a part of their corporate policy, it's clear that certain kinds of progressive values are becoming mainstream.

Whether these progressive values are anti-capitalist is another question entirely.

Free Love and Free Software

The radical free software movement was initiated by MIT researcher and UNIX guru Richard Stallman, an infamous hacker who wrote the powerful editor-and-compiler Emacs in the early 1970s. In the 1980s Stallman also founded the nonprofit Free Software Foundation (www.fsf.org) and wrote the GNU Manifesto, in which he noted satirically that free software meant "free as in free speech, not free beer." His widely used GNU General Public License (GPL) for software, often called the "copyleft," stuck a knife in the heart of private property. The GPL license begins,

> The licenses for most software are designed to take away your freedom to share and change it. By contrast, the GNU General Public License is intended to guarantee your freedom to share and change free software—to make sure the software is free for all its users . . . Our General Public Licenses are designed to make sure that you have the freedom to distribute copies of free software (and charge for this service if you wish), that you receive source code or can get it if you want it, that you can change the software or use pieces of it in new free programs; and that you know you can do these things.

In a nutshell, free software is software in which the underlying source code to a program is made freely available to the general public. It's a development methodology that sharply contradicts the way companies like Microsoft or Oracle do business. Stallman and many of his contemporaries like Eric Raymond, who later became one of the open source movement's chief evangelists, were heavily influenced by 1960s counterculture. Proto-free software hackers often met in the sexually liberated atmosphere of 1970s science fiction conventions, and shared their philosophies about free love as well as free code. The Internet, whose sexual content is legendary, was built on the code of early 1970s hackers, who were developing network operating systems on many of the same college campuses where students and professors were espousing radical new socio-sexual values as well.

At first glance, the idea that free love and free software would come together as smoothly as so many orgiasts might seem odd, but this combination of sexual and techno-liberation has its roots in historical and present-day radical movements. Even today, free software hackers aren't all that uncommon in the "sex" community, a group that includes people in open relationships, queers, S/M or kinky fetish fans, and anyone else whose sexual proclivities fall outside the mainstream.

Open sexuality might also have become a symbol of freedom for people developing free software and, later, open source software because coders suffer an unfortunate reputation for living disembodied, asexual lives; they are maligned for being passionate only about their computers and often deemed incapable of non-virtual lust. But the stereotype doesn't hold true—certainly the geeks I know are getting some, and not infrequently with utter disregard for conventional social mores. Most intriguingly, that subset of geeks who are passionate about free software may well be leading the way: Some of the same free software programmers who eagerly experiment with new methods for developing software are also gleefully dallying with alternative ways of developing sexual relationships.

Free software champions see no need to constrain themselves to a sexual status quo just because the boring majority doesn't know how to have fun. Likewise, many advocates of free and open source software describe themselves as nonconformists, rebels, or as

241

just generally more open-minded than your average person. In terms of software, that means that they delight in engaging in practices that challenge the staid old proprietary capitalist way of doing software business.

The ideals that underlie free and open source software are applicable to more than simply coding and business—they get at the very nature of what constitutes human community. Free software is a shared resource that nobody can selfishly hoard; open source software is an alternative form of production that involves groups of people who work together rather than in competition with each other.

When programmers see that software production is dramatically improved in a shared, non-competitive, free environment, wouldn't it be natural for them to apply what they've learned from coding to what they practice in their everyday lives—including their sex lives? And the logical extension of free and open source software in the realm of sex would certainly include publicly shared sex at a sex party, for instance, alternative ways of building relationships (such as queer sexuality), and non-monogamy (non-proprietary sexual affection).

Stallman himself notes that his moral intransigence about free software isn't limited to code. "I've been resistant to the pressure to conform in any circumstance," he says. And that includes sexual conformity. Stallman says he has never had a monogamous sexual relationship, and he's also observed that programmers tend to favor polyamorous or non-monogamous relationships more than people in other jobs. "It's about being able to question conventional wisdom," he asserts.

He confesses with a smile that he doesn't consider himself an expert on sex, but he recognizes that the unconventional choices he has made as a software engineer are analogous to the choices he's made in his romantic life as well. "I believe in love, but not monogamy," he says plainly.

Stallman's specific beliefs are his own, but the nonconformist, experimental nature that guides his work is shared by a not-insignificant portion of the coder community.

Open Source Goes Mainstream

Stallman is often dismissed by mainstream software developers as an oddball who is not to be taken seriously—so it wouldn't be surprising for defenders of the sexual status quo to do the same. But Stallman isn't unique in his hacker polyamory. Author and programmer Eric Raymond is an expert on geek anthropology whose credentials are second to none. "Hackerdom easily tolerates a much wider range of sexual and lifestyle variation than the mainstream culture," writes Raymond in *The New Hacker's Dictionary*. "It includes a relatively large gay and bisexual contingent. Hackers are somewhat more likely to . . . practice open marriage, or live in communes or group homes."

Raymond and several other hackers invented the term "open source" in 1998. The Open Source Initiative website (www.opensource.org) includes a description of the event. "We realized it was time to dump the confrontational attitude that has been associated with 'free software' in the past and sell the idea strictly on the same pragmatic, business-case grounds that motivated Netscape [to open their source code]." The use of the term "sell" is crucial here; mostly what motivated the open-sourcers of the late 1990s was a need to distance themselves from Stallman's free software foundation, which they considered "too confrontational." Instead, they foregrounded the way free software (as in "free beer") which released its source code could be "marketable." This was the first step toward selling out the values that had once energized the thousands of software developers the world over who had been contributing time to popular free software projects like the various distributions of Linux.

And yet, the selling out of free software via the hegemony of

243

open source in no way abated the countercultural thrust of the now-divided free software/open source community. Indeed, sex parties and erotic raves packed with open-sourcers were common in places like San Francisco and nearby Silicon Valley.

Of course, no one's been counting how many hackers frequent sex parties or calculating the percentage of open source contributors who also enjoy open relationships, but there does seem to be a crossover. "This [alternative lifestyle] group is a healthy contingent of the hacker culture, and has been even more influential than its size would suggest," says Raymond.

At the very least, it's safe to say that not only are many open-minded open source hackers unafraid of the anything-goes mentality of the experimental sex community, but that they also positively embrace it. There's even a crop of online open source pornography, memorialized in J. Stile's hoard of erotic "Linux slut" images, which you can find on his Webby award-winning Stile Project. The overlap between the languages of programming and kink is a source of humor on a bondage website known to fans as the BSD BDSM Site. As an advertisement for the "Cat5 o' Eight Tails" reads, "Light and fast, perfect for the home or office where multitasking is vital. Eight individual strands to transmit your message interference-free."

244

For some of the select group of techies who have devoted themselves to free software and open source projects, free love and creative sexuality are part and parcel of their dedication to communities that value openness, sharing, and collective pragmatism.

"There's no causal connection between being into open source software and being sexually adventurous. Let's dash the implication that open source causes bisexuality or anything else," laughs Eli Silverman (not his real name), a longtime programmer who worked extensively with the GNU Emacs text editor at a Silicon Valley company devoted to open source development. He is also a self-described "pervert" whose collection of gray-market lesbian fisting videos is much admired in the sex community. Adds Ed, a queer Apache developer working in San Francisco: "Just because you know other freaks in open source doesn't mean that being into open source makes you a pervert."

And yet both admit that the ideals that motivate a person to get into open source or free software might also motivate them to be sexually experimental. Open source "is not the textbook solution," Ed explains. "It's an alternative mode of economic production, and being queer or non-monogamous are alternative modes of having relationships. Perhaps people who can consider alternate modes of production are willing to consider other kinds of alternatives."

Even as the craze for free software saturates the market, spurring stock market public offerings and inciting fear and trembling in industry giants, opting to go the free or open source route is still difficult. Although in the late 1990s, free software hackers were more likely than not to get rewarded for their labors with stock options from aspiring Linux companies, the usual result was more intangible, like getting to build communities or creating better code just for the sheer joy of it. Therefore, it is no surprise that mavericks and free thinkers are the lifeblood of open source and free software development. And thinking outside the box is, of course, exactly what is required of anyone whose sexuality doesn't fit into cultural norms.

245

Yet the notoriously debate-prone open source and free software communities are as divided on the question of sexuality as they are on whether Debian or Red Hat is the better distribution of GNU/Linux. While people like Raymond and Ed see the communities as open to alternative lifestyles, others disagree.

Deirdre Saoirse, a former employee of Linuxcare and founder of a Bay Area users group for people who use the Python scripting language, feels strongly that people involved in open source can be just as conservative and closed-minded as any other part of the population. "Some of my female and/or queer and/or transgendered friends have felt very out of place in the Linux," she says emphatically. "I've seen a lot of sexism and not a lot of openness to alternative lifestyles among the community as a whole, even in the Bay Area."

Questioning Family Values

Goolie, a programmer who works on open source community-development projects at a San Francisco start-up, warns that an ability to connect open source sensibilities and open-mindedness about sex "would take a particular type of coder, one who felt that open source gets at some basic, fundamental expression of humanity."

Richard Stallman, of course, is just this sort of person. Free software is not a business model for Stallman, nor is it a technically superior method for creating software. Stallman has made his point of view very clear—he doesn't care if the software he uses is actually technically inferior; for him, free software is a moral imperative based on the principle that people who share code are ethically better people. His commitment to an unorthodox romantic life extends even into the realm of family.

He says he distrusts the idea of traditional families and criticizes the idea that having children is necessarily a positive contribution to an already overpopulated civilization. "As a child, I rebelled against parental authority," he recollects. In his view, traditional family structures are predicated on the opposite of freely given love. His point of view is shared by many people in the queer community, where "family" often means longterm friends rather than biological relations, and having children isn't regarded as the logical outcome of marriage.

Like many social renegades, Stallman has had to create a home life out of his work and friendships. He remembers that back in the 1970s he flirted with the idea of joining a commune devoted to creating "families" who practiced polyfidelity (committed, but non-

246

monogamous relationships). But he was concerned that he wouldn't fit into any of the families.

Instead, he created his own family of sorts with his Free Software Foundation, a nonprofit devoted to the sharing and creation of free software resources and information. Rather than sharing food and shelter with a biological family, Stallman shares his famous GNU software with an international group of like-minded individuals.

When queer San Francisco network consultant Richard R. Couture launched a Linux-based Internet cafe known as CoffeeNet, one of his wishes was "to create the kind of space where socializing and sexuality and an interest in computers could come together." And yet Couture, who also founded the Linux user group now known as the Linux Mafia, mourns the fact that Linux users seem so, well, straight. "People call me a pervert jokingly in the Linux cabal," he laughs. "It's because I'm openly homosexual and I sometimes enjoy freaking everybody out by commenting on sex. I do it to shock everybody."

Couture's friend Rick Moen, also a network consultant and member of the Linux Mafia user group, contends that the connection between hacking and open sexuality goes back to the 1970s. In a free zine called *The Node*, published by San Francisco's now-defunct Kerista commune, he found a "mix [of] articles about computers and technology with pieces on polyamorous/community living and all sorts of other oddities. I read it whenever I could find it," he says.

247

"Geeks are introverts, we read a lot of science fiction, and we have bizarre socialization," says Muffy Barkocy, a non-monogamous bisexual working with Apache and Perl at Egreetings.com. She believes that a geek's stereotypical lack of socialization encourages a more experimental sexual life. "Because of our lack of socialization, we don't learn about the monogamous imperative. It just doesn't occur to us."

Barkocy's point about science fiction bears examination. Speculative fantasizing has always been a passion for geeks of any kind. For some free software enthusiasts, there is a clear link between the bold visions common in science fiction and a tendency toward experimentation in both coding and sexual practice. Lile Elam, a member of Linux Chix, a women's user group, suggests that many proto-free software geeks grew up imagining a world where societies weren't necessarily driven by the profit motive—or by compulsory heterosexual monogamy. Elam adds that many hackers are also pagans—yet another data point indicating an openness to alternative ways of living.

Adds Stallman: "A lot of programmers are science fiction fans, and there's a tendency in science fiction fandom to accept nonstandard relationships." Science fiction is a genre sometimes known for its utopian musings on what a more liberated society would look like. And reading about alien or unknown worlds can inspire fans to go beyond the realm of imagination and explore alternative realities and social arrangements in everyday life.

Not all free software geeks are science fiction fans, of course, nor are all open source software developers likely to be ready to strip down and join a three-way at the drop of a Red Hat. But that's not the point. Part of the essence of the open source and free software communities, ideally, is that they are open to experimentation of all kinds, both in terms of practical engineering—the compilation of efficient code—and social engineering—the construction of new ways of being in the world. And these new ways of being are certainly not limited to the sexual variety. Open source enthusiasts are likely to see applications for open source strategies in a vast number of arenas, including politics, the creation of literature, and even hardware design.

"Computer people talk about two things: code and sex," says Barkocy. "You discuss alternatives to what your company can do with code, or alternatives to sexual norms."

Open sexuality is no alternative to capitalism. It's easy to mix smutty talk, no matter how enlightened, with talk of how your company can fatten its bottom line. And yet it's undeniable that the free software and open source movements have changed the way people do business and, for that matter, what kinds of people are allowed to do business. Free software found its place in the market when many of its adherents became open sourcers, but Stallman's vision of free software remains unassimilated, an anti-capitalist thorn in the software market's side. So many programs have been released under the GPL that this source of anti-capitalist sentiment isn't likely to go away any time soon.

Interview with Tom Frank
Charlie Bertsch

*F*ame is relative. Ask most Americans if they've heard of *The Baffler* and they'll respond with a blank stare. But in some circles, reading this publication is practically a requirement for membership. For the largely over-educated and under-paid individuals who still resist the idea that mainstream media conglomerates know what's best for us, *The Baffler* is a beacon in the nation's cultural darkness. And a lot of the wattage comes from its co-founder and present editor-in-chief Tom Frank, whose beautifully worded rants are an integral part of the magazine's identity.

250

A wide-ranging thinker with a Ph.D. in History from the University of Chicago, Frank challenges the division between scholarship and journalism that fragments leftist thinking. His first book, *The Conquest of Cool* (University of Chicago Press, 1998), explored how advertising culture in the 1960s borrowed from the nascent counterculture to sell goods to a new generation of consumers. His second book, *One Market Under God* (Alfred A. Knopf, 2002), tackled the marketing of the market in the 1990s, as seemingly everybody under the sun touted the superiority of unfettered commerce. Now, Frank is preparing to author a new volume about the fate of the New Economy. But he continues to be devoted to *The Baffler*, which at the time of this interview was putting together its fifteenth issue.

Interview conducted in two parts: October 1999, April 2002

CB: You built your reputation in the mid-1990s with your powerful critique of alternative culture in *The Baffler.* You've moved on to different topics since then, but have continued to remind us that we should be wary when ideas and goods are presented to us as "radical" or "revolutionary." Has your perspective changed in the wake of the events of September 11, 2001?

TF: I had my first op-ed in the *New York Times* in late December, 2001. The right-wingers were hopping mad about this "Teen Taliban," the traitor-boy John Walker Lindh. They were trying to blame him on liberal permissive upbringing. And so it occurred to me that I've never thought of Marin County as being particularly liberal. I pointed out that, at the time when they started making these accusations, they didn't know anything about this guy except that he was from Marin County. I argued that blaming him on liberalism was just preposterous. I said you might as well blame him on TV advertising that promotes "extreme" culture: extreme fishing rods, extreme meat loaf sandwiches, extreme cordless drills—you know the routine. It was satirical.

CB: But you have a point. You could argue that John Walker Lindh was simply an extreme tourist who ended up in the wrong place at the wrong time: a latter-day Rimbaud. To my mind, the most interesting aspect of his trip to Afghanistan is the sense that he was desperate to find a meaningful alternative to middle-class American existence. His search reminded me of something that *Baffler* contributor Stephen Duncombe wrote in *Notes From Underground*, his book on zine culture from a few years back. "The powers that be do not sustain their legitimacy by convincing people that the current system is The Answer. That fiction would be too difficult to sustain in the face of so much evidence to the contrary. What they

251

must do, and what they have done very effectively, is convince the mass of people that *there is no alternative.*"

TF: Duncombe puts his finger on a really interesting part of the big PR operation and that is to talk about the infinite amount of choice under capitalism, and also to present obsolescence as this liberating thing. I don't know if you read much management theory, but the people who write it were all hot and bothered about Joseph Shumpeter during the New Economy bubble. These people hadn't read his book or anything, but there's this one quote from him that they all repeated—they got it from each other—and it's about "creative destruction." That has been the big buzzword in capitalist theory recently, the idea being that products are evolving much faster than ever before and obsolescence is speeding up and that all this is very wonderful. But even the people who believe this recognize that it's only part of the story. A good example is Tom Friedman, the *New York Times* columnist, who talks about the wonders of everything speeding up, but at the same time says that our political choices are by necessity constrained. And it's not a surprise that both major parties in the U.S. nominate candidates who say exactly the same things and that all the western countries, with a few exceptions, are moving to the American model because the market will tolerate no dissent in politics.

252

CB: No alternative to itself. But there are plenty of alternatives within that no alternative.

TF: *[Laughs]* Right. You can go snowboarding, you can go skiing, you can go rollerblading—but you can't vote for a socialist.

CB: Obviously the existence of *The Baffler* and other subcultural commodities like it—if you're following Duncombe's reading— testifies to the potential for there to be a meaningful alternative. But in the case of your writings in *The Baffler* it's very much implicit as opposed to something that you state outright. Your tone can be dauntingly severe.

TF: That's definitely true. But one of the reasons that I write in the way that I do is because I think that we live in a time of monstrous public error and foolishness. I mean, there's so much out there to correct and to disagree with and to dissent from that I really think that it's the main task at hand. One kind of writing that I look back to as an inspiration is the crusading, journalistic style of the Populists and the people right after them, the Muckrakers. The Muckrackers were pretty much straightforward journalists, but always with this incredible outrage to their writing, like Lincoln Steffens going around looking at what was wrong with American cities.

CB: "Graft everywhere."

TF: He would present this unbelievable panorama of corruption. And he would for the most part keep his authorial voice under control, but occasionally break out in these expressions of anger that were very justified. The Populists tended to be a little bit more apocalyptic about it all. But both of those traditions were explicitly political and involved. They made this kind of critique as a prelude to political action. When you're criticizing and doing that kind of muckraking, obviously that's not when you're making specific policy proposals.

CB: At this point, *The Baffler* has become something of an institution in the post-1989 left. It's hard to remember that it wasn't always there, that it is itself a product of the "do-it-yourself" ethic. How did it get started?

TF: It started in 1988—even pre-'89, what do you know about that!—and at the time some guys and I at the University of Virginia thought we would start a literary magazine. I think every kid in college thinks at some point that he is somehow destined to found a great literary magazine. And we were among the deluded. We did one issue. It was nice—nice cover, nice paper—but I really can't say too much about the contents. Although there is one very funny thing in it, in the manner of the hoax Sokal pulled on *Social Text*. We were using some really over-the-top jargon and footnotes to analyze a comic strip. Have you ever seen *Mark Trail*? It's a really, really square comic strip. But as we wrote it, we got more and more interested in analyzing this comic strip and it actually wound up being kind of serious. Anyhow, that first issue wasn't much to speak of and the second issue wasn't either. It didn't come into its own until later. We were all really involved in the punk rock scene. And all the stuff that happened in 1991 and 1992 really started to make us think. There was this huge thing going on with all the "alternative" crap that was not what it said it was, that was just plain wrong. Somebody had to write about it, somebody had to point out that the emperor had no clothes. So we did.

CB: The "we" in that last sentence reminds me of something I noticed while looking through back issues of *The Baffler*. There was a time when you used the first-person plural a lot, particularly in reference to what you call the "culture trust." A good example is the conclusion to your piece "Alternative to What?" from issue #5, where you offer an "us" versus "them" call to arms for the independent music scene: "They seek fresh cultural fuel so that the machinery of stupidity may run incessantly; we cry out from under that machine's wheels. They manufacture lifestyle; we live lives." Or the piece "Twenty Nothing" that you co-wrote with Keith White for issue #4. Even if your words have an ironic edge in these pieces, they are still imbued with the aura of the barricades. By contrast, in your more recent pieces you seem to have moved away from a "we" that is localized in a particular community. When you deploy the first-person plural now, it seems more rhetorical.

TF: "Twenty Nothing" was sort of a stab at a manifesto. That's why it was written like that. And we went way too far in that particular piece. We obviously don't write very much in that style anymore or use the first-person plural.

254

CB: Is there a sense that you had a community back then which is lacking now?

TF: I think about this a lot. One of the things that is not that frequently remarked about *The Baffler* is its regionalism. It has a very distinct and intentional regional flavor to it. We're all Midwesterners. We write about Chicago as though it were the most normal thing in the world to have a literary magazine coming out of Chicago, when in fact it's very, very strange. And I think that's one of the things that annoys certain critics of ours. There's definitely still a sense of localness. As for whether there's a sense of community, some group of people I'd have a reason to speak for, I have a lot more doubts about that.

CB: The building in which *The Baffler*'s office was housed burned down recently. Did that experience change the way you think about community at all?

TF: It definitely did. The fire was a terrible thing. We lost a large chunk of our back issues. And they were very important for us. But our readers have been generous. They've given us everything from money to dictionaries to computers. They were very, very kind and we are so grateful to them. And the local community was also great. Our building had a number of businesses in it: a bicycle shop, an artists' shop, and a furniture shop in addition to our offices. Locals patronized them. One of the things that the city required us to do after the fire was to stand guard outside the building around the clock. The people in the neighborhood really rose to the challenge and helped us.

CB: I wanted to ask you something about your critique of cultural studies, to which you devoted a chapter in *One Market Under God*. It seems like you're trying to show some sort of convergence

255

between right-wing populism and the work that people have been doing in cultural studies. I'm thinking particularly of your comments on the rhetoric of anti-elitism.

TF: Right. One of the many things that annoy me about cultural studies is that its practitioners present their work as something "radical." I quoted some good examples in the chapter you mentioned. A lot of the "cult studs" sincerely believe themselves to be on the vanguard of leftist thought and practice. And what's astonishing to me is how little distance there is between their critique, their way of understanding culture, and the libertarian, free-market critique. Both speak in this populist vein, it's just that one openly embraces the market and the other has nothing to say about it. Now some cult studs—I've been keeping track of this—have been changing their tune and saying that the market can actually be a force of liberation. In which case I would say that they have to stop pretending to be leftists. It's kind of like the whole alternative problem.

CB: It almost seems as if the ire you exhibited toward mainstream alternative culture has been displaced onto cultural studies.

256

TF: In a certain way. Everybody wants to be a radical. Hell, Dodge wants you to think its cars are radical. It's the weirdest damned thing. Everybody wants to be a radical and everybody comes out and says the same libertarian stuff. What most bugs me about it is that the cult studs won't acknowledge this similarity. They never talk about it. And I've gone through so many cultural studies books and articles, I've searched databases, looking for references to right-wing things, to libertarian things, and there's nothing. The only right-wingers the cult studs tangle with are Family Values types. They're a complete straw man. And, big surprise, the libertarians also take craps on these same people. Another shared enemy is the Frankfurt School, which even Rush Limbaugh has slagged. Everybody hates the Frankfurt School.

CB: I cut my critical teeth on the Frankfurt School, particularly Theodor Adorno—I wouldn't be doing what I'm doing right now if I hadn't read him—but there was a time back in the early 1990s when it was important to me, as a student of popular culture, to distance myself from the Frankfurt School. And for a while there, I had the same reaction to your writing in *The Baffler*. I loved to read it. But it made me mad. It seemed too self-righteous, too absolute to me. At one point I accused *The Baffler* of being too "Adornoan."

TF: Believe me, this has happened a lot. And the ironic part is that I read some Adorno in graduate school and was not impressed.

CB: He does sound like a *Baffler* contributor sometimes . . .

TF: Maybe if he was writing nowadays. But the critiques of his work are correct. His writing is very heavy-handed. He doesn't allow for a lot of distinctions. And he tends to just want to wash his hands of the United States.

CB: There are a few passages where he almost seems to be blaming fascism on the Americans.

TF: *[Laughs]* I like the United States! So it's not an exact match-up. But this comparison comes up in the strangest places. I was on a radio show once and a caller accused me of being a latter-day Frankfurt School disciple. The Frankfurt School, because it's so mysterious—these guys with German names—has sort of replaced the talk about communist conspiracy that the right-wing used to use. You find the funniest references to the Frankfurt School now.

CB: It actually goes back a long way. There's a *Playboy* interview with John Wayne from the late 1960s in which he explains how Herbert Marcuse is ruining America.

TF: Really? That must be where it comes from. I've always won-

257

dered what the source of it was. It's amazing how widespread the conspiracy theory has become. A few years back, someone even had the nerve to blame the Columbine massacre on the Frankfurt School! *[Laughs]*

CB: I'm sure the Frankfurt School was a big influence on Osama Bin Laden as well!

TF: Let me tell you, I was very glad to have a child after September 11. One of the groups I felt sorry for right afterwards were the daily and weekly newspaper columnists, the people who were on a writing schedule and had to say something about it. Many, many people made fools of themselves. They said stupid things that you just knew they would be embarrassed about later. One of the good things about writing the way I do, being a complete freelancer, is that I didn't have to say anything. I just played with my daughter and worked around the house for several months.

CB: It will be interesting to see how well the new populism you excoriate in *One Market Under God* survives the present economic downturn. It's harder to speak of the wisdom of the marketplace when people are going bankrupt. But maybe I'm underestimating capitalist ideologues' force of persuasion. In your piece from *The Baffler*'s issue #14 last year, you focus on their almost religious conviction in the market's infallibility. At one point, you write that, "the market only fails us, it seems, when we fail it, when our piety is somehow incomplete, when we don't give the market enough power, when we balk at entrusting it with our last dime."

TF: I was referring there to the disastrous deregulation of the energy business in California. The libertarians have tried to blame everything on the state for not deregulating enough, which I found very intriguing. That was the starting point for me. But if you look at the legacy of the Chicago School of Economics, that's always the response when things go awry. The error is always that we don't deregulate enough, that we don't entrust enough to the market. One of the adages at the Chicago School is that the way you figure out what's causing a problem is to look where the government intervention is. That's their standard answer. It's always the government. And even when the government involvement is minimal, it's always there. So you always have something that you can blame. But you never blame the market. I'm starting a new book about the New Economy on the defensive. The Enron meltdown at the end of 2001 would give you an idea of the kind of thing I want to pursue in the book. And this is a point I'll be making in it. You have all these libertarian and conservative thinkers who will do anything to avoid talking about what used to be called the business cycle. For example, in the current recession they simply will not acknowledge that this is systemic to capitalism, that this is what capitalism does: it has ups and downs, it has fat years and it has lean years, it has booms and busts. They won't acknowledge that. Recession is always the fault of the Federal Reserve or Congress or the President. It's never, ever because of business itself. I think that attitude is fascinating, because it's so clearly in defiance of the facts.

CB: I was talking to someone from New Zealand recently about the role that the Chicago School of Economics played in the privatization of government services there in the 1980s. In this person's estimation, their theories screwed the country up so badly that it still hasn't recovered.

TF: I didn't know anything about that. That's one of our biggest shortcomings on the left. We don't know the stories from other countries. I'm up in Canada right now, where they're having a debate about their National Health System. And a bunch of premiers from the western provinces are in favor of some form of privatization, changing it pretty drastically. They're using the same language to make their case that we saw in the United States during the deregulation of electrical utilities, talking about the inevitability of privatization and the need for a wider range of choices in the marketplace, without any sense that these ideas have been badly discredited in the States in recent years. The critics of these proposals are no better informed, because they read Canadian newspapers instead of American ones.

CB: The Enron debacle certainly comes to mind when you talk about this discredited language. I think it's interesting, reading the press coverage and hearing interviews with people in the street, to see how many people failed to connect Enron with the New Economy. The fact that it's not a dot-com colors their perception.

TF: Enron was very high-tech. By the time of their collapse, they didn't own very many power plants or gas pipelines anymore. They had tried to get themselves out of that business and become a company that lived on abstraction, the buying and selling of energy contracts. And they wanted to go into the buying and selling of contracts in other fields as well, among them bandwidth. I still don't really get that one.

CB: It's a pipeline!

TF: All of the fields that they went into were fields that you would think of as natural monopolies. How can you buy and sell bandwidth? It's a classic natural monopoly where there just isn't room for a lot of competition. The other great example is electricity. In every one of these fields, Enron had figured out some way to privatize distribution and make a profit off the buying and selling of contracts. So in that sense Enron was the perfect example of a New Economy company. It didn't have bricks and mortar.

The Enron people used to deride factories as "Big Iron." They were all about creativity and entrepreneurship: pure will and idea. A big part of what the company did was ideological. Pushing privatization was a huge part of their operation. Deregulation would not have happened without Enron. What's funny is that, if you go back to the days when deregulation was sweeping the country in the late 1990s, the language that its proponents used to describe it was a classic example of New Economy thinking: markets are coming, markets are inevitable. They used the word "inevitable" all the time. And that was largely Enron's doing. They had figured out this ideological spin.

CB: It's interesting to compare Enron to Bechtel. Bechtel is a privately held civil engineering firm from the San Francisco Bay Area. They're the antithesis of the stock market–driven company. Everything they do is highly secretive. They have a track record of following in the wake of American intervention in other nations, rebuilding what our weapons and troops have destroyed. The best example is the Gulf War. Once the fighting was over, Bechtel was the first in the door. I'm sure they'll show up in Afghanistan. The security-minded folks in the U.S. government have always loved Bechtel because they can rely on their discretion.

TF: Sounds like one of those companies owned by the CIA.

CB: There have been rumors to that effect, actually. The reason I bring up Bechtel is that the people in the current Bush administration have this schizophrenic identity where, on the one hand, they want absolute deregulation of the market, and, on the other, they want companies they can trust to comply absolutely with their policy directives.

TF: Conservatives have never really had any trouble with being hypocrites. They'll say whatever needs to be said to get the job done. And, in some ways, I admire that about them, the fact that ideological fighting in the intellectual world is strictly to get something done, whereas for people like you and me it's something very different. Because the job that we want to get done is never going to happen! *[Laughs]*

CB: In a way, it would be good for people on the left to start thinking more like conservatives.

TF: You're completely right. This is one of the huge differences between foundations on the left and right. The conservative foundations—much to their credit, I think—have really approached the world of ideas in a very pragmatic manner. There are no comparable institutions on the left.

Portions of this interview originally appeared in Bad Subjects: Political Education for Everyday Life.

Yes, Information Wants to be Free, But How's That Going to Happen? Strategies for Freeing Intellectual Property
Rick Prelinger

Why Worry About Intellectual Property While Chaos Rules?

As I write in late February 2002, the United States has declared itself to be in a state of war. But even as our government asserts anti-terrorism as its first priority, corporations hustle to make the world safe for business. The courts are clogged with intellectual property (IP) lawsuits. Lawyers are busy churning out cease-and-desist letters to alleged copyright infringers. Entertainment conglomerates are consolidating their control over the fibers, cables, and switches on which programming is distributed. Hackers have even been equated with terrorists and are forced to defend their ability to explore, reengineer, and retool hardware and software. Content and advertising continue to combine into a tediously promotional happy meal. The limits of permissible speech in the mass media tighten every day. Not a quiet time, not a happy time, and under wartime cover decisions are now being made that will affect all our futures as producers and consumers of information, culture, and the arts.

Today, products of the intellect are copyrighted at the moment

263

of creation, patented before release to the world, and trademarked before sale, born not as contributions to a shared body of knowledge or heritage, but as "intellectual property." Wars are raging over the ultimate control of IP, and the terms of engagement seem to change almost weekly. This conflict is likely to envelop us for a long time, and as such it's hard to know how it will play out. But this isn't an excuse for waiting to act. If there's any chance that anti-capitalist models for the distribution and control of content will ever work, we need to be thinking beyond today's ruling paradigms.

This essay contends that although a critique and restructuring of copyright law (and the concept of copyright in general) is immensely valuable, focusing exclusively on changing copyright law is a smokescreen. Copyright reformism focuses on fixing copyright law, rather than articulating a more fundamentally radical vision about how information, ideas, art and culture might be produced and exchanged. It constrains us into thinking in limited terms, terms that might not necessarily be our own, and most especially forces us into defensive positions. When copyright "infringement" is equated with stealing, when the free exchange of content is criminalized, and when intimidating legal letters fly freely, it is easy to behave reactively. When we are obliged to defend ourselves against assaults motivated by someone else's agenda, we are fighting for freedom of expression on unfriendly turf, and are unlikely to win what we deserve.

Reformism is one of the first questions that arises when we think about anti-capitalist ways of seeing intellectual property. Is it really worth our time trying to solve problems created by capitalist economics while capitalism still prevails? What do we stand to gain by challenging capitalist control over IP while other kinds of property remain under the same owners? Why even bother trying to synthesize a new theory of IP, a progressive version of copyright law, or a strategy to overturn the carefully woven net of legislation that benefits the "owners" of IP over the rest of us? Perhaps most important, does liberating IP benefit the many, or just the relatively few heavy content users in the developed world looking for free music and movies?

There are in fact good reasons to develop anti-capitalist perspectives on intellectual property. We might, for instance, think of freer content as an end in itself, as a radically different way of thinking about the distribution of knowledge and culture, and as a utopian wedge that might lead to more liberated ways of circulating other goods and services. We might imagine a future where content functions to increase consciousness, improve the quality of our lives, and integrate culture into daily life, and consider how we might get there. And, even as most high-demand IP remains under corporate control, there are a few equalizing tactics that could tip the balance toward a different kind of IP landscape. Imagine a shared, profit-free body of knowledge, culture, and entertainment whose very existence might challenge long-lasting concepts of property ownership and control and stimulate popular alternatives to winner-takes-all thinking. We might even conceive of content that is not simply created to distract or entertain (though distraction and entertainment can be noble objectives, too). Culture can illuminate and demystify property relations. Changing the way that culture is distributed can lead the way to changing how property is distributed.

265

And all of us have an interest in halting current trends toward increased corporate control over IP. The arguments are familiar by now to most of us. By commodifying and asserting ownership over ideas, art, culture, and inventions, corporations control much more than just intangibles. While asserting that they stand for the protection of authors' and creators' rights, large corporations quite often bind creators to coercive contracts that cause the lion's share of royalties to remain in corporate hands. Creativity, innovation, problem-solving, and all kinds of social change are fostered and encouraged by the free exchange of ideas and inventions. A society that places impermeable barriers on the movement, exchange, and appropriation of IP, such as we are now doing, sets frightening limits on its ability to evolve and progress. In some instances, control over IP actually poses life-threatening issues, as in the case of patented drugs that are not available at affordable prices to residents of developing countries. Finally, the lack of a free (not a free-trade!) regime for the exchange of IP that still fairly compensates individuals for their efforts tends to prevent developing regions from building their own content industries that have a chance of competing for their own people's attention.

Copyright Seeks (and Gets) Eternal Life

Copyright law is not likely to disappear all by itself. It may be under siege by new access technologies, but it is far from dead. The "copyright-based industries"—publishing, entertainment, and software—contribute hundreds of billions of dollars to the U.S. economy. Intellectual property is our second most valuable export, and more and more of us labor to create, manage, distribute, sell, and shrink-wrap what passes for "content" these days. It is essentially inconceivable that the large corporations controlling intellectual property rights will stand by as the fences separating their holdings from the public domain melt down.

Copyright law states that works of the intellect are copyrighted at birth—beginning at the moment when they become fixed in tangible form. But unlike organic creatures, copyrights enjoy what seems to be an infinitely extendable life span. Congress' original intent in drafting copyright law was to grant exclusive rights for limited terms, linked to the life spans of authors, in order that they could enjoy the fruits of their labor. Until 1978, copyrights generally lasted twenty-eight years and could, if formalities were strictly followed, be renewed for another twenty-eight. Publication without proper copyright notice threw a work into the public domain. This is why so many older U.S. works are out of copyright, unlike works that originate in most other countries. After 1978, the U.S. "harmonized" its copyright laws with those of most other countries, extending the term of copyright for new works created by individuals to the span of their lives plus fifty years, and new works created by corporations to seventy-five years.

In 1993, renewals for older works became automatic. The tragic death of John Lennon at age forty was cited in congressional testimony, as paid lobbyists warned that his young son Sean might outlive the terms of his father's copyrights and see John's works exploited without proper compensation. In 1998, the largely undebated Sonny Bono Copyright Term Extension Act further "harmonized" our copyright laws with our European trade partners, extending terms to life plus seventy and ninety-five years respectively. These laws have collectively kept hundreds of thousands of U.S. works out of the public domain, and restored copyrights to perhaps millions of foreign works. Such lengthy periods lock works up for an inordinately long time. But then, corporations often live longer than people do.

In February 2002, the U.S. Supreme Court agreed to hear arguments in *Eldred v. Ashcroft,* a challenge to the Sonny Bono Act. Plaintiff Eric Eldred, aided by a host of lawyers, scholars, librarians, and archivists, argued that continual extensions of copyright law violate the constitutional specification that copyright should exist for a limited duration. The Court's agreement that a constitutional question is involved here has sent waves of concern through Hollywood and the rest of the community of IP proprietors, and has excited many others. In contrast to the comparative silence surrounding the original legislation, debates over the fairness of lengthy copyright terms are now widespread. Though it's impossible to predict how the Court will rule, it is exciting to see generally arcane IP issues discussed in the mainstream press, and the increased growth of skepticism around the question of corporate control of IP.

267

Corporate copyright holders have also pressed to limit the definition of "fair use" and now, under the Digital Millennium Copyright Act of 2000 (DMCA), to prevent just about all unpaid copying, performance, distribution, and collection of digitally based works. The DMCA encourages copyright holders to build protection mechanisms into technology, and then criminalizes "circumvention"—attempts to reengineer the technology, however well-intentioned (and necessary) they may be.

Beyond Copyright Consciousness

Many commonly circulating ideas about IP predict the end of copyright, following two major threads: technology killed copyright, and copyright is anachronistic in networked culture. Both of these notions are simplistic and ahistorical, and I believe, shortsighted. What we really ought to be talking about is *access* to works. Though access is related to copyright, it's really more fundamental to our freedom to think and experience. Trying to debunk the idea that technology killed copyright is a tiring chore. Yes, the proliferation of new tech tools makes it harder to control the unauthorized duplication of copyrighted works, and such tools are certainly sustaining another thrilling chapter in the arms race between geeks and suits. But people are still renting videos and buying DVDs. Yes, millions of people used Napster and now other peer-to-peer services to collect semi-degraded music files, but the record companies were able to cut Napster off at the knees. As soon as Napster's successors become big enough to pose a threat, the record companies will go to court to protect their oligopoly. (Interestingly, the judge who essentially closed Napster down has just opened the way for them to sue the large record companies for conspiring to control the recorded music business. Stay tuned.)

Many prominent individuals have lined up behind the notion that we live in a post-copyright age. They try to convince us of the total irrelevance of copyright, that "information wants to be free." Others posit that the disintermediating characteristics of the Internet will empower individual authors and artists by permitting them to sell their work directly to their audiences. People like John Perry Barlow and Esther Dyson imagine an era in which creators are compensated in a royalty-free realm, where reputation, expertise, consulting chops, and sales of collateral products almost magically generate income. This isn't completely beyond the realm of possibility, because this model works for some people, notably the proponents of those ideas themselves. Like so many economic schemes today, it presumes a winner-takes-all model. But how many writers can give away their texts and survive on honoraria from guest slots on CNN? And, ultimately, who cares enough about most creative people to help provide them with a living? As long as IP is bought and sold as a commodity, market rules will continue to apply.

Perhaps copyright needs to be reincarnated in some modified form. I see nothing wrong with a system that protects the rights of individual creators, especially if it helps to equalize their position with regard to the entities that may help distribute their work. But what should those rights be? I'm not yet prepared to say. In many ways, copyright law has outlived its social and economic function. And this is why I am sympathetic to those who support formative chaos, those who rhetorically call for total and complete disobedience of copyright law, rather than cloaking their efforts under a veil of disingenuous "responsibility." If we're to transform authoritarian copyright laws into social practices that protect creators and benefit society in general, a period of flux and experimentation will be essential.

Experimentation may be essential for yet another reason, too. Other kinds of rights are asserted in cultural works, rights which are harder to dismiss than copyrights held by anonymous corporate entities. These are rights claimed by stakeholders who don't hold

269

copyrights: unions seeking to protect their members against exploitation; creators who hold "moral rights" guaranteeing that their work will not be performed or distributed in mutilated or incomplete form; individuals whose creativity may make up part of what we see, hear, or read in a particular work. How can an anti-capitalist framework for IP compensate the writer, director, composer, or actor for their work in a film over that film's life? How can such a framework guarantee that someone's work won't be replayed in a distorted form? Should such compensation or guarantees even exist? These are difficult questions.

Copyright law is hundreds of years old. Its long history and densely structured system of legal precedents would itself be enough to harden it against anyone who would dare to reject or ignore its power, and that doesn't take account of the power held by the world's largest copyright owners. Copyright—or, more accurately, the restriction of the right to copy and redistribute—is believed to be the base of the content industry, rapidly growing into one of the world's largest and most profitable businesses. It is possible that one day IP-based industries will together form the largest economic sector of all. It is widely believed that copyright is necessary for these industries to flourish. It is also commonly felt that interference with or infringement of copyright constitutes interference with the well-being of the present and future capitalist economies. And since the concept of IP labels products of the intellect as "property," unauthorized appropriation or movement of IP constitutes theft. Advocacy of theft earns no friends for the advocate. These terms trap those of us who believe in true freedom of expression.

Perhaps instead we should think of IP as "born free," which runs directly counter to the U.S. Copyright Act of 1976, which declares that all human works capable of being fixed in enduring form are copyrighted at the moment of their creation. But beyond that, we should also consider whether the struggle over copyright is really the most meaningful struggle for us right now.

Access and Authorship

"Access" to works of the intellect doesn't just mean being able to read, listen, watch, or feel them. Today, it also means being able to incorporate other people's works into ones own: to quote, resynthesize, recontextualize, sample, appropriate, or plunder. Today's reader is also a writer; today's listener, a sampler; today's spectator, an editor or director. Many of us are no longer content with simply reading, listening, or viewing works—we want to appropriate material from other works and make something that is more than the sum of its parts. This is a pretty obvious point, and it's also obvious that unyielding copyright law limits freedom of expression for all of us. Less obvious are the other ways of limiting our ability to quote, cut up, and recontextualize.

In order to be an active reader/listener/spectator, we need access to materials. Yet aside from pop culture products widely available in American superstores, such access is currently quite difficult. One reason for the popularity of peer-to-peer technologies is the sheer diversity of music and sound that they've made available. Much of this audio was hitherto inaccessible, locked in record company vaults, private collections, archives, and radio station libraries. In this sense, the stuff that's online and available via p2p functions constitutes a virtual archive that's available to all.

271

Quite the opposite is true in other media. Our history and culture are increasingly becoming private property rather than public resources. Consider still photography. Hundreds of millions of historical still images are now controlled by two large corporations, Getty Images and Corbis, which are actively competing for top market rank. Unfortunately, these collections are generally inaccessible without payment of substantial research and licensing fees. In other media, textual material, music, and works of art are now owned or controlled by a dwindling number of rights-holders. It is now highly probable that most access to cultural and historical materials will follow the paradigm of "billable events," with few exceptions or discounts for nonprofit or public users. E-commerce, of course, makes it much easier for rights-holders to charge for the experience of listening to or eyeballing content.

The function of not-for-profit entities like libraries, museums, and archives is also changing. They no longer exist simply to offer reference or read-only access to their holdings. With the proliferation of authoring tools in all media and the vast increase in various modes of cultural production, many access requests now anticipate the reproduction of materials for reuse and public distribution, and this trend is running headlong into the limitations of copyright law. Although the Internet is dramatically increasing the population of creators and publishers, there is less preexisting content available for reuse.

The access problem exists for both copyrighted and non-copyrighted works. Many public-domain works exist only in libraries, archives, or private collections, and their custodians charge for access. Though fees may pay for storage, preservation, cataloging, and the production of viewing copies, it ultimately defies common sense for public domain works not to be freely available. If we act to lessen or to end copyright's authoritarian control over access to culture, we must make sure that other controls don't take its place.

Guaranteeing Access Through Preserves and Conservancies

One transitional means for making content and culture more readily available may be the "intellectual property conservancy" or "IP preserve." To think about strengthening public access to cultural resources is to consider basic questions of property and its privatization. It's worth looking to history and landscape for precedents and a possible solution. In the late nineteenth and early twentieth centuries, private corporations exerted unprecedented pressures on the "public domain"—American land and natural resources. They owned or controlled key tracts of productive land, often as a result of government giveaways or favoritism. The aggressive pursuit of extractive interests such as mining, logging, and agriculture threatened to destroy public lands and encroach upon naturally or culturally significant sites. In response to this threat, the conservationist movement lobbied to organize a system of national forests, parks, and monuments. By preserving a limited public sphere not subject to the exercise of private property rights, the benefits of some wilderness and cultural sites were preserved for all.

In much the same way, an intellectual property preserve might house content and protect it as public property. The preserve would contain textual material, still and moving images, works of art, sounds and digital information of all kinds, plus the rights to reproduce and disseminate them. These assets would be acquired in two ways. First, the preserve (supported by private or government funding) would purchase certain key resources to build up a core collection of content. Second, the preserve would solicit donations of content. These donations might not necessarily include the physical materials representing the content, but would definitely include copyrights or rights to reproduce.

Why would copyright owners (or owners of public domain materials) ever cede their properties to the preserve? First, and perhaps most important, tax incentives. Amend the tax code to allow substantial deductions or tax credits for donating valuable copyrights or materials. Second, following the precedent of public land acquisitions, key donors might be compensated with private funding. Third, promote public recognition that an act of donation is a prestigious deed benefitting the world cultural heritage. Active efforts to create such organizations are now underway. One, called Creative Commons, has been announced and is set to open in the near future.

There is nothing particularly radical about the practice of a

273

preserve. It's an attempt to work within the system, a voluntary expropriation, a creation of incentives for property-holders to do the right thing. Ultimately, though, its goals are to rebalance private vs. common property for mass benefit. The preserve aims to make a significant portion of our intellectual and cultural property available to one and all—both individuals and corporations—for nothing more than the physical costs of duplication and transmission. Its concept supports freedom of inquiry and freedom of expression by preserving the right to quote, to duplicate, to appropriate preexisting material. Though it might require the support and expertise of elite elements to organize, a preserve could mount a fundamental challenge to our definitions of public and private property. In so doing, it would be a greater force for change than any possible reform of copyright law.

Other Models

The open source model is rooted in communitarianism and the hacker ethic. Though the details of open source philosophy are beyond the scope of this essay (but easily available online; see also "Peace, Love, Linux" by Annalee Newitz, included in this volume), it points to a possible future where copyright owners might no longer assert a stranglehold over creativity and innovation. Open source software, text, music, movies, or any other kind of content are released under a license, sometimes known as the GPL (General Public License), permitting anyone to use, modify, distribute, or publish the content in original or modified form. The catch is that whatever anyone might add to the original material itself becomes open source and available for free use in the same way. Rather than being compensated for simple ownership of copyright, people or companies in the open source world are rewarded for the value they add. If a person adds significant functionality to a piece of program code, writes a good manual, corrals an unruly collection of

274

software tools into a coherent package, people buy it and hopefully the creators make money. Extending this model to other kinds of collaborative creative work, such as music and movies, opens up fascinating possibilities.

Then there's simply refusing to recognize the authority of copyright. In recent years, anti-copyright artists and musicians have built a rich and entertaining tradition of appropriation, collage, uninhibited quotation, and sampling, much of which has coalesced as part of the Plunderphonics movement. Work of this kind is simultaneously a harking-back to a much simpler world of hunting and gathering and a fast flash-forward to a smarter utopian society in which artists are free to quote and manipulate the stimuli that inspire them. While prominent challengers to corporate IP control like Napster get nailed, most individual artists fly under the horizon of corporate legal departments (or are sufficiently marginal to dodge cease-and-desist letters). Their work is refreshing and, from an anti-capitalist perspective, points the way toward a crisis of legitimacy for copyright, as it encourages individuals to disobey a law to which their conscience objects.

Libraries are one of the last remaining deeply democratic institutions in Western society, providing access to arts, culture, and ideas. At their best, they stand for and actively support freedoms of speech and inquiry, and impose no property or income qualifications upon their patrons. As access institutions, they are unequalled. Their freedom to continue providing these resources to all (and even to preserve digital information for public access) is currently under attack by publishers and copyright holders who would like to make every access to their works into a billable event. We should defend their ability to continue doing what they have done for hundreds of years. Libraries should be able to loan material as they have always done, but with the assistance of access technologies such as the Internet, so that they serve a worldwide community with a minimum of difficulty.

275

Another thought that has recently emerged recalls once again the idea of IP preserves. What if certain cultural resources were, by popular agreement, placed squarely within open territory? There has been discussion in Europe about placing historical moving images from the World War II period into the public domain, so that they will be free for use by all without the sense that anyone is profiting from their exploitation. Moving concretely in this direction, the German government-chartered foundation that controls the copyrights to films produced under the Third Reich has reportedly begun to forego charging license fees for reuse of clips from certain key Nazi propaganda films. Though this is certainly a reformist idea, it is easily scalable to encompass ever-increasing areas of content—if there is pressure to make it happen.

Conclusion: Scenarios of the Intangible

To help frame possible tactics for freeing IP, I offer three non-exclusive scenarios for the future of intellectual property. All have come true already, at least in part.

276

1. The dystopian scenario. The current content-grab escalates. Greater territories of ideas and culture come under ever-tighter corporate control. The distribution infrastructure itself comes under the control of copyright owners. The "model of scarcity" rules: every cultural microevent (reading, listening, watching, browsing online) becomes a billable event.

2. The diffuse scenario. This most closely describes where we are now. The dystopian scenario is well on the way, but there is still considerable "public space" for IP to circulate freely, largely because of an active culture of resistance to tighter and more centralized control. The coexistence of public and private spaces is uneasy, though, and highly stratified: content with "mass appeal," whatever its ultimate worth, is in general under private control and requires money to access. Since alternatives to the present public/private standoff are underdeveloped, many creators choose the default option of letting major corporations "protect" them.

3. The utopian scenario. This evolves out of both previous scenarios. Essentially, control over IP collapses under it's own weight. People reject (or cannot afford) authoritarian and unwieldy systems that limit their access to arts, culture, and entertainment. Fringe cultures move to the mainstream as mass cultures become too expensive or too difficult to access. A "model of plenty" evolves: new means of rewarding creators emerge that do not require the intervention of corporations.

Anti-capitalists seeking to free IP might think about how their tactics fit into each of these scenarios. Should we acknowledge today's diffuse situation, acting incrementally to increase and defend public territory within a mixed landscape of public and private IP control? Should we reject corporate control altogether, even though it might render us marginal for some time? Should we organize and build alternative structures for the exchange of IP, structures that might help us transition into a post-corporate era? Should we do all of the above?

277

Resources

More detailed information on the issues mentioned in this essay can be found in the books listed below. Here also is a list of some websites that offer frequently updated information on fast-breaking IP issues.

Chris DiBona, San Oakman, and Mark Stone, *Open Sources: Voices from the Open Source Revolution.* Sebastopol, Calif.: O'Reilly & Associates, Inc., 1999.

Lawrence Lessig, *The Future of Ideas: The Fate of the Commons in a Connected World.* New York: Random House, 2001.

Jessica Litman, *Digital Copyright*. Amherst, NY: Prometheus Books, 2001.

Creative Commons, an intellectual property conservancy.
http://www.creativecommons.org

Kembrew MacLeod, *Owning Culture: Authorship, Ownership and Intellectual Property Law*. New York: Peter Lang Publishers, 2001. Kembrew MacLeod trademarked the phrase "freedom of expression" as a prank.
http://www.kembrew.com

Center for the Public Domain, a nonprofit foundation supporting the growth of a healthy and robust public domain.
http://www.centerforthepublicdomain.org

Copyright's Commons, a "coalition devoted to promoting a vibrant public domain."
http://cyber.law.harvard.edu/cc/

Detritus.net, a site devoted to recycled culture in all its manifestations.
http://www.detritus.net

The Negativland site has an excellent IP resources section.
http://www.negativland.com/intprop.html

Interview with Colin Robinson (formerly of Verso Books)
Joel Schalit & Charlie Bertsch

Started in the UK in 1970, Verso Books is one of the largest and most influential publishers of radical literature in the world. Originally founded as the publishing wing of the *New Left Review*, Verso first made its mark by issuing titles from the most important European Marxist thinkers of the twentieth century: Theodor Adorno, Walter Benjamin, Raymond Williams, Herbert Marcuse, Jean-Paul Sartre, Terry Eagleton, Stuart Hall, and Louis Althusser.

As much as these thinkers might epitomize the radical edge of intellectual chic, their respective influences can be felt throughout the history of Cold War–era leftist politics. Indeed, the great majority of them helped define the intellectual parameters of the 1960s New Left, echoes of which can still be heard today in the cries of anti-globalization protesters attacking international financial institutions in Europe and North America. Verso Books was essentially the first publisher to gather together all of these diverse radical thinkers and expose their significant publications to a wider audience.

Simultaneously issuing fresh translations of older works as well as brand new titles, Verso's impact upon leftist intellectual life over the past thirty years is profound. Moving all the way from Marxist theory to human-rights activism, gun-toting Latin American revo-

279

lutionaries to economists such as Nobel Prize–winner Rigoberta Menchu, revolutionary poster-boy Ernesto Che Guevara to *Wall Street* author Doug Henwood, Verso has been a virtual university for radicals of all conceivable progressive stripes.

For nearly twenty years, Colin Robinson served as one of Verso's chief editors. This interview was conducted the year before Robinson left the Verso staff to become an editor at The New Press.

October 2000

JS&CB: It seems that Verso has had more "crossover" titles recently, at least in the States, than years previously. We're thinking of Che Guevara's *Motorcycle Diaries,* and the 150th anniversary edition of Marx and Engels's *Communist Manifesto.* Not to mention Doug Henwood's *Wall Street.* Does this seem like an accurate perception?

CR: Yeah, I think so. Through the '70s and the '80s, Verso was a publisher of theory, mainly European theory. In the last ten years we've definitely branched out into publishing a lot more stuff that appeals to a more general audience, mainly within the field of culture, I suppose.

JS&CB: What was the rationale for making that transition?

CR: Well, I think that partly it was just a question of necessity. The sorts of theory that we were publishing, mainly European Marxism, just dried up. But so did the audience, to some degree.

JS&CB: How much do you attribute that to changes in the political climate since the end of the Cold War in 1989?

CR: Obviously through the '80s and the '90s, the political situation was not very sympathetic. That affected the market for the sort

280

of books we were publishing, so we had to try and branch out a bit. I think we did that pretty successfully.

JS&CB: It's interesting from our perspective, having unfortunately been graduate students for most of the last decade. For us, Verso's Marxist publications were particularly indispensable items in most of the households that we've rotated in and out of. And being narcissistic, of course, we thought that everyone bought what we did.

CR: You know, we still do sell quite reasonable quantities of Theodor Adorno, Walter Benjamin, and Louis Althusser. Actually, the biggest selling backlist titles now, apart from Benedict Anderson's *Imagined Communities* and Rigoberta Menchu's book, are *The Motorcycle Diaries* and the *Communist Manifesto*, which are obviously being used in courses. I can't imagine what kind of courses they're using *The Motorcycle Diaries* in!

JS&CB: Let's talk a little bit about the *Communist Manifesto*. You took some heat from some of the more "pure" people on the left for releasing the *Manifesto* in a glossy, red bookmark form. We heard that *The Monthly Review* folks weren't pleased. [*The Monthly Review* is a longstanding Marxist journal and press associated with the Trotskyite International Socialist Organization.]

CR: Yeah, *The Monthly Review* weren't too complimentary about our edition, it's true.

JS&CB: A lot of people got to know Marx through the brittle yellow pages of political pamphlets. It was quite a contrast to see this nice book prominently displayed next to the coffee-table volumes at the best independent bookstores. But at the same time the book's elegant packaging helped win it some new publicity, not to mention a lot of new readers. Can you tell us about the thought process that led you to do such a republication?

CR: The idea for republishing it came from Robin Blackburn, one of the editors at Verso who used to be the editor of *New Left Review*. He found out that Eric Hobsbawm was writing an introduction to a Spanish edition of the *Manifesto*. So we decided to ask Hobsbawm if we could have his introduction. Then we thought, "It's the 150th anniversary of its publication, why don't we try and present this as a kind of modern edition?" And then, I just thought that maybe it would be fun to play with the idea of doing an upscale version of the *Manifesto*.

The idea was reinforced by a piece in *The New Yorker* by John Cassidy saying that Marx was going to be the "next big thing" in terms of economic theory. It struck me that if the upscale *New Yorker* audience was being told this, maybe we ought to, in a sort of to slightly tongue-in-cheek way, present an edition of the *Manifesto* precisely for those sort of people.

It was partly ironic and partly not. I think there was an acknowledgment in the way that we published it that the proletariat is not the "horny-handed sons of toil" any longer. Most of the people who are workers these days are in offices, especially in the United States. And they have quite a developed aesthetic. In that sense, it wasn't entirely ironic. There was some feeling that presenting the book in a nice, attractive, designerly way would relate to where the modern proletariat actually was. But we did play around with it a lot once we got Komar and Melamud to do the cover. They gave us a big red flag for the cover, which was very nice of them. Then I thought maybe we should put a little *red* ribbon in it, and put *red* end papers inside, and start to make it into a sort of Sybaritic edition.

JS&CB: You had a lot of fun publicizing the *Manifesto*, didn't you?

CR: I was talking with a journalist from *New York* magazine, because they were doing a little feature on it, and I said that we were going to try and sell it through upscale clothing and furniture stores. The writer asked which ones, and of course I don't really know any upscale clothing or furniture stores. I mean, I'm a left-wing publisher. So I said Barneys. The writer then asked if she could ring Barneys and ask them what they thought of the idea. I told her, "Go ahead, that would be great." A half-hour later she called me back and said, "You really ought to get in touch with Barneys. They're very keen on this." I was kind of shocked by that.

JS&CB: So you actually got an appointment to talk to Barneys about selling Marx books?

CR: Yeah. I went up to see the creative director, this guy called Simon Doonan. We had a meeting, and he asked what I wanted to do. I told him that it would be great if we could have the mannequins on Fifth Avenue marching across the window with big red flags wearing little Prada dresses. In their purses would be copies of the *Communist Manifesto*. He said he thought it was a great idea. Doonan said, "I can see lipstick displays in the corners, with lots of red lipstick around the *Manifesto*." So I came away fairly nonplussed by this. I was surprised.

Then we sent out a press release that Barneys was going to do this. The media went really crazy. There was a lot of interest from television. They wanted to come down and film the windows. A lot of newspapers carried reports about what Barneys was going to do. But it became such a big thing that in the end, Barneys decided not do it. They were getting a lot of comments from people saying, "This was the book that was responsible for the Gulag," you know. In the end they backed out of it, but by that point it didn't really matter because we'd had so much publicity that we were up and running. Then it was really just a question of trying to think of other things along similar lines that we could do.

JS&CB: How on earth could you top that?

CR: The next place we tried was the Royalton Hotel on Forty-

283

fourth Street in New York, which is a very groovy, Phillipe Stark kind of hotel. All of the bellhops in there dress like Maoist guards. They're all so fabulous looking; when they come to the door, you feel like *they* should be staying in the place's fabulous rooms and you should be the one bringing them a drink.

We asked them if they'd like to put our Sybaritic edition of the *Communist Manifesto* in the bedside table where you'd normally find a Gideon's Bible. Again, to my astonishment they said yeah; they thought it was a pretty cool idea. They could see that it might work quite nicely for them. So again, we got into discussing it in detail with them, and released the information to the media. And again, we got a lot of media coverage. However, once they realized how much attention it was going to attract, they chickened out and didn't do it. But again, it didn't matter because by then we'd gotten a lot of press out of it.

JS&CB: A virtual spectacle!

CR: Then we thought that we really ought to try and do something on Wall Street with it. One of the things about the *Manifesto* is that there are a lot of passages in it where Marx and Engels praise the dynamism of capitalism.

JS&CB: Absolutely. It gets rid of that halo.

CR: Right. It's this modern system sweeping away the old kind of feudalism. They're into the energy of the new order. So we got the bookstore that's closest to Wall Street to give us a couple of big windows. We blew up all of the little passages from the *Manifesto* where Marx and Engels are praising capitalism, and put them in the store's windows in the hope that we could lure Wall Street guys in to pick copies up.

JS&CB: *[Laughter]* How obnoxious.

CR: It didn't really work, though the store ordered hundreds and hundreds of copies because they thought it was such a cool idea. And also because they thought it was going to pan out. But it didn't really. Basically, I've realized over the years of trying to shock Wall Streeters into taking notice of what we're doing in order to attack them that they just ignore you. The only thing they're interested in doing is working hard all day, making serious amounts of money, and getting shit-faced at night. They don't really do anything in between. But ABC went down there and filmed outside the store and asked investors walking by what they thought of the *Communist Manifesto*, so we got quite a lot of television and media coverage out of it just being there.

JS&CB: Aside from honoring the anniversary of the original *Manifesto*'s publication, what were the political reasons you decided to publish it?

CR: We hope that shorn of the dead weight of Stalinism, which both myself and Verso have always been implacably opposed to, Marx will get a new lease of life.

JS&CB: Globalization sure has been a big help.

285

CR: Yeah. At the moment there's only one game in town, which is globalization. But on the other hand, there's only one other game that you can really turn to. There's not really anything in between. If you're not going to accept capitalism as a way of running the world, what system are you going to accept? A planned economy under worker control of some sort or another. That's the only alternative. The *Manifesto*'s republication was a first shot at trying to win a new audience who are beginning to understand the terrible shortcomings of globalization, back to some sort of socialist perspective.

JS&CB: This certainly makes sense given the very strong critique of capitalism that's been offered by the anti-globalization movement at the last three anti-capitalist gatherings in Seattle, DC, and London. Yet they don't seem to be totally schooled in any particular leftist tradition such as socialism. They appear to be offering a synthesis that spans Marxist, Anarchist, and environmentalist thought, among other things.

CR: Without sounding too fuddy-duddy about it, while I think that what happened in Seattle and DC was very uplifting, it seems that what's motivating a lot of people is a kind of moral stance, not something which is underpinned by a deep understanding of how the world's working. Or how alternatives to the way it works might be constructed.

JS&CB: Sure. It's a little bit like saying, "Money is bad."

CR: In the '70s, when I was in my twenties, the core of the left was made up of revolutionary organizations. For all of their shortcomings, and they had many, they put a lot of effort into education. We used to read enormous amounts of stuff to try and understand what was going on. It was part of the internal democracy of the organizations we were in. People in their twenties today are generally not coming out of that kind of background.

286

JS&CB: At least in the States, if people are going to read any of that kind of literature, it's going to be through more traditional academic paths. Two or three weekends ago, the *New York Times* ran an article in which a number of radical professors, like Homi Baba, who specialized in post-colonial studies took credit for partially inspiring the intellectual current of the anti-globalization movement.

CR: I'm more inclined to see it the other way around. I generally believe that theory comes out of practice. You get drawn into these things because you feel as though you've got to do something because of your material circumstances. Then, when you're in, you're forced to try and understand what it is you're fighting against and what it is you're fighting for. But I think that in this case, it seems pretty evident to me that action is preceding theory. I hope that when people want to begin to understand in more depth what its they're up against, the Verso list is one of the things that they'll be able to turn to.

JS&CB: As far as your plans for the future, is there some thinking that you're going to try to appeal to this new progressive political current here, however amorphous it may be, with more accessible titles aimed at this particular kind of audience?

CR: There's no question about it. I'd certainly like to do stuff on direct action. We've been talking about doing a book with the Ruckus Society if we could. I think it would be good to do more accessible stuff on globalization and global structures like the World Trade Organization, the World Bank, and the IMF. I also think it would be good to do books on political movements that have been precursors of the sort of action that these anti-globalization protests involve. For instance, I think the Situationists are quite important in terms of their understanding of the way in which you can mount symbolic protest, which is what's going on now. We're about to publish a book on the Zapatistas, which again, I think is a very good example of people who've understood the importance of being able to develop symbolic forms of resistance.

JS&CB: One of the reasons we asked that is because we're both avid collectors of out-of-print New Left readers from Grove Press in the 1960s. We've got a couple here right now, like *The New Left Reader* . . .

CR: By Carl Oglesby.

JS&CB: Yeah, exactly. It's really interesting to see how publishers like that, who were independent back then, immediately engaged the New Left.

287

CR: Grove was certainly independent then. Now it's owned by Atlantic. Yeah, in 1970, that sort of radical publishing cut right across the industry. Even big houses like HarperCollins and Simon and Schuster were publishing titles by Jerry Rubin and Yoko Ono. It was a reflection of the spirit of the times. These people were not going to allow their political prejudices to get into the way of making money. I find it astonishing. It bears no relation to what it's like now.

JS&CB: Other than repackaging books like the *Communist Manifesto*, what does an independent leftist publisher like yourself have to do in order to survive in such a market?

CR: Obviously we carry much lower overheads than large corporations. We aren't paid as much, and the offices aren't as grand. We don't lash out on big advances in the way that the big houses do. It'd be very rare for us to pay an advance of over $20,000. I'm not saying that we don't publish books well, because we publish them better than anyone else could. But I think we ask writers to discriminate in our favor, and it happens. People who could get much bigger sums elsewhere stay with us. And it isn't just because they share our political commitments and do it for philanthropic reasons. It's because they think that we will probably produce the books more beautifully than anyone else.

JS&CB: Certainly the style of Verso's presentations of its books has set an aesthetic standard for a lot of other independent publishing houses, the last ten years in particular.

CR: There's no economy of scale in producing beautiful books. Anyone can produce beautiful books if they want to. Especially if they have a discriminating eye and use people who are talented enough to do it. I know a lot of the designers that we use do it because they want to see their work in the Verso list, and they're

288

going to have to subsidize it with the work they do for Phillip Morris or whomever. And you know, sometimes they can't do that. But often enough, even people who aren't that political, but like the feel of what we're doing, offer to do a few books for us. So we can get them to do it very cheaply. Authors genuinely know that their books will be produced beautifully. And I think they know that they will be marketed in an imaginative way.

I don't really think that radical publishing is just publishing books with radical ideas in them. Obviously that's a large part of it. But there's a way in which you can apply radical ideas to all aspects of the publishing process, like the design, which we really try to push to the edges. Certainly in marketing we try and do things in unusual ways, like the sort of things we were doing with the *Communist Manifesto*, where we quite openly borrowed Situationist techniques to market it. We've done other things where we'll slip-stream our marketing on someone else's, which is probably very annoying for them. But, you know, when we put out Christopher Hitchens's *The Missionary Position*, we made sure that we published it about the same time that Mother Teresa's own book called *A Simple Path* was published by Random House.

JS&CB: *[Laughter]*

CR: It was a huge book with a million first printing and a full page ad in the *New York Times,* and so on. We issued a press release saying, "A Simple Psychopath?" Basically, everywhere that Random House went with *A Simple Path*, we were turning up with *Missionary Position*. It must have annoyed the hell out of them. But on the other hand it got us a lot of coverage that we couldn't otherwise have drawn. I think we're going to do the same thing this autumn, actually. Perhaps the biggest book being published in the U.S. this year is the *Beatles Anthology*, which is coming out from Chronicle Books in October. We've just bought the rights to John Lennon's interviews with Jan Wenner in *Rolling Stone* from 1970.

They're great. This was Lennon at his most radical. He was pretty radical when he was a radical.

JS&CB: He had a little Vladimir in him . . .

CR: Right, exactly. At a certain point in the interview, Jan Wenner says, "Surely a revolution would be the worst thing that could ever happen." And Lennon replies, "Everyone says that. There'd be a lot of uproar for a little bit, then things would settle down. It would be cool. I'd like a revolution. I've got nothing to lose now." He's very political in these interviews. He talks about the break-up of the Beatles, his favorite songs, what the Beatles' tours were like, his use of drugs, Bob Dylan, and the Rolling Stones. It's great stuff.

The *Beatles Anthology* that Chronicle is doing is the story of The Beatles written by George, Paul, and Ringo. We have the missing Beatle. Everywhere that they go, with their, god knows, several-million-dollar publicity campaign, there's going to be this incredibly annoying little book by John Lennon published by Verso hanging around on the edges like the skank of the garden party.

You can do that if you don't really care too much about the established etiquette of the business. It's the easiest thing in the world. On several occasions people have offered to buy Verso, not to mention lure our employees away to go work at mainstream companies. The reason why we don't do that is because there is some value to being independent. In the end, particularly in cultural production, the record of people who've been taken over—generally what happens is that they're given enormous assurances at the time that they're taken over that the purchaser has always respected what they've done and will do nothing to compromise their independent stand. And then, a year or two down the line, some financial crisis comes up and the whole thing just gets folded into whatever conglomerate they're a part of. That's sort of sad. We're very resistant to that.

JS&CB: How do you see Verso in relation to other leftist presses, like AK Press, Pluto, and South End?

CR: I've certainly got a lot of time for all of them. I definitely hope they grow and prosper. I know the guys at AK in particular. I think they do a great job. I suppose the thing I'd say about Verso is that we've never ever had any particular political line beyond being broadly on the left. We'd never turn down a book because we disagree with its politics.

JS&CB: But Pat Buchanan wouldn't pass muster?

CR: No, of course not. We'd never publish anything that's homophobic or racist. But what I mean is that I certainly know of left presses where they've turned down a book because it had a different political line on, for example, what went on in Nicaragua. I'm talking about that kind of very specific political line that certain kinds of left organizations espouse. We've never done that. There'd be huge disagreements amongst Verso authors—quite a number of whom if you put in a room with one another, you'd end up with a fight on your hands. Nonetheless, within the framework of being a left publisher, we've always had a very non-dogmatic approach to what we publish.

291

The other thing is that Verso is not interested in being a *small* publisher. In 1990, we won the small-publisher-of-the-year award in the UK. For the year that we were fated as that, I was aware of the double-edged quality of that compliment. It never seemed to me that being small had anything going for it at all. I think that we would like to be a mainstream radical publisher. Both of those words are pretty vague, but there doesn't seem to be any particular advantage to always being seen as marginal. And we wouldn't be interested in being seen as not being political. It's all a question of how you combine those two together.

JS&CB: The point is to make *leftism* popular.

CR: If we could have the front cover of *Publishers Weekly* four times a year in order to publicize audacious, radical books, that would truly be a wonderful thing.

Portions of this interview originally appeared in Punk Planet.

Anti-Capitalist Taste
Charlie Bertsch

*W*hat would the revolution taste like? The question sounds strange. But it puts us on the front line of our struggle to imagine a better world. Taste is fundamentally conservative. When we like something new, it is usually because it is like what we already like. The problem of taste is the problem of identity. When we say that we like something, we are, in a sense, saying that it is like us.

It's easier to understand this in reverse. When we express distaste, whether it's for a book, film, or type of food, we indicate that it's not part of our world. If I don't like seaweed, it's probably because I wasn't raised in a culture where people eat it. If I hate jazz, there's a good chance that I haven't been exposed to much of it. Of course, there's always the possibility that distaste can turn into its opposite. I can learn to like California rolls or California rock. But if that metamorphosis does occur, it will almost always be the result of a connection that I make—or that gets made for me—between the thing I'm developing a taste for and a taste I already have. Sometimes this connection is direct and intuitive, as when I decide that I like the independent rock band Pavement because they sound like a cross between two of my faves, the Velvet Underground and Sonic Youth. In other cases, the connection may be more abstract, as when I start eating sushi because I have a thing

293

for Japanese design and desire a more comprehensive experience of the culture that produced it. The main point here is that it's hard to imagine a person suddenly developing a taste for something in the absence of this connection between past and present. That's what makes our tastes so resistant to revolutionary transformation. And this, in turn, explains why the problem of taste matters so much for radical politics.

This is something that Marx overlooked. In order to make his point that the economy drives history, he downplayed the power of culture. Although his position on the relative importance of the "superstructure" of society—politics, philosophy, art—shifted over time, his most famous and forceful description of it makes the transformation of culture an afterthought. In *The German Ideology*, Marx used the metaphor of a camera obscura to show that the superstructure is only a reflection of the economic base. More dubiously, his metaphor also implies that the superstructure can only present an inverted image of reality. From this perspective, culture simply turns the world upside down, making the revolutionary's job simple: to set things right. The value of this approach is clear, particularly when the people around you seem to believe—as most of Marx's contemporaries did—that the economy is a mere reflection of culture. His simplest formulation drives the point home: "Life is not determined by consciousness, but consciousness by life." Or, as that latter-day proponent of Marxist thinking, James Carville, put it while managing Bill Clinton's 1992 campaign for President, "It's the economy, stupid."

Yet as useful as it may be to ground our flights of fancy with this admonition, the fact remains that a whole lot continues to happen, not because of the actual state of the economy, but because of how people *feel* about the economy. The bursting of the "New Economy" bubble in the aftermath of George W. Bush's disputed electoral victory in 2000 exemplifies this paradox. The economy may be paramount, but it is not driven by hard numbers alone. As the scandal surrounding Enron's spectacular collapse in late 2001 demonstrated, even the data that analysts prize for its apparent objectivity is susceptible to all kinds of manipulation.

It is worth recalling that Marx himself repeatedly insisted that human labor provides the foundation for civilization. Humans "distinguish themselves from animals as soon as they begin to *produce* their means of subsistence." But if they are "the producers of their conceptions, ideas, and so on," as Marx argues, then, they also must be the producers of the economy. To imagine that the economy is a force beyond human intervention, with the status formerly reserved for gods, is to miss what really matters in Marx's critique of his contemporaries.

The distinction between base and superstructure, while it may be strategically useful, has the potential to lead our political thinking astray. In an effort to address this danger, the post–World War II French thinker Louis Althusser developed a more complex theory of ideology. Abandoning the framework of the camera obscura metaphor, he argued that "ideology has a material existence." Our ideas aren't a distortion of reality. They *are* reality, every bit as much as our bodies are. As theorists working in Althusser's footsteps have postulated, there may be nothing more "ideological"—used here in the more limited, negative sense of *The German Ideology*—than the move to divorce mind from body. The products of our minds matter no more or less than the products of our hands.

This insight has profound consequences for our understanding of taste. Nowhere do our mind and body overlap more completely than in our tastes. Taste is the domain of some of our most abstract thinking—"What do these two things have in common?"—and of our most visceral reactions—"That makes me sick!"—yet we have no trouble fitting these extremes under the same concept. And taste is conservative for precisely this reason. Even if we are able to recognize that our distaste for country music, broccoli, or Jackson Pollock has no solid intellectual basis, we still have the recalcitrance

295

of the body to deal with. As anybody who has tried to quit a "non-addictive" substance like coffee or ice cream will tell you, resisting the tide of desire requires a massive force of will. We would do well to learn from outmoded medieval philosophers here. The only way to break free of bad habits is to displace them with good ones. Sit and pray for ten hours a day and you won't have much time to play around with the boys in the rectory.

There's something depressing about this realization. Sure, the old left tried to instill virtue in workers, but this led to incompatibility with the new realities of the post–World War II era. The freedom to act like everyone else takes the life out of the party. That's what made the New Left so compelling for people raised with all the privileges of the middle class. It promised that the revolution could be fun. And, for a little while, it delivered. The radicals of the late 1960s were a lot happier than their counterparts of the previous decade. The hard part was figuring out a way to sustain that happiness. It's hard to make bliss a habit.

This may be the key to understanding the disintegration of the New Left. Some of its leaders returned to the academy to pursue their goals by more subtle means. But a great many radicals burned out, turning to violence, drugs, and religion as a way of securing the happiness that conventional politics could not provide for them. By the time this move started to pay diminishing returns, they were hooked. Ironically, the least self-destructive path out of politics was free enterprise. Think of all those artisans and organic farmers, bookstore owners and restauranteurs, software developers and stock market pundits, who got their start in the student movement. While making money may not be as personally damaging as becoming a terrorist or heroin addict, it can represent a more dramatic political shift. The man who sells vitamins with the same techniques he used to sell the revolution has sold out, unless he never wanted to move beyond capitalism in the first place.

The point here is not to repeat the timeworn cry of "sellout!"

In a world structured by the global marketplace, it is almost impossible to avoid buying and selling. The problem lies with the conviction that consumerism can deliver a better life. Who can forget the experience of eating Ben and Jerry's ice cream for the first time? Most people love the taste. And there's nothing wrong with that, until you convince yourself that it tastes like the revolution. Unfortunately, this sort of delusion is the principal legacy of the New Left. And while it's easy to poke fun at the Baby Boomer who beats out the rhythm to the Rolling Stones' "Street Fighting Man" while driving his new Lexus SUV home to the suburbs, it's important to realize that this legacy has proven more insidious than the taste preferences of the generation that gave it to us. You need only recall the debates on "going major" in the independent music scene of the 1990s to recognize that, while the taste preferences of twenty-somethings may have changed, the problem of taste has not.

What is to be done? Marx loved to read Shakespeare and Greek philosophy. And that didn't stop him from coming up with a comprehensive critique of capitalism. Maybe we should worry less about taste and more about politics. To be sure, there are plenty of commentators on the left who will tell you that people would be better off reading the classics than listening to music that ironizes classic rock. But, for better or worse, we no longer live in Marx's world. To promote Shakespeare in a society where most scholars confined themselves to classical Greek and Roman works is one thing. To promote him today, when his name has become shorthand for the classics, is another. Even teenagers who prefer *Othello* to Tupac Shakur still live in a society saturated by mass culture. It confronts them in the packaging of everyday life—not just in entertainment, but on the news, in the grocery store, and even in schools. The taste for Shakespeare is cultivated by and through the consumerism that it seems to repudiate.

Like God and the Dallas Cowboys, the topic of Shakespeare pushes people's buttons. For this reason, it may be more fruitful to pick a different example. The *Utne Reader* is one of the bright lights of American publishing. By reprinting articles from the alternative press in an attractive format, it lends authority to voices that the mainstream media tends to ignore. In particular, it helps to legitimize leftist discourse. Because its mission is to package, however, it is prone to being criticized for dumbing down the ideas it presents. This seems uncharitable, since the magazine never seeks to hide its "sampler" approach and provides readers with the resources to pursue a subject in greater depth. A more serious problem with *Utne Reader* concerns its role of tastemaker. As a publication that relies on advertising to stay in business, it can't help but play on the desire of consumers. Because many of its readers are self-consciously searching for alternatives to the status quo, the marketing it makes possible takes on more significance.

In addition to *Utne Reader's* conventional advertisements, the back of each issue features three separate sections targeted at the alternative consumer: "Smorgasbord" displays ads for everything from organic tea to high-tech toothbrushes; "Culture Shop" touts books, music, software, and video; and "Off the Newsstand" highlights the sort of publications from which the *Utne Reader* culls articles. Taken individually, the product descriptions on these pages aren't particularly noteworthy. Anyone who reads magazines like *Utne Reader* knows what to expect: lots of organic goods, books on New Age spirituality, primers on improving sexual performance, "thoughtful" publications for grade-school children. The disconcerting aspect of these pages is the impression they make as a whole. They present the same logic as a shopping center. And that can make a critical reader wonder if the content of the magazine is somehow analogous to the merry-go-rounds, holiday events, and cultural displays found in the average mall.

This spillover effect is most pronounced when the contents of the magazine tackle the subject of taste. A cover feature from late 2000 on the "wisdom of wabi-sabi" is a case in point. In the lead article, originally published in *Natural Home* magazine, Robyn Griggs Lawrence traces the history of this concept. "Emerging in the 15th century as a reaction to the prevailing aesthetic of lavishness, ornamentation, and rich materials, wabi-sabi is the art of finding beauty in imperfection and profundity in earthiness." In Japan, she adds, the idea "is now so deeply ingrained that it's difficult to explain to Westerners; no direct translation exists." While she acknowledges the concept's cultural specificity, she also wants to promote it to an American audience. Her task requires translating what can't be translated literally.

Noting that "wabi-sabi is everything that today's sleek, mass-produced, technology saturated culture isn't," she reels off a series of images. "It's flea markets, not shopping malls; aged wood, not swank floor coverings; one single morning glory, not a dozen red roses." Lawrence places particular emphasis on the idea of decay. Wabi-sabi understands "the aching elegance of an abandoned building or shed. It celebrates cracks and crevices and rot and all the other marks that time and weather and use leave behind. To discover wabi-sabi is to see the singular beauty in something that may first look decrepit and ugly."

Presumably, Lawrence needs to "sell" us on the idea of wabi-sabi because it is foreign to our way of thinking. But it doesn't take a Ph.D. in art history to realize that weather-beaten wood, delicate wildflowers, and domestic ruins have been popular in the West for a very long time. A look at seventeenth-century Dutch landscape paintings, one of Wordsworth's lyrical ballads, or Arts and Crafts–style homes from the early twentieth century demonstrates how thoroughly the search for a beauty based in "character" saturates our aesthetics. So why must it be repackaged as an exotic foreign concept?

This question reveals the difficulty of imagining life beyond the marketplace. Perhaps we recognize that "distress" is merely one effect among the many that are built into our household goods to

299

increase their desirablity, no harder to achieve than any other look. But even people who seem only partially aware of this fact are drawn to the sort of culture you can't buy at a big-box store. We need only consider the popularity of PBS's *Antiques Roadshow* and the eBay shopping website to realize that life under present-day capitalism inspires a longing for what it has trouble providing. To be sure, collectibles are sold for profit. Yet their value depends less on the production process than what happened to them once they left the workshop or factory. The paradox is that we confront this history as novelty.

If you look closely at the language used in advertisements in *Utne Reader* and similar "alternative" publications, you will see how many products are marketed the way Lawrence promotes wabi-sabi. One vendor in the "Smorgasbord" section "puts the funk into functional" by creating coasters, magnets, and journals that "combine retro images from the '40s and '50s with witty text." A conventional advertisement invites you to "experience natural hot tubbing" by purchasing a bath heated by burning wood. Another advises readers "caught up in the hectic place of western living" to follow in the footsteps of over 100 million people in the developing world who "sleep in hammocks nightly," because "these people are among the poorest on our planet, yet the joy and luxury they derive from their hammocks is immense and their hammocks become their refuge from their everyday struggles." What the language in these advertisements conveys is a sense that we would be better off returning to a simpler time and place, where we can work off our stress "naturally."

This mode of nostalgia holds undeniable appeal. But it also reminds us how conservative taste can be. It is far easier to make someone long for the comfort of the past than the ambiguity of the future. We see this not only in the alternative consumption promoted in *Utne Reader*, but in the taste for Shakespeare as well. The line between watching *A Midsummer Night's Dream* and shopping for steak-on-a-stick at a Renaissance Faire is blurrier than you might think. That's why leftists need to be particularly careful when they present their vision of a better world. We can only return to a time before capitalism in our fantasies. And what's worse, we will probably have to pay twenty-five dollars for the privilege. What will the revolution taste like? We better make sure it doesn't taste like the past.

An Interview with Ramsey Kanaan of AK Press
Megan Shaw Prelinger

The AK Press Collective has been publishing and distributing anarchist and other radical literature for over a decade. Through this political literacy project, they disseminate classic and current radical literature, as well as other politically relevant books, both fiction and nonfiction, plus spoken-word CDs. At their Oakland warehouse, they also host readings and get-togethers where authors present their work and discuss their ideas with readers. Originally organized in Britain, the AK Collective expanded across the pond in 1994 and has since been organized into two interdependent publishing collectives. Their catalog is a comprehensive tour of some of the most interesting works available to politically educate the curious.

November 2001

MSP: What do you know about the recent downscaling of the U.S. office of Verso Books in New York?

RK: My understanding is that it is an editorial decision, not necessarily an economic one. They're not closing the American office because of a horrible lack of sales, or because there's no market anymore for radical literature. I think it was an editorial disagreement. What Colin Robinson wanted and what the London branch wanted differed, but I don't think he was fired or sacked or anything like that.

MSP: I'm not here to discuss Verso per se, except in the context of the future of radical publishing. I want to get a sense from you of what kinds of market and social forces AK Press is being impacted by right now.

RK: Well, the main problem that's faced by all independent publishers and distributors, not necessarily radical, has been the rise of the chains in the last ten years: primarily Barnes & Noble, Borders, and the Internet chains like Barnesandnoble.com and Amazon.com. What that has meant, and continues to mean, is the wholesale destruction of independent booksellers. That has been an accelerating trend over the last decade. And that doesn't seem to be slowing at any particular rate.

The chains have quickly and aggressively set out to put independent stores out of business, and they've been pretty successful in doing so. To some extent we've been inured against this by the bookselling/bookbuying network in the San Francisco Bay Area. And we've been lucky that there are several excellent bookstores, such as City Lights and Cody's. Chances are, they're not going to go out of business. Other major cities haven't been as lucky. Three or four years ago we were selling to three or four different stores in Austin, Texas. I believe that now there are no independent bookstores left in Austin. This has been disastrous for independent literature, insofar as independent bookstores are the natural home for it. I'm choosing the word "independent" deliberately, because I'm not talking about just radical literature. Independent bookstores are more likely to carry independent literature. They're more likely to take a chance, they're more likely to be responsive to local desires and needs. They're more

303

likely to take a local history book on that particular area than the chains, which would all be buying the same books.

The raison d'être of chain bookstores is to make a profit. And they don't make money just by selling books. They make money out of selling space in their stores. They don't actually have to sell any books. If you walk in to Barnes and Noble or Borders, what's displayed on their front table is not decided by chance. It's not staff favorites or what's currently hot. The books that are on the front table are there because publishers have *paid* to position their books there.

For example, a large distributor that sells to chain stores offered to carry AK Press books. We were offered that program—the chance to get our books on the front table at either of the big chain stores. But it would cost us four dollars per book. And that's on top of what we pay our distributor. If we are giving our distributors a fifty-percent discount on a ten-dollar book, we are already giving the book to them for five dollars each. In other words, we would receive one dollar per book on a ten-dollar book.

MSP: So they're in the real-estate business.

RK: Yes, that's how the chains actually make their money. If we have paid to place five books on the front tables of a hundred different stores, the bookstore doesn't care if they sell or not, because they've already been paid $2000 to take those five hundred books. This is the way they drive independent bookstores out of business. Initially they will offer to sell independent literature. They will offer radical literature. They will offer to sell gay literature, or so-called "marginal" literature. Typically they will open across the street from the local independent bookstore. Then once the store that they're competing with has gone out of business, you'll find their "marginal" section or their gay and lesbian section has been discontinued.

MSP: Has AK Press been demolished by this reality?

RK: Actually, since we've been in America, since 1994, we've been expanding, and we continue to expand.

MSP: Even in the face of the current economic downturn?

RK: Exactly. In spite of the shrinking market for independent books, we continue to expand. I think we grew fifteen percent last year, and I think we're growing even more this year. The growth has been in a variety of areas, and it's still problematic.

The beauty of bookstores, as opposed to mail-order or the Internet, or even tabling at conferences, is that bookstores are permanent institutions. They are infrastructures where people can go and actually browse. The beauty of the bookstore environment is that it provides a place where people can happen upon a book, take a chance upon a book. For all its convenience, for all its benefits, people definitely do not browse the Internet for books. If you know the book you're after, or you are looking for a particular author, or perhaps even a subject matter, if you're lucky you might be able to find what you're looking for. But you don't stumble across something totally unexpected on the Internet the way you can looking at bookstore shelves.

MSP: How is your experience of business growth problematic?

RK: Although we've managed to increase sales in other areas, our sales at independent bookstores have gone down. That's because there are fewer such stores. We think that's a disaster, in general terms, for the dissemination of literature. Coming across radical ideas in a bookstore is one very real way that people do that. And having that opportunity taken away is a disaster, not just economically for us, but also politically. The lack of a real infrastructure that supports radical literature is a huge problem. I don't think the other ways we've developed to sell books are a replacement for that. They are a replacement in the sense that we're selling more books than ever before. But in terms of building something that's permanent,

no. I'm a firm believer in infrastructural institutions that can be
built upon, that can be expanded upon.

It could be argued that, yes, we're finding many ways to get radical literature out there, which is great. And we've seen a huge
increase in our sales through the Internet. We have also seen an
increase in finding other ways to sell directly. Other people are doing
a lot of tabling at events such as conferences, concerts, demonstrations, and book fairs. Bands take our books on tour with them.
There has been a huge increase in sales through these channels.

MSP: How has your work been impacted by the changing global
political unrest?

RK: Since September 11 our sales have rocketed. We've got an
upsurge in orders on the things you would expect, such as books
by Noam Chomsky or anything to do with the Middle East or
American foreign policy. But whether we're better servicing those
that are already interested or reaching new converts, I'm not sure.
There have been many more opportunities to reach a potentially
interested audience. Every other week there have been rallies,
teach-ins, and events. We're tabling as much of those as we can.

306

MSP: I think there has been an appalling lack of response to this
war.

RK: Oh yes, if you compare the Bay Area's reaction to the Gulf War
ten years ago with the reaction to this current war against
Afghanistan, it's dismal. Ten years ago the Bay Area reacted spectac-
ularly. It wasn't ten thousand or two thousand people marching
here and there. It was 100,000 people closing down the Bay Bridge.
So in that sense the face of activism is way down. It has been ever
since the early 1990s.

MSP: I've noticed a contradiction in the course of activism recently.
It peaked with the anti-globalization protests of two years ago, and

it came to head at Seattle. But now that there's an economic downturn, there's not as much activism.

RK: I think that's a very good point. Being that we've been growing every year since we started in 1994, it's difficult to say that interest in radical ideas reached a peak at the time of the Seattle protests in 1999. But in general you can certainly see that post-Seattle, there was a great rise in interest in books relating to globalization. That's partly because a lot more books were being published, but it's also true that books that had languished prior to the Seattle protest became more popular. And certainly Noam Chomsky's book on the Middle East is selling better than it has sold in the past ten years. In the same way, books on the world economy and the world economic order always existed, but they definitely got a boost post-Seattle.

I have a lot of problems with the anti-globalization movement. I think a lot of participants in the anti-globalization movement can be summed up in their utter retreat from everything after September 11. The largest anti-globalization protest that would have ever been seen was scheduled for Washington, DC following September 11. But the main players in that demonstration, the Sierra Club and the Ruckus Society, Global Exchange, etc., actually canceled the protest. I think that's disgusting. It's terrible.

307

MSP: I think that's because of the fear of liberal politics to appear radical during a time of national crisis.

RK: I think it's a quality of liberal politics that they all scrambled and fell into the national unity. They wanted to show that in these dark times they are all standing shoulder-to-shoulder against a common enemy. I mean, it's utter rubbish. To a certain extent, I think the economy plays a part—to the extent that a majority of the footsoldiers at these demonstrations don't have the time and money these days to fly around the country or around the world.

Maybe their investments were wiped out when they invested in these dot-com companies. That's probably part of it.

But I think what's more telling is that the formal response of the Sierra Club, Ruckus Society, Rainforest Action Network, and those groups opposed to globalization was to cancel the whole protest. That really exposes the fundamentals of their politics, which are not anti-capitalist. Or maybe the weakness of their politics is that they're able to do an about-face due to their lack of analysis. Maybe they're incapable of seeing a tie between nationalism, war, and genocide, to see links between any of those and globalization. That's astounding.

If we believe in our politics, now more than ever we should be getting them out there. Rather than saying, "Oh, it's troubled times, and we might be in for a bit of repression. People won't like us so much so maybe we'd best crawl back into our holes." Or at worst say, "Well, we should all stand together and bomb Afghanistan." Or "Pull together as a nation and buy American!" I don't know what they're thinking, but it's ridiculous.

In terms of AK, we believe in our politics now more than ever.

MSP: Are you putting out any new books in direct response to September 11 or the war in Afghanistan?

RK: Yes, insofar as we're doing what we can in terms of writing and editing and production. It's very difficult to do instant books.

MSP: I don't mean instant books. I mean, is there a general trend of authors being available and inspired to produce new interpretive works?

RK: Yes, we're working with a group called Just Cause to produce handouts and do trainings on how to handle encounters with law enforcement. That would be a timely book at any time, but we're trying to get it out in January. As a publisher, that's our response to these difficult times. Activists should be armed with the best information about how to cope with law enforcement. We're also talking about doing a CD, because we can do those quicker than books.

MSP: Do you know if anyone is planning to write a book on the new anti–civil rights legislation that passed this week?

RK: Well, the best response to this legislation is the same as dealing with law enforcement in general. You should never speak to them, never make a statement, never sign anything. Given what little rights we do have, if you don't say anything, that limits what they can do to you. The reason that law enforcement asks you questions and asks you to make statements is because they don't know what you're doing. Ninety-nine percent of people that are convicted are convicted because of statements that they made.

What I find disappointing and depressing in general is that lack of infrastructure. Without that, I think the most important thing is to keep on doing what we're doing. Whether it's publishing, whether it's building, whatever. To me, the weakness of the left in responding to September 11 showed me starkly how important it is to have that infrastructure, to have organization, to have something you can build upon that can react to these events from a position of strength.

309

MSP: Can you see a crisis occurring in capitalism as a result of economic depression and war that will create new opportunities for the left to re-motivate?

RK: Well, typically the left doesn't grow in times of crisis. It's more likely to wither away and get smashed because people don't react well under pressure. Typically, change comes about when there's an expectation of something better. Historically, periods of war have not been good for the left. I mean, the time when the left was strongest in the U.S. was before the First World War. The First World War was used as a pretext to smash the left. The IWW was at its strongest, the unions were huge. So I don't think that a period of recession or even depression is a good time to be organizing. It's unfortunate that the left is so weak it can't fight against that right now.

MSP: There was a viable socialist America before WWI.

RK: The war was used as a pretext to smash that, very successfully. Radical literature was not totally destroyed, of course, but it was largely derailed by the anti-sedition acts which prohibited sending anything through the mail that campaigned against the war. So socialist newspapers that had circulations of hundreds of thousands suddenly couldn't be distributed anymore.

MSP: I'm aware that you've had turnover in your group. How's the health of your collective?

RK: It's okay. I mean, the fact that we are unable to pay ourselves a living wage or health-care is the problem. We get no subsidies, no grants, and we're not a nonprofit. And even if we were, I doubt that very many people would give their money to a specifically anarchist revolutionary project. The FBI hasn't sent us any money, either. We haven't been able to exploit enough revolution, sales-wise, to pay ourselves a living wage. That's a perennial problem. Virtually everyone who works at AK has a subsidy. Either they have a partner or spouse who has a better-paying job and can subsidize them, or they have a lucky living situation here in the Bay Area. I happen to live in a house where I pay $275 rent. So I'm able to live on AK's wages. On that fundamental level, AK is still not economically viable, no matter what our growth in sales has been.

That's still the biggest problem that we face. It's the main problem we've always faced. Most other left presses and independent publishers have some form of subsidy. Verso is subsidized by Stalinist millionaires. Virtually all literary presses and some progressive presses are subsidized by their archives, or are supported by

310

private moneys. Which is great. I wish more millionaires would get interested in radical culture. But we don't have that. I wish we did. If anyone's reading this who would like to finance the revolution, come on down.

That's the ultimate irony for us, that for AK Press to exist as a specifically revolutionary anarchist anti-capitalist venture, we have to be successful capitalists. We have to ship units at a good profit. That's a contradiction we are constantly struggling with.

MSP: Can you talk about how you negotiate that contradiction on a daily basis?

RK: Other than the great personal financial sacrifices, it's through what we choose to distribute. In a different world, we would make different decisions about what we choose to distribute. Everything we choose to publish or distribute has to meet two criteria: politics, and how well we think we can sell it. There's always that balancing act.

Of course, if we think something is garbage, we don't publish it. But there are many things we know we can sell well which we think are questionable in terms of political merit. To give a non-contentious example, it could be argued that Beat literature is very important. However, no one in AK has a particular love for Beat literature. We can debate its importance in the revolutionary trajectory, but the reality is that it sells very well. So we sell it, and it literally subsidizes the sales of other kinds of books. We sell bucketloads of Bukowski. If we didn't sell bucketloads of Bukowski, we would be more restricted in what else we could sell. Now that's not a comment on his literature. Unfortunately, Kropotkin doesn't sell very well, but we think it's very politically important. So on that basic level, Charles Bukowski subsidizes Peter Kropotkin.

MSP: Say more about the mechanics of how you integrate the capitalist model into an anarchist revolutionary publishing project.

311

RK: I think in terms of one's politics, one always has to be realistic. I'm a firm believer that people should do what they're able to do and what they're comfortable doing. I think certain politics of guilt are rubbish. I don't believe in that. Until we can destroy capitalism, we'll have to live within capitalism. We pay sales taxes, we pay state taxes, we pay federal taxes; we pay evil corporate bastards like PG&E as well as whoever our phone company is. We pay our landlord, we pay commercial printers. We have to do that to exist, and that doesn't bother me, as such. I don't feel bad about it.

We take part in all sorts of business practices that you could argue are cutting our own throats. We sell to chains. If Barnes and Noble ordered a copy of either Charles Bukowski or Peter Kropotkin from us, we would sell it to them. Even though it could be argued that we'd be putting ourselves out of business by doing so, even in a strict capitalist model of business. These are all contradictions that we have to face. Such is life.

MSP: As a collective, how do you make these kinds of economic decisions?

RK: We talk and argue about these things all the time. That's a continuous process. For example, we had a debate and we made a decision not to distribute books published by the major publishing companies. That was a political decision that we feel comfortable with, though I could make a very strong argument against that decision. And our decision to do that was largely based on the economics of AK rather than, say, a conviction that major corporations are evil scum. *Manufacturing Consent* by Noam Chomsky and *A People's History of the United States* by Howard Zinn have both been published by evil corporate scum. But if we bought books published by Rupert Murdoch, the chances are we would pay for those books sooner than we would pay for the independent-press books because the large corporations are more likely to put the screws on you. They are better at harassing people for money. Our decision not to carry those kinds of books was based on the fact that those people would have to be paid first. And we'd rather not be put in that situation of paying the big scumbags before the little people—who may or may not be scumbags. Being independent doesn't mean that you're great. But nevertheless, we'd rather pay the independents.

I do think a lot of it comes down to having morals and having a set of politics, but it also comes down to being realistic. I don't think politics are moral in and of themselves. The fact that I am currently wearing Converse shoes and Levis jeans doesn't make me feel bad. Or the fact that my sweatshirt, although it doesn't have an American flag on it, was probably made in a sweatshop. As I said, I believe—we believe—people should be what they can, as and when they can. And until sweatshops are abolished, and until we can destroy the capitalism that produces sweatshops, the chances are we'll have to wear clothes that are made in sweatshops. That doesn't mean you shouldn't campaign against sweatshops or seek out alternatives. But to live well within capitalism implies that you have a choice and have power. Most people, in most circumstances, including AK and the way we conduct our business, don't have a choice. We don't have any choice not to pay our landlord, not to pay PG&E. I think people should be encouraged and praised for doing what they can, not attacked for not doing what they can't.

Another example is, we print with a local screen-print shop lots of T-shirts that say "AK Press" on them, and some other slogans that we like. And all the artists who design the T-shirts we sell are paid royalties. However, those T-shirts are bought from warehouses by our screen printer. He came to us one day and offered to get us American-made T-shirts, as opposed to your typical T-shirt that is manufactured in Guatemala or El Salvador or Mexico. He said the American-made shirts would cost a dollar more for each shirt. So we had this debate within AK. Do we want to pay a dollar extra per

313

shirt? That would cut into our profit margin because we weren't prepared to drop the price of the shirts.

We had to decide whether it is worth it to play what we think is the politics of illusion. Because the American-made T-shirts are not union label. If they're made in America that means they're made in a sweatshop in L.A., as opposed to a sweatshop in Guatemala. We had to ask ourselves, is that good? Is that better capitalism than the sweatshop in El Salvador? And are we playing this game of having our T-shirts *appear* more credible because they say "Made in America." And we decided that, no, we couldn't afford it. And we couldn't afford to play that game, that politics of illusion or politics of appearance. We were not willing to do that. (We couldn't afford to do that.)

A friend of ours who publishes a magazine—I won't mention any names—told us that his subscribers gave him all kinds of angry phone calls and letters because the baseball caps he was selling were made in Indonesia. So he told us he just cut the labels off them and he hasn't gotten any more complaints. That's playing the game of the politics of illusion. We prefer to think that people understand that rightly or wrongly we live within capitalism and we do what we can.

314

MSP: Say a word about your internal organization.

RK: We are a flat organization where everyone is paid the same and everyone has equal decision-making power. And that's one way that we can work within capitalism. It's very important that we build the new within the shell of the old—that our practice mirrors our politics. And that's notable because most organizations around, even those that advocate for revolutionary change, are not organized that way.

There are several other publishing companies and activist organizations that are anti-capitalist but who organize in hierarchical ways. To me, that seems a little bizarre. And I'm not trying to be holier-than-thou or accusatory. But I guess for us, we wouldn't have it any other way. We *couldn't* have it any other way. And not because we're so wonderfully politically and morally pure, but because it's a practical way of organizing and a very successful way of organizing.

If we're not beholden to the motivation of the boss or of the board, then we're working together toward a mutually held goal that we can all agree on, more or less. I'm at a bit of a loss to understand why anyone would organize in other ways. Even capitalist business orthodoxy is now saying that decentralization is better and top-down isn't so good. For us, our organizational structure not only makes sense politically but it makes sense economically. Parts of it may be unwieldy, but overall it's more efficient. Yes, we meet every day to talk about our project. But having an informed workforce who actually know what they're doing and share general views is a lot more efficient than having an uninformed workforce—I would guess!

315

Conclusion

The screen is black. Emerging from the distance, the sound of a single voice: *"This is what democracy looks like."* The well-worn phrase is repeated, accumulating voices. Again and again. It's hard to say at what point, but eventually we're aware that the words have dissolved into the surface noise of the tape recording. There is a high-end whisper and at the bottom, the muted pounding where once voices shouted, *". . . what democracy . . ."*

The screen floods with the sun-drenched view of the Pacific. It might calm us, fill us with the warmth of its tropical vista, were it not for an ominous black wall of rusting metal cutting the surf in half.

The din of voices chanting, all distorted, harsh, and cavernous, reminds us that it's a long way from the tumultuous streets of Quebec City to the sands of Imperial Beach.

Imperial Beach
A Soundtrack with Images
Ultra-red

"We have a great vision before us: a fully democratic hemisphere bound by goodwill . . . the benefits of dignity and freedom."
—George W. Bush, speaking at the Summit of the Americas, Quebec City, Canada, April 12, 2001

Beneath the Barbed-Wire, the Beach:
Free-Trade and the Unruly Classes

On that Saturday afternoon, April 21, 2001, the distance seemed at once a matter of perspective and something more critical. We heard over cellphones the sounds of chanting voices ringing down the Côte d'Abraham. The cascade of 4,700 tear gas canisters. The marching of 6,000 police. Someone announced one affinity group was using a catapult to breech the 2.5-mile-long, ten-foot-high security fence used to shield the Summit of the Americas from its opponents. Another added that the catapult was launching stuffed teddy-bears. "The fence has been torn down in several places," a speaker reported to the crowd. We cast a glance around us. The wall between us and Mexico stood unassailable.

Gathered near the doubled walls and no-man zone of the U.S./Mexico border, about 2,000 activists came to the San Ysidro Border Crossing to express their support for the Quebec City protests against the Free Trade Area of the Americas. Touted as a hemispheric expansion of the North America Free Trade Agreement, the FTAA loomed disastrous for anyone paying attention to the border regions between the U.S. south and Mexico. Massive economic destabilization in Mexico and Central America has sent tens of thousands of refugees across the border searching for work. *Maquiladoras* dotted the arid landscape, fueled on the cheap labor of mostly women from rural Mexico displaced by a tide of agricultural consolidation. Working for Matsushita, Zenith, Hyundai, and JVC, these women work without a living wage and without adequate job-safety guarantees. Many turn to prostitution in Tijuana's red-light district, hoping to achieve that standard of living promised them by the industrial life.

Across the border, the U.S. sends mixed signals with its hunger for cheap migrant labor contradicted by a calamitous sanctions policy that punishes workers when it's convenient for employers. As soon as workers demand decent wages, job safety, or the right to join a union, employers call in the INS, clearing the shop floor for a new crew of cheap laborers. Concurrently, millions of dollars are poured into the border region, building up medieval fortress walls, thousands of security cameras and movement sensors, and a military zone that forces migrants deeper into the hills and deserts. As of that Saturday afternoon, April 21, in the year 2001 alone, over 300 men, women, and children had died attempting to enter the U.S. from Mexico.

Military offensives like Operation Gatekeeper are proven failures in curbing migration. The stakes are too high for those desperately searching for better economic conditions. They accept the risk of the passage (often having been lied to about the exact nature of those risks), eager for work in the U.S. to support their families and communities back home. Those who make it across rarely benefit from the labor rights granted under U.S. law. Few discover a better life than what they had in Mexico. The real beneficiaries are the employers hiring them, and, to a lesser degree, the people receiving the dollars at home. With a few exceptions, those who come north would rather remain in their own communities. However, as a person crosses the border, he or she becomes a social, economic, political, cultural, and ideological resource for their home community and family. At a cost. And at risk for their own lives.

A member of Ultra-red speaks. We'll name her Elizabeth. Besides her video work within the collective, Elizabeth is also a community organizer with the public housing residents' *Union de Vecinos* in East Los Angeles.

"In several of our discussions we've talked about whether the mass protests of the last couple of years are an effective way of organizing for change. In my opinion, they are not. When organizing mass mobilizations, we have to ask ourselves to what effect. The protests (or, more precisely, the instances of violence at the protests) have drawn media attention to the issues, but that is not enough."

The time came for the protest to march toward the San Ysidro Border Crossing. Faced with the uncertainty of passing through the gate, members of the Black Bloc retreated, opting instead to bang on the fence separating the sidewalk from the freeway. A few U.S. Marshals got excited, but really, where were the Black Bloc to go should they have succeeded in tearing down the fence? A dash across eight lanes in solidarity with their sisters and brothers in Quebec City? The absurdity of the notion would later find resonance in much of what occurred up north along that other perimeter fence.

321

"I wouldn't argue for surrendering the momentum behind the mass mobilizations. However, we must do what we can to integrate these actions into a larger strategy with goals that are defined and measurable.

"If we're talking targets, I think it would be enormously beneficial to call for a blatant disregard for certain economic structures: i.e., banks and credit companies. Imagine if people started closing their accounts and refused to use banks. Card-holders can refuse to buy on credit on a mass scale. Luddite or not, we need to begin thinking of ways in which on a personal level we can act out our refusal of the current market system. Refuse to use it. I know it means sacrifices and changes in lifestyle, but the alternative is to live, use, and support a system that we know is benefiting a few and oppressing many.

"Personally, I believe the greater test of our resolve to transforming globalization from the bottom up would be to organize a mass protest denouncing the militarization of the U.S./Mexico border. Such an action, disciplined and committed to nonviolent tactics, would result in a glorious confusion, making it impossible for the Immigration Naturalization Service and border-patrol agents to distinguish protesters from border crossers. At that point, all would be deserters of the present barbarism."

Eventually, the Black Bloc abandoned their struggle and parted ways with those protesters willing to risk entering Mexico. Those of us who did venture across were met on the other side with Mexican Border Patrol, who stripped us of our stickers, our pamphlets, posters, puppets, T-shirts, and banners. Although the members of Ultra-red were able to get through with our video-camera, we did have our audio-tape confiscated. When it would later come time to produce the "Imperial Beach" video, we were left with the conundrum of high-quality audio from Quebec City but none from the Tijuana solidarity action. The reverse was true with video images. This fact would compel us to produce a video combining the audio from the Canadian mobilization with images from the border. It seemed an appropriate juxtaposition as we collectively began to wrestle with the matter of fences, borders, walls, and perimeters. Are we so oriented toward temporary barricades that we have ignored the everyday reality of more permanent borders?

This was the question that filled our thoughts as we took a bus from the border crossing to *Las Playas*. When we arrived, we found a large sound-truck set up on the cliffs overlooking the ocean. The nearby lapping of the Pacific did little to dull the grim understanding of what the massive fence meant in the life-and-death struggle for freedom. How crass and fitting that the beach on the U.S. side should be named "Imperial." The border wall, constructed from the landing tracks used during Bush Senior's Gulf War, traveled down the cliff side, across Imperial Beach, and far out into the Pacific surf. While the landscape bears this scar, the ocean was more forgiving. Waves flowed between the two sides. Children followed the water's example, skipping back and forth between the two countries through the gaps in the wall. Border-patrol agents surveyed the scene from their perch on the cliffs. The transgression of the children didn't provoke them. Still, the agents watched the porous wall.

Ultra-red's Canadian operative approaches the microphone. A radio artist and activist based in Winnepeg, David (not his real name) recorded over twenty hours of audio over the four days of anti-FTAA protests in April 2001. By year's end he was active in the grassroots organizing effort to defeat Canada's sweeping anti-terrorism bill, Bill C-36.

"I remember distinctly the confusion of that moment where the Wall of Shame did come down in Quebec City. Disoriented and aimless, the protesters seemed to embody something representative or revealing of the larger confusion of where this movement is going, particularly in terms of practices and goals. Can an event be radical enough if the cops don't show up? If the barricades and perimeters and riot cops are only the most blatant manifestations of institutions that don't go away when the fence comes down, where is 'the wall' when the cops don't show up?

"Declaring an action ineffective implies that specific goals were not achieved. Can the presence of these temporary militarized zones facilitate

323

the achievement of certain goals? This seems at least possible: They certainly do lay bare the nature of bourgeois public space as social control."

Between the Beach and the Wall of Shame: Free Trade and the Wings of Death

"Post-Genoa or post–September 11, what has changed? Any changes to come will disproportionately effect those that are consistently disproportionately effected. We see this in how the object of the present anxiety may be directed at one ethnic group but in practice is effecting immigrants from the south with a massive escalation of deportations. Border agents at both the northern and southern border of the U.S. are targeting any and all persons with histories of political dissent. (Perhaps these developments will provide ground for new alliances between economic refugees from Mexico and Central America with those anti-globalization activists who might have before supported stricter borders.)

"I doubt that the spaces of resistance encircling the IMF or the WTO will become Santiago circa 1973. I think that it will still be a whole different kind of danger than the reality of what people live with daily in Columbia or Indonesia. The borders hemming in the underdeveloped world are still so much more permanent than are the temporary and metaphorical ones—even as those barricades are manifestations of the same institutions."

324

★ ★ ★

This is my home
This thin edge of
barbwire
—Gloria Anzaldúa,
Borderlands/La Frontera: The New Mestiza

While the spectre of terrorism clips the wings of liberty in the northern democracies, a date appears at the bottom of the screen, just outside the margins of a long shot of border-patrol guards riding cowboy-style on horseback along the wall: September 11 . . . 1979.

It was six years ago to the day that the democratically elected socialist government of Salvador Allende was overthrown in a U.S.-supported military coup. To celebrate the sixth anniversary of his dictatorship, General Augusto Pinochet appeared before the Chilean people announcing the embrace of market liberalization. Also known as an economic "shock treatment," the liberalization plan was the handiwork of the Chicago Boys, a group of former disciples of Milton Friedman's free market religion. Jumping directly from the boardrooms of private industry to the top posts in Pinochet's government, the Chicago Boys introduced a program of "seven modernizations" designed to reshape government to that of client-state for foreign investment, facilitating massive privatization and strict limitations on labor protections.

Pinochet's dictatorship flew on two wings: political and military terror (with intelligence assistance from the CIA), and the economic dictates of the Chicago Boys. What was chilling about Pinochet's speech of September 11, falling as it did on the anniversary of the coup, was the call to extend the free market model to all aspects of society, a total "shock treatment." For the north, champions of the Chilean economic miracle found themselves caught in an epistemological conundrum as they struggled to disconnect their admiration for Chile's economic marvel from its UN-condemned record on human rights.

325

★ ★ ★

"Earlier enemies learned that America is the arsenal of democracy. Today's enemies will learn that America is the economic engine for freedom, opportunity and development. To that end, U.S. leadership in promoting the international economic and trading system

is vital. [The Free Trade Area of the Americas] is about more than economic efficiency. It promotes the values at the heart of this protracted struggle."
—U.S. Trade Representative Robert Zoellick, *Washington Post,* September 20, 2001

Puffed up with moral authority, Zoellick would arrive in Miami on November 27, 2001 to meet with his free trade counterparts of the now-democratic Chile. The purpose of the closed-door meeting was to resume talks on the proposed Free Trade Agreement between Chile and the U.S., largely seen as a precursor to the Free Trade Area of the Americas. As U.S. free traders tout any and all free trade agreements as the economic front in the war against terrorism, again it is important to recall Chile. Not just for its present role in the post-Pinochet free trade juggernaut, but also for the role of its Pinochet-era economists in advocating the U.S. drift toward neo-liberalism.

Only a few years ago, the Cato Institute launched a tour of the United States with Dr. José Piñera, former Chilean Minister of Labor and Social Security (1978-1980). Speaking of the glories of privatization in Chile, Piñera diplomatically omitted from his presentation that it was his own labor code that launched the "seven modernizations" Pinochet announced September 11, 1979. Scanning Piñera's resume is like reading an abridged history of military despotism in Latin America: advisor on pension privatization and "the process of economic liberalization [to] the presidents of Argentina, Colombia, Bolivia, El Salvador, and Peru . . . [as based on] the Chilean model." Fully expunged from his self-portrait are the decades-old ties between himself and his policies and the half-dozen authoritarian military regimes which employed his services. The suggestion being that his policies and vision for radical economic liberalization find realization independently from the brutality and state-orchestrated terror of those states which follow his guidance.

And yet specifically in the U.S., one gets the sense that boosters like U.S. Trade Representative Zoellick sincerely believe the advance of free trade possible without resorting to military and police-state terror. In terms of confronting the complacent assumptions of the free trade juggernaut—whose own advance is far from inevitable—about the passive compliance of the north, here it can be said the Battle in Seattle shot that fallacy to hell. One can't help but wonder if the escalation of militarism following the events in Seattle—and now enjoying an enormous boost after September 11—is not in fact a steady retreat to that other wing in the Chilean model: military rule.

★ ★ ★

Another member of Ultra-red takes the floor, a man we'll refer to as Pablo. A musician and desublimator of sound, Pablo is also an educator, leading Ultra-red's "School of Echoes" Popular Education Initiative in Echo Park, Los Angeles.

Throughout the soundtrack we hear protesters rallying their comrades to "bring down the wall." "It's coming down," one gas-masked rebel announces triumphantly as the chain-linked Wall of Shame comes crashing down in front of her. "The fence belongs to the people now!" declares another, as he and his affinity group rush down the street with the liberated section of fencing. Within minutes, a hailstorm of tear-gas canisters rain down on the scene. The constant volleying of shots nearly overwhelms the chorus of coughing where seconds before was heard a chorus of victory: "We just brought down the fence!"

"Listening to these sounds I keep thinking about Elizabeth's suggestion of a mass mobilization at the border. Whereas protesters in Quebec were tear-gassed, showered with pepper-spray, arrested, and many brutalized at the hands of the police, the plight of those attempting to cross the U.S./Mexico border face these dangers plus the threat of perishing from the elements, from murderous coyotes, or trigger-happy vigilantes.

327

"Most of us would certainly shrink from the suggestion of a Quebec City–scaled protest at the U.S./Mexico border for these very reasons. However, I think fully appreciating the difference between these two spaces is the key to the development of a resistance to the FTAA and free trade in general. In other words, are our actions attempting to transform a virtual barrier, one symbolically empowered through the temporary military occupation of space? Or, are our actions more effective when directed at those structures—ideological, geographical, economic—empowered through their unassailable permanence? Perhaps in considering these questions we might give a critical look at the Seattle template as increasingly ineffectual and even detrimental to any expressed targets for social change.

"Can we at some point move beyond the parasitic protest of world-leader assemblies in order to do the work of organizing ourselves and our allies? Can our movements prove dynamic enough, dangerous enough, to no longer need their calendars to do the work of movement building?"

Sistema de Valor: Strategies For Deserting Empire

As the forces of neo-liberalism redirect their might, albeit defensively—always defensively—against its dissenters, advocates of democracy should pause to consider our own strategies and tactics. In some respects, our next move will be decisive not just in terms of our own success as a movement but also in forcing the all-too-often brutal hand of capital. When we consider just how much of capital's own actions are defensive in nature—defensive against the autonomy of labor, of desire, of social relations independent of exchange value—we realize our own power to dialectically impact the course of our opponents.

Taking advantage of the pause in the narrative, Ultra-red's Leonardo (not his real name) begins to speak. An immigrant himself, Leonardo is both an artist and an organizer with the community-based Union de Vecinos.

"Frankly, even within Ultra-red there is little consensus about the sig-

nificance and potential of the anti-globalization movement in the present time. What is agreed is that, in reviewing the timeline from the third to the fourth Ministerials of the WTO, the peak of the anti-globalization movement in the north has been Seattle. The forces of capitalism were caught off guard. Inside the Ministerial, delegates representing Third World countries were aligned on their demands and ready to fight for concessions; outside, they found support in the 50,000 people who flooded the streets opposing the talks. Both movements leveraged each other to the point that the talks were not what the major capitalist countries expected. This coordination— some of it calculated, some of it accidental—proved a decisive blow against the Seattle Ministerial.

"The broad coalition to emerge from November 30 was soon weakened, however, by Labor's withdrawal from the active struggle. Organized Labor, quick to reduce politics to the electoral bureaucratic arena, decided to have a more mellow approach so they wouldn't alienate their Democratic allies. There was concern about the coming elections and popular support for the Democratic Party.

"Labor's retreat was not the only thing to weaken the forward momentum established in Seattle. On a tactical level, while the police declared with each subsequent action, 'This is not going to be another Seattle,' and prepared for it, the sentiment of anti-capitalist activists promised, 'This is going to be another Seattle,' and they didn't prepare for change. We moved from the offensive to the defensive.

329

"This defensive turn becomes manifested in a basic mistrust of the process. This can be seen in the handling of internal dissent to the more basic issue of violence. Regarding the latter, rather than defining the values and common interests within a group, people resort to ideological mystifications. By defining themselves nonviolent or with the purpose of violence against property, groups must make themselves vulnerable to scrutiny in terms of the goals and purposes of the struggle. Instead, there is a tendency toward the swift dismissal of practices even before the goal and target is defined.

"During revolutionary struggles in Latin America and in South Africa, nonviolent movements and their armed counterparts engaged in open

dialogue. This manner of coordination was essential in reducing the danger facing those very persons the revolution meant to benefit. By covering our ears and shielding our eyes to the possibility of property damage and the like, we only create the conditions for everyone to be put at risk. We can learn from the Black Bloc, which does not hesitate making a distinction between themselves and others at protests. They have a very clearly identifiable mode of presentation and set of principles. These kinds of distinctions are helpful because they actually engage diversity functionally.

"*The point of a spokescouncil and that kind of structure is to then coordinate amongst the many principles and groups and produce a space where everybody can participate according to his or her abilities and desires. Openness is at the core of this process. One of the principles of nonviolence and civil disobedience is that you announce your objectives and your actions. During the civil rights struggle, when the Student Nonviolent Coordinating Committee organized the lunch-counter sit-ins of Nashville, all the residents of the city, black or white, knew what those acts of protest were about. Civil disobedience has to be connected to the objectives and goals of the struggle. Sitting at a lunch counter was at that time a civilly disobedient act. At the same time, in the same space, it was also a disturbance of the prevailing ideology of racial apartheid. In the end, the concern is not whether someone will subvert our actions, but to what extent we are committed to achieving our goals.*"

The camera returns one last time to Imperial Beach.

A man leans on the fence, gazing across to where an indifferent ocean washes up on U.S. soil. He is a young man, like one of the tens of thousands who have crossed the border in the past, like one of the tens of thousands debating whether to cross it in the future. As the man looks down the sands of Imperial Beach, our own view of the scene is disrupted by the incongruent sounds around us. There is a call for radical action and the command to bring down the wall. We hear the chanting of the women and the rattling of the fence as if it were a cage.

But are these the sounds of Quebec City? Whether spring or

the deepest winter, individuals and entire families participate in a form of civil disobedience more radical than anything witnessed in Quebec. The sounds of the fence-rattling persists. The man on the beach remains still. He imagines taking that first step, free from obstacle, without risking his life or seeing others losing theirs. The fence vibrates with the man's dream. It is a dream planted along that barrier everyday. Just across from Brownsville, Texas to Calexico, California. From Imperial Valley to Imperial Beach.

331

Contributors

ALI ABUNIMAH (www.abunimah.org) is a writer and commentator on Middle East and Arab-American affairs living in Chicago. His articles have appeared in the *New York Times*, the *Los Angeles Times*, the *Chicago Tribune,* the *Financial Times*, the *Philadelphia Inquirer*, the *Jordan Times,* and *Ha'aretz*, among others. Abunimah is a frequent guest on local, national, and international radio and television, including NPR, CNN, and the BBC. He is a contributor to *The New Intifada* (Verso, 2001) and *Iraq Under Siege* (South End Press, 2001). Ali is also co-founder of *The Electronic Intifada* website, a resource for media activists and journalists, www.electronicintifada.net.

CHARLES ANDERS (www.charlesanders.com) is the author of *The Lazy Crossdresser*, a how-to manual and manifesto of liberation for cross-dressers, published by Greenery Press. His/her writing has appeared in a number of magazines, newspapers, and anthologies, and he/she's the creator of www.godhatesfigs.com.

CHARLIE BERTSCH is an Assistant Professor of English at the University of Arizona, Tucson, where he specializes in post-1945 American fiction, critical theory, and popular culture. He is a regular contributor to *Punk Planet* magazine and a co-founder of *Bad Subjects: Political Education for Everyday Life*.

BLANK SLATE SERIES, 2002
LISA KNOWLES

JOHN BRADY is a University of California faculty fellow in Cal Berkeley's Department of Political Science. He can be contacted at jsbrady@socrates.berkeley.edu.

GIUSEPPE COCCO studied political science in Italy and social history in France. He currently teaches in the Federal University of Rio de Janeiro in Brazil.

DOUG HENWOOD is the editor of *Left Business Observer*, a newsletter on economics and politics (www.leftbusinessobserver.com). He is the author of *Wall Street* (Verso, 1997) and *A New Economy?* (New Press, 2002), and serves as a contributing editor to *The Nation*. Henwood also hosts the Thursday edition of "Behind the News," a talk show covering politics and economics on New York's WBAI (Pacifica Radio), and contributes commentary and analysis for a variety of publications.

NAOMI KLEIN (www.nologo.org) is an award-winning journalist and author of the international best-selling book, *No Logo: Taking Aim at the Brand Bullies* (Picador U.S.A., 2000.) Her articles have appeared in numerous publications including *The Nation*, *The Guardian*, *The New Statesman*, *Newsweek International*, the *New York Times*, the *Village Voice*, and *Ms. Magazine*. Klein writes an internationally syndicated column for *The Globe and Mail* in Canada and *The Guardian* in Britain. She lives in Toronto.

MAURIZIO LAZZARATO studied political science in Italy and sociology in France. He is currently a researcher in the University of Paris, Matisse-Isys.

JOE LOCKARD is an Assistant Professor of Early American Literature at Arizona State University and writes on issues of human rights and literature. He is an editor in the *Bad Subjects* collective.

334

J.C. MYERS is an Assistant Professor of Political Science at California State University, Stanislaus, and has lectured at the University of Cape Town.

ANALEE NEWITZ was an academic once upon a time, working as a lowly lecturer at a large public university. Now she's a muckraking technology journalist who sometimes writes about sex (www.techsploitation.com) and an editor at the *San Francisco Bay Guardian*.

RICK PRELINGER (www.prelinger.com) is a film archivist and cultural historian. He is currently working on a book about the history and culture of radio monitoring and a film on menace and jeopardy in American culture.

MEGAN SHAW PRELINGER is an independent scholar whose work focuses on the interaction between geography and social history. She is the author of numerous essays that analyze the political implications of human land use and landscape interpretation. She also practices as a wildlife rehabilitator, and is a member of International Bird Rescue's oil-spill response team.

SCOTT SCHAFFER is an Assistant Professor of Sociology at Millersville University of Pennsylvania. His research focuses on the relationships between resistance, ethics, and everyday life, and he currently serves as managing editor of the *Journal of Mundane Behavior* (www.mundanebehavior.org), and on the production team of *Bad Subjects*.

335

JOEL SCHALIT is co-director of *Bad Subjects: Political Education for Everyday Life*, and associate editor of Chicago's *Punk Planet* magazine. His first book, *Jerusalem Calling: A Homeless Conscience in a Post-Everything World* (2002), is available from Akashic Books. Schalit is a contributor to the *San Francisco Bay Guardian* and edits musical waveforms in the Elders of Zion. He lives and works in San Francisco.

PAUL THOMAS teaches Political Theory, Marxism, and American Cultures at the University of California, Berkeley. He is the author of *Karl Marx and the Anarchists* (Routledge, 1980), *Alien Politics: Marxist State Theory Retrieved* (Routledge, 1994), *Rational Choice Marxism* (with Terrell Carver, Macmillan/Penn State University Press, 1995), and *Culture and the State* (with David Lloyd, Routledge, 1998).

Founded in 1994, **ULTRA-RED** is an audio activist group producing radio broadcasts, street actions, performances, recordings, and installations. The group's work radicalizes the conventions of electro-acoustic and ambient music. The essay included in this volume was written by the following Ultra-red members: Elizabeth Blaney, Pablo Garcia, Dont Rhine (musician, activist, Pride At Work/AFL-CIO), David Shulman, and Leonardo Vilchis. Thanks to Nathan Britton (poet, organizer, California Peace Action) and Rubén A. Tamayo (musician based in Mexicali, Mexico) for contributing to this project.

INDEX

A

Abu-Jamal, Mumia, 95
Academic Consortium on
    International Trade, 45
Acteal massacre, 97
    see also Zapatistas
Adbusters, 158
Adorno, Theodor, 116, 257, 279, 281
    modernity and, 203-6
    see also Frankfurt School
AFDC (Aid to Families with Dependent
    Children), 119-20, 123, 129
Afghanistan, war in, 137, 140, 251, 261
    opposition to, 306, 308
Africa, 82, 148, 151, 329
African National Congress (ANC), 82
Ain't I a Woman (hooks), 126
AK Press, 291, 302-15
Allende, Salvador, 325
Alsop, Stewart, 150
"Alternative to What?" (Frank), 254
Althusser, Louis, 279, 281, 295
anarchism, 168, 310-11
    anti-capitalism and, 44, 45, 286
    organizational principles, 44, 72, 73-4,
        98, 161, 312, 314-5, 330
    state socialism and, 29, 53-4, 72
    see also anti-capitalism, Black Bloc
Anderson, Benedict, 281
"anti-" movements, 41, 49
anti-capitalism,
    contemporary, 26, 33-4, 46-8, 58-66,
        141-4, 161-4, 186-96, 285
    electoral politics, 62-3, 130, 144,
        168-9, 192-4
    fragmentation, 159-60
    intellectual property and, 264-5,
        273-4, 277
    language, linguistic tasks of, 60-1,
        64-5, 68-9, 213-7
    local currencies and, 182-3
    open source and, 248-9
    past, 29-34, 49-54, 279
    education and, 286
    language and, 55-7, 214-7

negative legacy of, 61, 67-8
New Left, 48, 130, 133, 197, 213,
    279, 287-8, 296-7
Old Left, 213, 296, 310
religion and, 198
    see also anti-globalization movement,
        specific ideologies
anti-colonialism, 30-1, 133, 148
anti-statism, 114-5, 161, 168, 169
    see also anarchism, libertarianism
anti-globalization movement, 41-5, 46-7,
    160, 161, 175, 193, 219-20, 287,
    307, 324
    anti-capitalism and, 26, 41, 279, 285-6
    criticisms of, 219-20
    demonstrations, 44, 60, 162
    effectiveness of, 193, 321-2
    future of, 162-3, 307-8, 329
    see also anti-capitalism, globalization,
        demonstrations
Anzaldúa, Gloria, 324
Apache server, 238, 247
Apple Computer, 112-3
Argentina, 38, 175, 326
    parallel economies in, 177, 178
Ashcroft, John, 46
Autonomia movement, 133
autonomous Marxism, 161, 168
    see also Negri

B   337

Baba, Homi, 286
*Bad Subjects: Political Education for
    Everyday Life*, 156
Baffler, The, 43, 159, 250-8
Baker, James, 78
Baran, Paul, 39
Barkocy, Muffy, 247-8
Barlow, John Perry, 269
Barnes & Noble, 303, 304, 312
Barron's, 37
Barton, Mark, 128
Barzun, Jacques, 230
Beat movement, 311
Beatles, the, 290
Beatles Anthology (McCartney, et al),
    289-90

338

339

341

345

Y

Z

Also from Akashic Books

Jerusalem Calling by Joel Schalit
218 pages, trade paperback, ISBN: 1-888451-17-13
$14.95
"This remarkable collection of essays by an astute young writer covers a wide range of topics—the political ethic of punk, the nature of secular Jewish identity, the dangerous place, according to Schalit, that politicized Christianity plays in the U.S., and the legacy of the Cold War in the ability to imagine freedom. Schalit almost always hits his mark . . . This is the debut of a new and original thinker." —*Publishers Weekly* (starred review)

We Owe You Nothing: Punk Planet, the Collected Interviews
Edited by Daniel Sinker
334 pages, paperback (6" x 9"), ISBN: 1-888451-14-9
$16.95
"This collection of interviews reflects on of *Punk Planet's* most important qualities: Sinker's willingness to look beyond the small world of punk bands and labels and deal with larger issues. With interview subjects ranging from punk icons Thurston Moore and Ian MacKaye to Noam Chomsky and representatives of the Central Ohio Abortion Access Fund, as well as many other artists, musicians, and activists, this book is not solely for the tattooed, pierced teenage set. All of the interviews are probing and well thought out, the questions going deeper than most magazines would ever dare; and each has a succinct, informative introduction for readers who are unfamiliar with the subject. Required reading for all music fans." —*Library Journal*

R&B (Rhythm & Business): The Political Economy of Black Music
Edited by Norman Kelley
338 pages, ISBN: 1-888451-26-2
$24.95
"In this anthology, perhaps the first to deal solely with the business of black music . . . [t]he history of the modern recording industry . . . is dissected in several eyeopening contributions that should be required reading for anyone interested in popular music." —*Library Journal*

News Dissector: Passions, Pieces and Polemics; 1960–2000
by Danny Schecter
297 pages, trade paperback, ISBN: 1-888451-20-3
$16.95
"Danny Schecter, a kind journalist without borders, has shaken up public broadcasting, among many other media institutions, in the course of his career as a self-styled 'News Dissector' and human rights advocate . . ." —*The Nation*

Falun Gong's Challenge to China: Spiritual Practice or "Evil Cult"?
A report and reader by Danny Schechter
288 pages, trade paperback, ISBN: 1-888451-27-0
Price: $15.95
The only book-length investigative report on this severe human rights crisis that is affecting the lives of millions. "[Schechter] offers a persuasive analysis of this strange and still unfolding story . . ." —*New York Times*

Heart of the Old Country by Tim McLoughlin
216 pages, trade paperback, ISBN: 1-888451-15-7
$14.95
"Set in a crummy corner of present-day Bay Ridge, Brooklyn, this sweet, sardonic, and by turns hilarious and tragic first novel opens with a no-hoper named Michael going through his motions . . . The novel's greatest achievement is its tender depiction of Michael as a would-be tough guy, trying to follow his father's dictum of 'Give them nothing,' while undergoing a painful education in the real world." —*Publishers Weekly*

Adios Muchachos by Daniel Chavarría
(*Winner of a 2001 Edgar Award*)
245 pages, paperback, ISBN: 1-888451-16-5
$13.95
"Daniel Chavarría has long been recognized as one of Latin America's finest writers. Now he again proves why with *Adios Muchachos*, a comic mystery peopled by a delightfully mad band of miscreants, all of them led by a woman you will not soon forget—Alicia, the loveliest bicycle whore in all Havana."
—Edgar Award-winning author William Heffernan

These books are available at local bookstores. They can also be purchased with a credit card online through www.akashicbooks.com. To order by mail send a check or money order to:

Akashic Books
PO Box 1456
New York, NY 10009
www.akashicbooks.com • Akashic7@aol.com

(Prices include shipping. Outside the U.S., add $3 to each book ordered.)